# British Volunteers in the Spanish Civil War

During the Spanish Civil War of 1936–1939, almost 2,500 men and women left Britain to fight for the Spanish Republic. This book examines the role, experiences and contribution of the volunteers who fought in the British Battalion of the 15th International Brigade, asking who were these volunteers? Where did they come from? Why did they go to Spain? And how much did they actually help the Spanish Republic?

The author begins with an analysis of the composition of the British contingent, before turning to an examination of the motivations of the volunteers. The volunteers' experiences within Spain are traced, from the first few who fought with the militia units in the defence of Madrid in the late summer and autumn of 1936, to the creation and development of the International Brigades in early 1937.

Finally, some of the more contentious issues surrounding the role of the volunteers in the British Battalion in Spain are tackled. The organisation of the brigade and the role of the Comintern, the maintenance of discipline, desertions, and the execution of volunteers are all closely examined. The book concludes that discipline was indeed tough in the International Brigades, particularly as all the members of the battalion were, after all, volunteers. However, *British Volunteers in the Spanish Civil War* argues that recent studies which purport to 'prove' that the brigades were the pliant instrument of the Comintern and/or Soviet policy have over-played the extent of 'Stalinist' control within the battalion, by showing that discipline was driven overwhelmingly by military, rather than political, necessity.

**Richard Baxell** studied history as an undergraduate at Middlesex University, before taking an MA in Computer Applications for History at the Institute of Historical Research. This book developed from research while reading for a PhD at the London School of Economics and Political Science. He is currently researching into the British volunteers' attitudes and experiences during the Second World War.

# Routledge/Cañada Blanch Studies on Contemporary Spain

Series editors: Paul Preston and Sebastian Balfour
*Cañada Blanch Centre for Contemporary Spanish Studies, London*

# British Volunteers in the Spanish Civil War

The British Battalion in the
International Brigades, 1936–1939

**Richard Baxell**

 Routledge
Taylor & Francis Group

LONDON AND NEW YORK

First published 2004
by Routledge
11 New Fetter Lane, London EC4P 4EE

Simultaneously published in the USA and Canada
by Routledge
29 West 35th Street, New York, NY 10001

*Routledge is an imprint of the Taylor & Francis Group*

© 2004 Richard Baxell

Typeset in Baskerville by
BOOK NOW Ltd
Printed and bound in Great Britain by
TJ International Ltd, Padstow, Cornwall

*British Library Cataloguing in Publication Data*
A catalogue record for this book is available from the British Library

*Library of Congress Cataloging in Publication Data*
A catalog record for this book has been requested

ISBN 0-415-32457-2

# To the veterans of the International Brigades

The British Battalion banner, held in the Marx Memorial Library, London.

# Contents

# Plates

# Figures

# Maps

# Tables

# Acknowledgements

My thanks go first to Paul Preston, Professor of International History at the London School of Economics, without whose constant advice, support and friendship this book would never have been started, let alone completed; also to Martine Morris and Clive Fleay of Middlesex University, for reawakening my interest in history in general, and for this subject in particular. The kind assistance given to me by the veterans and their families and members of the International Brigade Memorial Trust has, of course, been crucial, and I would particularly like to thank Sam Russell, Dave Marshall and Marlene Sidaway, Bob Doyle, John Dunlop, Chris Smith, George Wheeler, Dave Goodman, and Fred and Sadie Thomas. The staff of the Marx Memorial Library, the Imperial War Museum and the Public Record Office in London, the National Museum of Labour History and the Working Class Movement Library in Manchester and the Russian Centre for the Preservation and Study of Recent Historical Documents in Moscow all went out of their way to help me in my research.

A number of other historians have also assisted me in my research and writing, principally Martin Blinkhorn, Tom Buchanan, Helen Graham, Angela Jackson, Barry McLoughlin, Michael O'Shaughnessy, Robert Stradling and Natalie Suart. Likewise, David Leach, and the information he uncovered during the making of his documentary *Voices from a Mountain*, has also been extremely helpful. My thanks go to my mother who acted as proof-reader, to Iván Pliego Moreno and Beatriz Anson as impromptu translators and to Heather Barnett and Jeremy Scott, who very generously donated their skills and precious time to preparing the illustrations. Lastly, I would like to thank Jim Carmody, who has provided me with invaluable assistance throughout my research and devoted enormous time and trouble to helping eliminate any mistakes. Those that remain are mine alone.

Excerpts from James K. Hopkins, *Into the Heart of the Fire: The British in the Spanish Civil War*, Copyright © 1998 by the Board of Trustees of the Leland Stanford Jr. University. Used with the permission of Stanford University Press, www.sup.org.

All plates used with the permission of the International Brigade Archive at the Marx Memorial Library, London, with the exception of plate 7.1 (photograph by the author).

All maps by Jeremy Scott.

# Abbreviations

| | |
|---|---|
| BUF | British Union of Fascists |
| CPGB | Communist Party of Great Britain |
| IBA | International Brigade Archive, Marx Memorial Library, London |
| ILP | Independent Labour Party |
| IRA | Irish Republican Army |
| IWMSA | Imperial War Museum Sound Archive, London |
| LBC | Left Book Club |
| NMLH | National Museum of Labour History, Manchester |
| NUWM | National Unemployed Workers' Movement |
| POUM | Partido Obrero de Unificación Marxista |
| PRO | Public Record Office, Kew |
| SWMF | South Wales Miners' Federation |
| TUC | Trades Union Congress |
| WCML | Working-Class Movement Library, Salford |
| YCL | Young Communist League |

# Introduction

In November 1996, 400 elderly men and women, including a number from Britain, gathered in a ceremony near the Spanish capital of Madrid to pay homage to their friends and comrades who had died fighting in the Spanish Civil War of 1936–1939. These were the surviving members of the International Brigades, the volunteers from around the world who had rushed to the country between 1936 and 1938 to fight for the Spanish Republic against its enemies from both inside and outside Spain. For many of these men and women, this was their first visit to Spain since the civil war, for they had refused to set foot there whilst the regime of General Franco, which so many of their comrades had died to prevent, still existed. However, following the death of Franco in 1975, a new democratic government had replaced the old regime, and, as a gesture of gratitude to the international volunteers who had come to Spain to fight the military uprising of 1936, the Spanish government offered citizenship to the surviving members of the brigades. So what did these volunteers do that was so significant such that, 60 years later, the few hundred still alive would be offered the citizenship of Spain? Who were they? Where did they come from? Why did they go to Spain? And how much did they actually help the Spanish Republic? These are some of the questions that this study will attempt to answer. First, however, an explanation of the events within Spain preceding the outbreak of civil war is necessary, for, whilst it is undeniable that the war developed an international dimension, it is inside Spain itself that the causes of the war were to be found.

The military coup, launched by a group of army officers against the Spanish government on 17 July 1936, was the culmination of a struggle for supremacy between two political blocs within Spain that were united by little except mutual incomprehension and enmity. That the Spanish government should be confronted by an armed insurrection came as no surprise to many observers; in the five years that the beleaguered Republican government had existed, it had faced mortal threats from both left and right. A military rising led by General Sanjurjo in August 1932, and a revolution in the Asturias and Catalonia in October 1934, may have been crushed, but the political and social forces that had been behind them most certainly were not. Indeed, the history of the Spanish Second Republic had been one of ever-increasing political polarisation.

Spain's Second Republic, *la niña bonita*, had been proclaimed following the municipal elections on 12 April 1931 that had been taken to be a plebiscite on the monarchy, and had recorded an overwhelmingly hostile vote against it. The king, Alfonso XIII, realising that he had lost not just the support of the populace but, crucially, the support of the military, fled Spain. For many Spaniards the birth of the Republic was celebrated by exuberant public rejoicing; this seemed to many to signal the beginning of the end for the powerful Spanish elites, and to offer a relief from abject poverty for millions of landless peasants. However, the Republic's attempts to reform powerful institutions like the church and the army, at the same time as challenging entrenched economic interests in the landed, industrial and banking oligarchies, never achieved the success expected by its supporters on the left, whilst antagonising its opponents on the right.[1] Separation of church and state, modernisation of the top-heavy army and attempts to reform the deeply unequal distribution of the land were all regarded with horror by the established elites. In addition, attempts to meet the demands for regional autonomy from areas such as the Basque Country and Catalonia further outraged the Spanish army, who believed in their duty to preserve 'the true and indivisible Spain'.

The situation did not take long to escape from the government's rather tenuous control. Anarchist and other anti-clerical elements demonstrated their opposition to the Catholic Church by burning churches. The government, unwilling to use the forces of order against workers, some of whom were their own supporters, sat on its hands. If the government's reformist programme had not already alienated the army and church, its inability, or unwillingness, to control its supporters guaranteed their opposition.

The army's withdrawal of support was made explicit in August 1932 with General Sanjurjo's *pronunciamiento* (military rising). The coup was a poorly kept secret and easily suppressed, but the event clearly showed that the Republican government faced deadly opposition from sections of the right in Spain. When the Republican/socialist government lost the elections in 1933 and was replaced by a conservative/reactionary government, many of the reforms were, at best, shelved or, in many cases, overturned. The left was not long in voicing its outrage. In October 1934, in the mining areas of the Asturias in northern Spain and in Catalonia, a general strike rapidly turned into armed insurrection. It was brutally suppressed by the army, with the help of Moorish troops from North Africa used for the first time in mainland Spain.[2] In the ensuing repression, Republicans and socialists across Spain were imprisoned, including almost the entire leadership of the socialist trade union the *Unión General de Trabajadores* (UGT).

In the Spanish elections held 18 months later in February 1936, a coalition of socialists and Republicans united in a 'Popular Front' won a narrow victory over the opposing coalition of the right and prepared themselves to revive the reformist programme of 1931. Meanwhile, elements of the Spanish right, who had lost any faith in the Republic, prepared for war. The murder on 13 July of Calvo Sotelo, a prominent Catholic conservative politician, by members of the Republican Assault Guard (itself a response to the murder the previous day of one of their comrades, Lieutenant José Castillo) served as the perfect excuse for the leader of the plot, General Emilio Mola. On the evening of 17 July 1936 the garrisons rose in Melilla,

Tetuan and Ceuta in Morocco, and the revolt quickly spread to the mainland. In conservative areas of Spain such as Old Castile the rising was, in general, successful, but in other areas, including the major cities of Madrid and Barcelona, the generals met with bitter and effective resistance. However, though the coup was not successful in capturing Spain in its entirety, neither was it an outright failure. To a great extent the rebel and government forces were evenly matched: the Republicans held most of the navy, air force and territory, including the capital and the vital industrial regions of the Basque Country and Catalonia, whilst the rebels controlled the majority of the army, including the formidable Army of Africa – the Spanish Army's elite, battle hardened from the Morocco campaign – under the command of General Franco.[3] However, it was trapped on the wrong side of the strait of Gibraltar, and the Republicans controlled the vast majority of the navy.

At this point, forces outside Spain decisively altered the progress of the conflict. What began as a typically Spanish *pronunciamiento* quickly took on a significance beyond a domestic military rebellion against a constitutionally elected Republican government. Instead, it evolved from civil war into what Hugh Thomas referred to as 'world war in miniature', becoming 'the screen on to which foreigners projected their own concerns with such luminous clarity'.[4] Two events in particular had a profound effect on the development of the war. For the Nationalists, the airlift of Franco's Army of Africa by the German JU 52s and Italian Savoia-Marchetti S.81 bombers across the strait of Gibraltar was absolutely crucial,[5] whilst the involvement of the International Brigades in the battle for Madrid in the winter of 1936–1937[6] helped inflict the first real defeat on the rebels in their hitherto virtually unopposed march on the capital.[7]

These volunteers for the International Brigades came from countries across the world to help the beleaguered Spanish Republic, many of them with bitter experiences of fighting against fascism and with personal scores to settle. To these 'anti-fascists', Italy, Portugal, Austria and Germany had all fallen to fascism, and now Spain was similarly under mortal threat. Weary of this remorseless spread of right-wing ideologies through much of Europe, they felt that in Spain the tide might, at last, be stemmed. Thus many thousands volunteered to fight for the Republicans, the majority of whom served in the International Brigades.

The International Brigades were recruited and organised by the Communist International (the Comintern), which was quick to respond to the influx of foreign volunteers for the Republic. Originally reluctant,[8] Stalin was, by the end of September 1936, persuaded to support the idea of the formation of the brigades by Dimitrov, the head of the Comintern, and by several senior Russian generals, who realised the potential value of military lessons that might be learnt in Spain.[9] For Stalin, who was concerned at the extent of German and Italian help for the rebels and its potential severely to weaken France, the International Brigades offered an opportunity to support the Spanish Republican forces without intervening directly, thus reducing the risk of alienating Britain and France with whom he was trying desperately to establish détente. The recruitment of the International Brigades was coordinated by the Communist Party in France where, like Spain, a Popular Front government had been elected, and which was situated conveniently bordering

Spain. Besides, the French communist André Marty, who was later to play a central role as commander of the International Brigades' training base at Albacete, was a member of the executive committee of the Comintern.

This influx of foreign volunteers into Spain came despite twenty-eight countries signing up to an agreement of non-intervention in the war, initially proposed by France, strongly championed by Britain, and flagrantly ignored by, first, Italy and Germany and, later, Russia.[10] Meanwhile, the instigators of the agreement, determined to limit the war to Spain, set up the impotent 'Non-Intervention Committee' in London, under the hopelessly ineffective chairmanship of Lord Plymouth. The British government, fully aware that several countries were bypassing the agreement, turned a blind eye, and the Foreign Secretary, Anthony Eden, later remarked, 'better a leaky dam than no dam at all',[11] even though official documents confirm that the British government knew that the Nationalists were benefiting far more from the agreement than the Republicans.[12] As one commentator on the British government's reactions to the war has observed, 'the Foreign Office was less troubled by a war scare than a red scare.'[13]

Among the 3,000 foreign volunteers who had arrived in Spain to help defend the Spanish Republic in late 1936 were a number from Britain. Some are well known, such as the writer George Orwell, the Marxist intellectual John Cornford, and Esmond Romilly, the nephew of Winston Churchill; others are not so, such as William Gough, a metal finisher from Luton, and Phil Gillan, a lorry driver from Glasgow. Many more arrived in Spain to fight alongside them, and British volunteers were involved in many of the major battles in the conflict, from the defence of Madrid between November 1936 and March 1937 to the last desperate Republican assault across the River Ebro in July 1938. British casualties in Spain were to be high, with as many as one-quarter killed and over half of the total number of volunteers sustaining some kind of wound.[14] The last brigaders were withdrawn at the end of 1938 and returned to Britain in December just after the farewell parade in Barcelona, renowned for the impassioned speech of the communist deputy from the Asturias, Dolores Ibarruri, '*La Pasionaria*':[15]

> Comrades of the International Brigades! Political reasons, reasons of state, the good of that same cause for which you offered your blood with limitless generosity, send some of you back to your countries and some to forced exile. You can go with pride. You are history. You are legend. You are the heroic example of the solidarity and the universality of democracy . . . We will not forget you; and, when the olive tree of peace puts forth its leaves, entwined with the laurels of the Spanish Republic's victory, come back! Come back to us and here you will find a homeland.

For these British volunteers the task of joining the Spanish Republican Army was not necessarily an easy one, for the journey to Spain itself involved risking imprisonment, or worse. Before December 1936, when the Communist Party began recruiting in earnest, British volunteers with their own passports and money often travelled to Spain under their own steam.[16] However, following the British

*Map 0.1* Military actions of the British Battalion in Spain.

- ❶ Lopera, December 1936
- ❷ Boadilla, December 1936
- ❸ Jarama, February 1937
- ❹ Brunete, July 1937
- ❺ Belchite, August-September 1937
- ❻ Teruel, January-February 1938
- ❼ Segura De Los Baños, February 1938
- ❽ Calaceite, March 1938
- ❾ Ebro River, July-September 1938

government's implementation of the Foreign Enlistment Act on 9 January 1937 and the banning of volunteers under the Non-Intervention Agreement in February 1937, recruitment obviously had to become rather secretive.[17] Any person found guilty of an offence under this act could be punished by a fine and up to two years in prison,[18] though no one was ever actually prosecuted.[19]

For most of those who left for Spain from late 1936 onwards, the procedure for volunteering was very similar. Contacts would be made with the local Communist Party branch, which until February 1937, would send the volunteers to the party offices in King Street in London's Covent Garden, after which they were sent to a nearby office above what would later become the Dependents' Aid office at 1 Litchfield Street. Here they would be interviewed by R. W. Robson, known to all as Robbie, who would assess their suitability, in military and political terms.[20] Some potential volunteers were turned away for their lack of experience in either field, but political commitment was usually regarded as an acceptable surrogate for military experience. Volunteers were also turned away if they lacked credentials (membership of a trade union or appropriate political organisation), but if they returned they would usually be accepted, for, 'this would be taken as evidence of their sincerity.'[21]

Those accepted would be told to purchase weekend return rail-tickets from Victoria Railway Station to Paris, which did not require a passport. At the railway station somewhat ineffectual efforts by the British Special Branch would be made to dissuade the volunteers from travelling. One volunteer described how, 'Victoria

Station was as thick as flies on ground with special agent men and detectives, you could tell by their huge boots . . . But they could do nothing about it.'[22]

Some volunteers were followed, and the Communist Party and Dependents' Aid offices were kept under surveillance, but little was done seriously to prevent the volunteers from going.[23] Tommy James remembers that, though 'the CID fellows at Dover favoured us with a searching look', no attempt was actually made to prevent them leaving.[24] John Longstaff, who served as a runner with the British Battalion, remembered encountering a degree of hostility from a plain-clothes policeman, but little else.[25] These somewhat half-hearted efforts to thwart recruitment made little impact, for, as one of the British volunteers stated, they were confident that 'this was only intimidation. They had no legal right to do anything about it.'[26] As S. P. Mackenzie has shown, the authorities recognised that there were major legal problems in applying the 1870 Foreign Enlistment Act to volunteering for the Spanish war.[27]

At Paris they would be met by a Communist Party representative, who for a time in 1937 was Charlotte Haldane (under the pseudonym Rita),[28] wife of J. B. S. Haldane, the scientist, and mother of Ronnie Burgess, who served in the British Battalion.[29] In Paris the volunteers underwent a medical examination and further checks on their political reliability.[30] Volunteers would be given a stern lecture on the importance of avoiding establishments offering the temptations of sex and alcohol, though these warnings had a rather limited impact on some.[31] Care had to be exercised, for groups of volunteers would occasionally be arrested and repatriated after a stay in a French jail,[32] though many volunteers believed that the French police didn't make undue effort to catch them, and that many were sympathetic to their cause.[33] William Feeley, a glass-worker from St Helens in Lancashire, remembers being interrogated by a non-intervention observer in France who asked if they were on their way to Spain.

> They said, 'Well, where are you going?' So we said, 'Beziers.' 'And where are you going to after that?' 'Back to Paris.' He said, 'Not to Spain?' And they all had broad grins on their faces, [']cos they knew perfectly well where we were going. We put on an expression of horror at this, 'Spain, no, not likely!' And they all just burst out laughing and left us there.[34]

In any event, were a volunteer to be arrested and returned to Britain, his next attempt to get to Spain was likely to be successful.[35]

From Paris, until February 1937, they would travel to Spain by train, after which the usual route was to be smuggled in groups over the Pyrenees. The volunteers would be gathered together in groups from many different countries, 'Germans, Poles, Czechs, all sorts'.[36] Many volunteers describe the tough physical demands of the climb over the Pyrenees, which could last for up to 16 hours[37] – most of the volunteers were, after all, from an urban background – though some relished the climb, such as George Wheeler, who described it as 'exciting and exhilarating',[38] or Tom Murray, who managed to carry one volunteer, previously injured in Spain, for much of the journey.[39] Many volunteers describe how their eventual arrival was met with a mixture of relief and excitement that the exertion was finally over and they were, at last, in Spain.[40]

From the border they would then be taken by lorry a short distance to Figueras, the mustering point for volunteers entering Spain from the north, and then by train to the International Brigade headquarters at Albacete (roughly half-way between Madrid and Valencia), where volunteers would be processed and divided up by nationality. Until July 1937, British volunteers were then sent on to their base nearby at Madrigueras, after which it was transferred to Tarazona de la Mancha. At this point their military training, such as it was, would take place before they joined their comrades, the majority of whom fought as infantry on the front line. Here, as James Hopkins stated, the volunteers would find themselves in 'the heart of the fire'.[41] Few would escape unscathed.

# 1    Who were the British volunteers?

> Because they were so scattered, therefore, there are no statistics of the makeup of the
> English volunteers, nor is it possible to know exactly how many there were of them.[1]

Ever since the outbreak of the Spanish Civil War rather imaginative claims have
been made, by both supporters and opponents of the Second Republic, of the level of
foreign intervention for the Republic.[2] The following assessment written just after
the war by Arthur Loveday, a British supporter of Franco, is typical: 'General
Franco's staff put them at 100,000 men and other experts at from 50,000 to 150,000
. . . They were certainly as numerous and possibly more numerous than foreigners
fighting for Franco.'[3] Likewise, in 1952 the Spanish Foreign Ministry estimated the
numbers at 125,000, and Andreu Castells's work in 1974 on the Internationals put
the numbers at around 60,000.[4]

These generous estimates probably make the mistake of including the large
number of Spaniards in the International Brigades within the calculations. The
experiences of John Peet, a member of the British Battalion who worked in the post
office in the International Brigade base at Albacete, 'where all the names of the
members of the International Brigades were card indexed', support this. Peet
states that:

> There has never been, as far as I am aware, an accurate estimate of how many
> men served in the International Brigades . . . It wasn't easy to determine. I
> couldn't simply count the cards to determine how many men were there. The
> cards included not only the names of the International volunteers, but also of
> the very considerable numbers of Spaniards, who by January 1938, had
> volunteered or been drafted into the Brigades to make up the strengths.[5]

The International Brigades always included a number of Spaniards, 'the only way of
replacing casualties',[6] particularly after September 1937 when the Republican
government published a decree incorporating the International Brigades into the
Republican Army[7] and ruled that there must be a Spanish battalion in every
international brigade, a Spanish company in every battalion and a Spanish section in
every company.[8] Most estimates now accept that between 1936 and 1938 over
35,000 people from perhaps as many as 53 nations left their homes to join the

Republican forces.[9] However, it should of course be remembered that even the most generous estimates of intervention for the Republic are dwarfed by the numbers intervening on the Nationalist side.[10]

Charlotte Haldane, who later became the honorary secretary of the Dependents' Aid committee, alleged that all foreign communist parties had been assigned recruitment quotas for the International Brigades.

> The Communist Parties were charged with the local and national organisation. The number of recruits each party had the task of raising was assessed according to its membership man-power and its sympathisers. The assessments were high; in many cases higher than the local Party leaders could possible attain . . . The British Communist Party was also given a quota to raise. It was one of the smaller and more insignificant of the European parties . . . It had been at first decided only to send unmarried men over twenty-one. But the smallness of their numbers compelled the British C.P., under orders from the C.I. [the Communist International], to furnish its quota of volunteers, to extend its recruitment among married comrades and the youth of the Young Communist League.[11]

This allegation is cited in several other works,[12] though there appears to be no source to substantiate this claim. Furthermore, R. W. Robson, who was responsible for recruiting the British volunteers, states that, though fewer and fewer volunteers were turned down as the war progressed, 'There was never any real pressure for recruits.'[13] Nevertheless, there have been suggestions made that Britain's quota was 1,000;[14] if so, even by the most conservative estimates, it more than doubled this number, with more than 2,300 British volunteers arriving in Spain.[15] Despite the belief of some of the earlier volunteers that they were signing up for a period of three months (a belief that perhaps might have been more strongly debunked by recruiters), in reality volunteers signed up for an indeterminate time, and since many were not travelling with passports, or had surrendered them to the recruiters, any volunteers who were to regret their initial zeal found themselves in a difficult position when travel in and out of Spain was later made very difficult.[16]

Despite Robson's claim that there was no real pressure on recruits, it is nevertheless clear that, as the war progressed, the high casualty rate had a negative effect on recruitment.[17] The original number of enthusiastic volunteers who arrived in December 1936 and January 1937 were decimated at Jarama, and by the spring of 1937 many potential volunteers had grown understandably less enthusiastic to become 'cannon-fodder'.[18] As R. Dan Richardson states:

> That steady reservoir of political émigrés and Communist militants which had supplied the bulk of the early Internationals had been, by the Spring of 1937, substantially exhausted . . . and the generally growing awareness that joining the Brigades was less a romantic adventure than a good way to die young played a part in reducing the numbers of men who might otherwise have been tempted to join.[19]

Whilst recruitment never reached the levels of the winter of 1936–1937, when 40 a month were arriving (rather than the 40 a week following the battle of Brunete),[20] it is clear that, as Figure 1.1 shows, following Brunete in July 1937, the numbers entering Spain from Britain began to increase once again, before tailing off in the spring of 1938.[21]

The crisis in numbers following Brunete had severe consequences for the Communist Party in Britain, which was forced to suggest to some party members that they might consider volunteering for Spain[22] and to reconsider allowing important cadres to volunteer. Bob Cooney, a commissar with the battalion in 1938, who had originally been persuaded not to volunteer, describes how he was allowed to go to Spain and arrived in October 1937, 'after a crisis in the battalion, a loss of manpower and terrific losses in leadership'.[23] Billy Griffiths, a member of the Rhondda Communist Party committee, was also asked to volunteer, and rather resented being taken away from his party work in Britain: 'I resented being asked to go to Spain. Why me? Could I be spared? Alas for my conceit, everyone agreed that I should go. I was not indispensable.'[24]

Tom Murray, a Labour councillor (and at the same time an underground Communist Party member), was also asked to volunteer in 1938, following the retreats of the spring: 'A local official of the Communist Party asked me if I was prepared to go, and I said, "If it's the view of the Party that I should go, then I'll go."'[25] Nevertheless, Murray believed that this official had made a mistake, and indeed, when he arrived in Spain, Peter Kerrigan, the *Daily Worker* correspondent and erstwhile base commissar at Albacete, admitted as much, and tried to persuade him to return.[26]

According to Robson this policy of encouraging party figures to volunteer was abandoned in 1938, as the party became increasingly concerned about the number of senior party cadres killed in Spain. Thereafter, figures were no longer encouraged to volunteer.[27] As George Aitken stated, concerning the repatriation of the battalion commissar George Coyle, 'He was a valuable party cadre and [it was important] that we should try to protect such comrades as much as possible since we had already lost so many of our very best party comrades.'[28] However, K. W. Watkins's claim that 'A policy was pursued by which the really key men were never committed to dangerous participation in the struggle'[29] is not accurate. Many senior party figures did serve in Spain, usually as political commissars, but the loss of Ralph Fox in December 1936 encouraged the party to try to keep senior figures as base commissars at Albacete, rather than on front-line service. Nevertheless, senior party figures such as Tom Murray, Bob Cooney and Walter Tapsell all served at the front during 1938.

In attempting to establish the exact numbers of British volunteers for the International Brigades we are faced with a number of problems. First, though the documents that survive the war are often detailed and comprehensive, there are many missing records and, in any case, record keeping was understandably imprecise, so there are a number of contradictory entries. Phonetic or erroneous spellings, imprecise handwriting and a complement of general clerical errors ensure that many of the records are inherently unreliable, a problem which is exaggerated

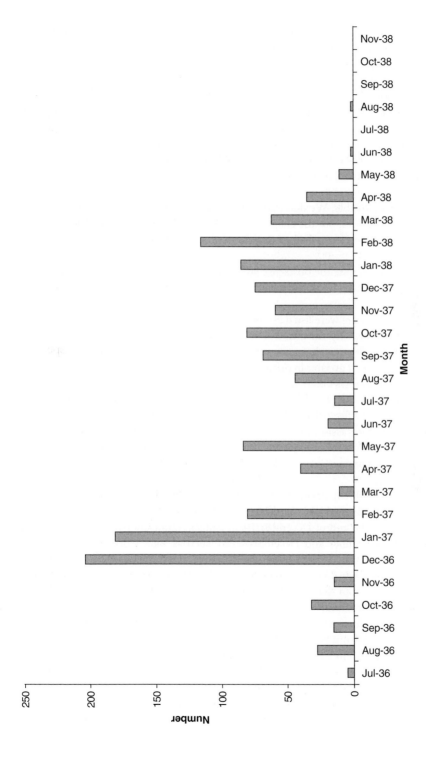

*Figure 1.1* Date of arrival of the British volunteers.

when working with mortality data. The Republicans spent most the war on the defensive and, in some cases, such as the spring of 1938, in outright retreat, so there was not always time to recover the bodies, or passbooks, of the deceased.[30] This is assuming, that is, that the volunteer was carrying any information, for 'there were no identification papers and etc. carried, by order.'[31] The confusion surrounding identification of casualties was further complicated by the Republican authorities' refusal to advise units if a member had been hospitalised, as a letter from the brigade base at Albacete to London admitted: 'We are not told by anybody when our men are sent to hospitals, or when they were killed. Nor are we supposed to divulge the information. Nobody knows.'[32] Thus establishing whether a missing soldier had been captured, killed or wounded was:

> often impossible. We don't know it and there is no way of knowing it. We find out in the lines, but the chaps here (and I myself) have no conception of dates, day of the week etc. Only approximate dates can be set in many cases.[33]

Nevertheless, despite the obstacles, attempts were made to keep track of the British brigaders in hospital, and by late 1938 lists of those in hospital were being compiled.[34]

Many volunteers were listed as 'missing in action' but, as the shooting of prisoners by the rebels was by no means a rarity, 'missing' all too often did mean killed. However, it is also true that some volunteers who were listed as 'missing' had simply deserted or turned up later in prisoner-of-war camps, such as San Pedro de Cardeña. For example, Francis Casey from Glasgow was listed as having been killed at Jarama in February 1937 in the International Brigade's records,[35] though records in the Public Record Office (PRO) show a Francis Casey appealing to the British Consulate in Madrid for assistance in returning to the UK in March 1937.[36] Similarly, the family of Jack Coward, a seaman from Liverpool, received a death certificate on 17 March 1939 claiming he was killed on 3 May 1938. In fact, he arrived home safely later in 1939.[37]

A further problem tracing those from Britain is that by no means all the British volunteers fought with the 'British' Battalion of the 15th Brigade, which was not founded until the end of December 1936. British volunteers who fought to defend Madrid in November and December 1936, such as John Cornford and Esmond Romilly, fought mainly with either the German Thaelmann Centuria or the French Commune de Paris (Dumont) Battalion, whilst others, such as Felicia Browne and the volunteers from the Independent Labour Party (ILP) such as George Orwell, fought with other militia units. More significantly, many of those who fought with the British Battalion were from various countries of the Commonwealth and, as the war progressed, from Spain itself.[38]

A further problem faces anyone trying to locate individual volunteers. Within the ranks of volunteers, there was a widespread use of pseudonyms.[39] Jewish volunteers often Anglicised their surnames; others changed around first and middle names, or dropped letters from their names. For example, David Soloman became David Loman, Frank Squires became Frank Antrim and Charles Gautzman became

Charles Boyd. Some changed their names completely: David Abrahams became Basil Minsk[40] and Manassah Lesser became Sam Russell.[41] No wonder, for most brigaders in Spain were under no illusions of the lack of sympathy towards them, either from the rebels or from the British establishment, especially after volunteering for the brigades was made illegal following the implementation of the Foreign Enlistment Act and the extension of the Non-Intervention Agreement to include volunteers in February 1937. Joe Norman, a Communist Party organiser with the British Battalion, described how a hostile British journalist questioned a group of captured brigaders: 'We did not feel better after we'd been sneered at by a reporter from *The Daily Express*. "You'll all be shot", he told us encouragingly.'[42] On more than one occasion, the reporter's spiteful words were to prove correct, and a false name did not necessarily guarantee any protection. James Rutherford, who was captured by the Nationalists at Jarama in February 1937 and repatriated to England after a prisoner exchange, later returned to Spain.[43] He was unfortunate enough to be recaptured and, even though using the pseudonym Jimmy Smalls, was recognised and shot for being in contravention of a League of Nations directive that barred foreign ex-prisoners of war from returning to Spain.

Though the various records on the British volunteers are, for the reasons mentioned above, incomplete and in some areas unreliable, this is not to say that a reasonably accurate estimate of various criteria, such as overall numbers, ages, occupations, geographical origins and political affiliations, cannot be reached. A combination of the files in the International Brigade Archive (IBA) and the PRO in London and the large number of memoirs and interviews does enable a coherent and meaningful picture of the makeup of the British volunteers to be reached. This picture is now considerably enhanced by the opening of the International Brigade Collection in Moscow, which contains a wealth of details on the volunteers, including biographies, assessments, and their responses to detailed questionnaires on their background pre-Spain.[44] It also reveals a great deal about the nature of the volunteers and the criteria applied to prospective recruits.

The most important criterion for potential volunteers for Spain, particularly during the winter of 1936–1937, was military experience, though political resolve might be considered a necessary replacement for a lack of the former.[45] A letter sent from Ralph Bates – a British intellectual who worked in the Republican government's propaganda and information services, and was the first editor of *Volunteer for Liberty*, the journal of the 15th International Brigade[46] – to the general secretary of the Communist Party of Great Britain (CPGB), Harry Pollitt, in London made this need explicit: 'Military experience is really essential and only a small proportion of those without should be allowed.'[47]

Many of the more middle-class volunteers had been in the Officer Training Corps at school and some, such as Sam Russell, chose to join whilst at university.[48] However, Ralph Bates argued that a year spent in the Officer Training School at public school or university was not sufficient experience and, with the exception of Bernard Knox and John Cornford, who distinguished themselves in the fighting in Madrid in the winter of 1936–1937, he did not seem to hold the student volunteers in high esteem.[49] A number of other volunteers had served in the Territorial Army, though not for 'conventional' reasons. As Phil Gillan, who fought in the battles for Madrid in late 1936, pointed out, 'Not out of patriotism, no way; it was the only way we could get a holiday.'[50]

Complaints about the poor quality of recruits resurfaced during the summer of 1937, following the heavy losses at Brunete. In a letter to Harry Pollitt in September 1937, Will Paynter complained that,

> Not only do we need and demand new forces but they must be better quality than the recent batches have been. I have reported to you the types that are finding their way out here. I may inform you that apprehension about this is not just confined to us. Some other people are expressing concern.[51]

Clearly, obtaining recruits with sufficient military experience was problematic for the recruiters in London. In the 600 or so records which list previous military experience,[52] over half claim to have none at all, suggesting that Bates's request was not an easy one for London to fulfil.[53] Furthermore, where volunteers had served in the forces, their experience was not necessarily relevant. Whilst ex-navy men such as Fred Copeman and Sam Wild could draw on their experiences, others could not. For example, George Brown asked Walter Greenhalgh, a fellow Mancunian he knew from the Young Communist League, to join up because Brown knew Greenhalgh had been in the Territorial Army. Unfortunately, though Greenhalgh did indeed possess experience of the Territorial Army, his time had been spent as a drummer. Thus the number of volunteers in the battalion with practical military experience was probably lower than it appears.

However, though militarily experienced volunteers were scarcer than the recruiters might have hoped for, there were undoubtedly many volunteers with extensive political experience and discipline. Most commentators describe the political background of the British volunteers for the International Brigades as overwhelmingly communist,[54] and there is no doubt that the British Battalion, like the International Brigades as a whole, owed a great deal to the work of the Communist Party. As one recruit admitted,

> The Communist Party have always played down their role in the Spanish Civil War. And I think I understand why. There are political reasons. But there was no doubt that the Communist Party was the driving force of the International Brigades.[55]

And, as can be seen from Table 1.1, of those for whom there is a record of political allegiance, clearly the majority were members of the Communist Party.[56] This agrees with Bill Alexander's estimate that over 60 per cent of International Brigaders were communists.[57] And whilst many volunteers did not list their political affiliation,[58] this does not necessarily mean that they were not communists, for it is clear that many communists listed their political affiliation as 'anti-fascist' on their International Brigade identity card, not wanting to be singled out if captured.[59] The International Brigade base at Albacete banned volunteers from carrying any

*Table 1.1* Political affiliation (where given)

| Political organisation | Number |
| --- | --- |
| Communist Party | 936 |
| Labour Party | 110 |
| Irish Republican Congress | 14 |
| Social Democratic Foundation | 1 |
| Young Communist League | 169 |
| Independent Labour Party | 15 |
| Socialist League | 6 |
| British Labour League of Youth | 5 |
| Irish Republican Army | 7 |
| Socialist Party of Great Britain | 1 |
| International Socialist Labour Party | 1 |
| None | 224 |

Sources: IBA Boxes 21, 21a, D-7 File A/2; and Moscow 545/6/89-94.

Note: if the Communist Party is combined with the Young Communist League, the total number is 1,107.

record of political affiliation for precisely this reason. As the Labour councillor Jack Jones observed, 'People didn't [flaunt] their membership of the Communist Party so much.'[60]

However, though the majority were clearly Communist Party members, this was by no means mandatory. Accounts from ex-brigaders such as Fred Copeman state that there was never as much pressure to join the Communist Party in the British Battalion as there was in others, such as the Yugoslavian Dimitrov Battalion.[61] As Albert Charlesworth, a volunteer from Oldham and a member of the Socialist League, not the Communist Party, described,

> This was never mentioned at any time. I mean, the Communist Party had nothing to do with it really, although the Communist Party sent me out. That was their role finished. I mean, we were anti-fascists out there. We weren't Labour Party members, we weren't communists or anything like that. We were anti-fascists and that was it.[62]

Thus there were many volunteers with other political affiliations. One hundred and ten British brigaders were recorded as members of the Labour Party (though several were also members of the Communist Party, such as Lewis Clive, a descendent of Clive of India, killed at Gandesa in Aragon in August 1938). That there are only seven members of the ILP listed as brigaders is, no doubt, due to the mutual mistrust between them and the communists. Most members of the ILP fought either with the Anarchist militias or with the Partido Obrero de Unificación Marxista (known as the POUM), such as George Orwell (fighting under his real name of Eric Blair), who was refused entry into the International Brigades for being 'politically suspect', and Bob Smillie, who died, probably of appendicitis, in a Republican jail in Valencia in June 1937.[63] Some of the volunteers declared themselves to have no political affiliation and a small number were relatively unpolitical, or uninterested, though those without strong political convictions appear to have served mainly with the various medical units. For example, Bruce Allender, who served as a first-aider with the International Brigade medical units in Spain, described himself as, 'vaguely liberal'.[64]

The large number of volunteers who were not Communist Party members is not particularly surprising. As Tom Buchanan suggests, the party was keen to recruit members of other political organisations because 'the party was confronted with the problem that, while its members were the best pool for recruits, as a small party it could not afford to squander its slender resources.'[65] There is little doubt that the party was also keen to involve those from other political organisations to justify their claim that this was a genuine popular front of volunteers fighting for Spanish democracy, 'the active representatives of the Peoples' Front of Europe',[66] rather than – as critics would have it – a feature of a communist plot to foment revolution in Spain.

In addition to military experience and political reliability, age was another criterion applied to applicants for the International Brigades. The aim of the recruiters was for volunteers to be between the ages of 25 and 35[67] and, from the 1,800 or so British volunteers in the sample who gave their ages, it would appear this aim was, in the main, achieved.[68] The average age of volunteers for the brigades was just over 29 years, though the most common age was 23, just outside the targeted age range for recruitment.[69] An overall picture of the ages of volunteers can be seen in Figure 1.2, which shows clearly that most recruits were between the ages of 21 and 35.[70] The ages of the British volunteers compared with those of the French and Americans may be seen in Table 1.2.[71]

This comparison suggests that the British were not as rigorous with their age limits as the French, for there are almost twice as many recruits below 21 and over 40; in both cases, however, four out of every ten recruits were over 30 years of age. There are few British recruits below the age of 21 years, and only a very small number under 18, for volunteers under the age of 18 were discouraged until February 1937, after which they were not accepted at all.[72] After this date those under 18 already in Spain were either sent home or, if they refused to leave, like a young volunteer from London, Charles Hutchinson, transferred to jobs away from the front line.[73] It should be noted that, as Tom Wintringham, the commander of the battalion at Jarama, suspected, a number of volunteers lied about their ages to avoid

*Table 1.2* Ages of volunteers by proportion

| Age | British (%) | French (%) | American (%) |
|---|---|---|---|
| Under 21 | 4.2 | 2.6 | 38.0 |
| 21–25 | 32.2 | 24.8 | |
| 26–30 | 23.6 | 32.6 | 26.0 |
| 31–35 | 20.4 | 21.9 | |
| 36–40 | 12.3 | 13.7 | 36.0 |
| Over 40 | 7.3 | 4.4 | |

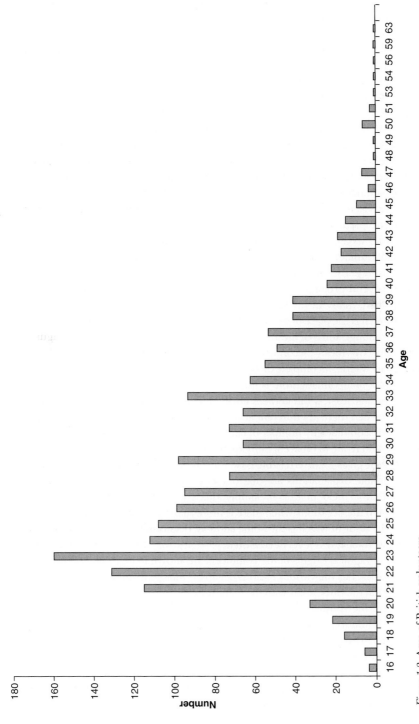

*Figure 1.2* Ages of British volunteers.

being sent home, so the ages of some volunteers may be unreliable.[74] Joseph May later admitted to be 63,[75] and both Thomas Patton[76] and John Longstaff,[77] who had claimed to be 19, were only 17.

Ethnic origin was explicitly not a concern of the recruiters for the British Battalion. As Bill Alexander stated, 'little attention was paid to religious or cultural background, and no one thought of keeping any record of Jewish volunteers.'[78] Nevertheless, Alexander still makes an estimation, based mainly on 'Jewish sounding names', that there were between 180 and 200 Jewish volunteers in the British Battalion.[79] This is considerably larger than an earlier estimate, which had suggested that only about 3 per cent of the British volunteers were Jewish.[80] In fact, it seems likely that both these estimates understate the number of Jewish volunteers in the battalion. Recent research suggests that the proportion was much higher, perhaps as much 20 per cent.[81] This should not really be regarded as surprising, for Jewish activists had been in the forefront of the opposition to Mosley and his Blackshirts, particularly in London and Manchester. Other religious origins are even harder to establish; at least 80 volunteers were Catholic (albeit lapsed) and a very small number stated their religion as Protestant.

Establishing the geographical origins of the roughly 2,500 volunteers also requires several problems to be overcome, again due mainly to the nature of the sources. First, many of the lists in the IBA do not always make clear whether the address given is the place of birth, the address of next of kin, or the volunteer's home address,[82] though some of the ambiguous addresses are clarified by details contained in the Moscow files.[83] Second, as one might expect, many of the entries in the archives are vague, incomplete or, sometimes, missing altogether.[84] For example, the address of a 'T. Connaughton' is listed as '? St. Helens' in one source,[85] though, in this instance at least, a full address appears in another.[86] Third, there are frequent occasions when there are different addresses for volunteers in different sources, for which there could be any number of explanations. It is theoretically possible that the records could relate to different individuals, but a combination of name, address and date of birth gives a fairly reliable base for linking records in a sample of this size. Other possible explanations are that one address could be the home address and another that of next of kin, or simply that the volunteer, or their family, had moved.[87] On the occasions when there is more than one address and it has been possible to establish which is the home address, details from one list have been given precedence to ensure a level of consistency.[88]

The geographical origins of the volunteers are shown in Figure 1.3, which, for the sake of clarity, has the various regions collapsed into geographical sectors. It should be noted that the three areas with the highest totals are all skewed by the inclusion of large cities: the south-east contains London, the largest city in the UK; Scotland contains Edinburgh and Glasgow; and the north-west includes Liverpool and Manchester. If the major conurbations were not included in the sector totals, the picture would look somewhat different, with Scotland as the largest sector with 259 volunteers,[89] nearly twice as many volunteers as the next largest area, the south-east. As Table 1.3 shows, the geographical origins of the British volunteers clearly display a strong urban trend.[90] Nearly half of the volunteers in this sample gave an address

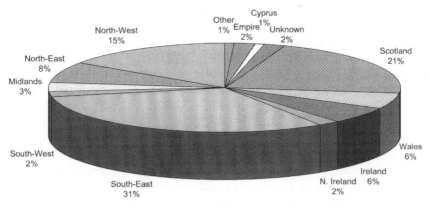

*Figure 1.3* Geographical origins of volunteers.

*Table 1.3* Numbers of volunteers giving an address in a major city

| City | Number |
| --- | --- |
| London | 520 |
| Manchester | 109 |
| Birmingham | 20 |
| Liverpool | 131 |
| Leeds | 21 |
| Newcastle | 21 |
| Edinburgh | 34 |
| Glasgow | 197 |

Source: based on data available in International Brigade archives in London and Moscow.

from the largest cities in Britain, with over 500 listing London. The number of volunteers giving their addresses as London is artificially inflated, however,[91] for many who gave a London address were from all over the British Isles and used a 'care-of' address such as the Communist Party offices.

Certain areas of Britain generated large numbers of volunteers, such as the north-east of England.[92] The ship-building areas of Tyneside and Teeside sent a large number, confirming the existence of a strong link between the shipping industry and the Communist Party.[93] Newcastle upon Tyne and Gateshead together sent more than 40 volunteers, with roughly the same number from South Shields, Sunderland and Middlesbrough combined.[94] There has as yet been no specific study of volunteers from the north-west of England, even though they numbered approximately 370. Two-thirds of the volunteers from the north-west came from the metropolitan centres of Manchester and Liverpool[95] and a number from other large towns such as Oldham.[96]

The contribution of Wales has been the subject of a number of academic studies. Such was the level of political ferment in South Wales in 1935 that one historian has drawn strong comparisons with the Asturian rising in Spain in 1934,[97] though it has also been pointed out that support for the Communist Party was concentrated in small localities and that, overall, South Wales remained overwhelmingly Labour.[98] Certainly, some areas were more militant than others; the Welsh mining district of the Rhondda had a fearsome reputation similar to that of the east end of London, and the other mining areas of Merthyr and Aberdare were also areas in which the Communist Party looked, and found, support.[99] Indeed, the Rhondda looked to be an area where the Communist Party might at last win a parliamentary seat, when A. L. Horner stood for Rhondda East in the by-election of March 1933 and gained 34 per cent of the vote.[100] That Harry Pollitt, the general secretary of the Communist Party, later chose to stand in Rhondda East in the 1935 election is clearly a testament to the radicalism of the Welsh mining region – a sentiment that ensured that more than 60 men from the Rhondda volunteered to fight with the International Brigades in Spain, more than a third of the total number of volunteers from Wales. Over 70 per cent of the Welsh volunteers came from the mining regions.[101]

Scotland as a whole sent over 500 volunteers to Spain,[102] of whom just under 50 per cent came from the two largest cities of Edinburgh and Glasgow. Dundee produced a particularly high number of volunteers, with almost twice as many as the capital,[103] and Kirkcaldy, a town lying on the north side of the Firth of Forth, also sent a number out of proportion to its size, for this was another area with strong communist sympathies. Willie Gallagher became the first communist MP in the election in 1935 following the Communist Party's adoption of Popular Frontism.[104] As in Wales, mining was an occupation on which the Communist Party could depend for support, and it is no coincidence that miners played a major role in the British Battalion in Spain.

Establishing the numbers of Irish volunteers is particularly difficult. Records in the IBA list only 75 volunteers from the Irish Free State within the British Battalion itself,[105] though a more reasonable estimate would be that Irish volunteers in the International Brigades numbered between 200 and 250, with a large proportion coming from the capital city of Dublin, in this case just under 25 per cent.[106] Around 60 came from Northern Ireland, with over two-thirds of this number coming from Belfast and all but a handful of the remainder coming from (London)Derry.[107] As with those from the rest of the United Kingdom, the picture is of recruits with overwhelmingly urban origins. Discrepancies in the varying estimates could be due to several factors. First, there was a tendency in official reports to play down the separate identity felt by the Irish. Instead, these portrayed the brigaders as a unified international working-class movement motivated almost exclusively by the desire to fight fascism, even though there was sufficiently strong feeling amongst some Irish volunteers in January 1937 to leave the British Battalion and fight with the Americans[108] in the Abraham Lincoln Battalion.[109] Many of the Irish volunteers had a history of (often armed) involvement in Irish Republicanism and were understandably less than happy fighting under English officers, particularly when it appeared that at least one, George Nathan, and possibly another, Wilf McCartney, had served with the notorious 'Black and Tans' in Ireland in actions against Irish Republicans.[110] Second, the names of the Irish who left to fight with the Abraham Lincoln Battalion do not always appear in the records kept by the British Battalion, which form the basis of the files in the IBA. Last, some Irish volunteers may have been born on the British mainland or elsewhere and not always listed themselves as Irish,[111] and, as has been shown, the widespread use of pseudonyms makes an analysis of this type extremely problematic.[112]

There were a number of volunteers in the British Battalion from outside the British Isles. There were a number of individuals who travelled from countries linked to Britain through the Empire and Commonwealth, including Cyprus, the Channel Islands, Canada, South Africa, India, Australia and New Zealand. More than 50 travelled from Australia and 12 from New Zealand[113] to fight with the British Battalion or serve in the medical services.[114]

As I have shown, the geographical origins of the volunteers were mainly urban and often associated with occupations such as mining and shipbuilding. Table 1.4 shows the 20 most frequent occupations drawn from the nearly 1,300 volunteers who have listed their employment.[115] As can be seen, there were a number who had been employed as clerks, salesmen and electricians and in other non-manual occupations, but, overall, the occupations are manual working class. The high number of miners confirms their reputation for being highly politicised, mirroring their Spanish brethren. After all, in the Asturias rising of October 1934, miners played a central role and bore the brunt of the repression that was imposed by the Foreign Legion and Moorish *regulares* led by General Franco, which, no doubt, helped fuel solidarity amongst the British miners who joined the Republican forces in such large numbers. Other popular occupations of British International Brigaders were labourers, drivers, seamen, painters, bricklayers, carpenters and steelworkers. The

*Table 1.4* The most commonly listed occupations

| Occupation | Number |
| --- | --- |
| Labourer | 149 |
| Miner | 92 |
| Motor driver | 60 |
| Seaman | 47 |
| Clerk | 37 |
| Painter | 28 |
| Engineer | 28 |
| Metal worker | 22 |
| Salesman | 21 |
| Mechanic | 21 |
| Bricklayer | 19 |
| Journalist | 16 |
| Student | 15 |
| Tailor | 14 |
| Electrician | 14 |
| Carpenter | 12 |
| Nurse | 11 |
| Ex-Army | 11 |
| Cook | 10 |
| Printer | 10 |

large number of volunteers from the maritime trades is due partly to their politicisation; like mining, shipbuilding was an industry on which the Communist Party could consistently rely for support.[116] Also, of course, sailors would have been able to work their passage on a ship bound for Spain, then jump ship in a port such as Valencia or Barcelona – at least until Franco's illegal naval blockade around Spain was accepted by the British navy, after which this became considerably more difficult.

A summary of the occupational makeup of the volunteers as a whole is shown in Figure 1.4, which classifies the occupations into their various sectors. The picture of the different sectors shows clearly the industrial working-class occupational profile of recruits. As Figure 1.4 shows, the four largest are manufacturing, transport, trades and mining, which, when combined, make up just over 80 per cent of the total number of recruits for whom there is occupational data available. As Table 1.5 shows, this picture is supported by a profile of trade union membership. With the possible exception of the Shop Assistants' Union, all of the ten trade unions with the largest numbers of members are also connected with manual occupations. Of the 500 volunteers who declared trade union membership, over half belonged to the five largest unions and well over a third to the top three. The large number of Welsh miners is again apparent in the 43 members of the South Wales Miners' Federation.

It is clear, then, that there is a distinct picture that can be drawn of the 'typical' British volunteer for the Republic in the Spanish Civil War. In the main, this picture conforms to that drawn in previous works, though there are some important revisions to be made. In Hugh Thomas's work on the Spanish Civil War, he states that most of the recruits were young, over 80 per cent were working class, many were unemployed and over 60 per cent were communists.[117] The above findings support his estimates of class background, though the average age of volunteers is slightly higher than Thomas estimated. The picture is clearly not one of 'young, naive and idealistic' volunteers, for well over a quarter of the total number of volunteers (where a date of birth has been given) were over the age of 30. Like many of the names given, not all the ages were necessarily truthful; however, it does

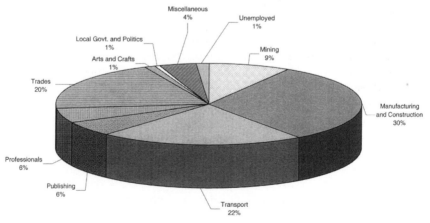

*Figure 1.4* Numbers of volunteers per occupational sector.

*Table 1.5* Trade union membership

| Trade union | Number |
| --- | --- |
| Transport and General Workers' Union | 122 |
| National Union of Seamen | 50 |
| South Wales Miners' Federation | 43 |
| Amalgamated Engineers' Union | 39 |
| National Union of Distributors and Allied Workers | 14 |
| National Union of Glass Metal Workers | 13 |
| Shop Assistants' Union | 13 |
| Electrical Trades Union | 11 |
| Amalgamated Union of Building Trade Workers | 11 |
| Amalgamated Society of Workers | 10 |

appear that there was a higher proportion of mature recruits than previously believed. The level of Communist Party membership – 62 per cent – is similar to Thomas's estimate. Both John Angus and Bill Alexander have remarked that there was no pressure to be a member of the Communist Party to join the brigades, though anecdotal evidence suggests that many did join whilst they were in Spain.[118]

Bill Alexander, who fought with the brigades as political commissar and later as the commander of the British Battalion, is rather critical of some of Thomas's views regarding volunteers for the British Battalion.[119] However, whilst he does agree that many of the volunteers had experienced unemployment, he also argues that it is impossible to determine any precise level of unemployment as the Communist Party kept no details. This claim is rather countered by questionnaires held in the Moscow archives which ask for these particulars; nevertheless it is true that the sources do not really shed much new light on the number of unemployed recruits. Only a small number of brigaders listed themselves as unemployed, but this is bound to be an underestimate. Unemployment can often carry a social stigma, even, perhaps, amongst communists critical of the role of capitalism in the economic depression and mass unemployment in the 1930s. This problem is a familiar one to historians, where trying to establish the numbers employed within so-called low status occupations is notoriously difficult. Many volunteers, rather than declaring themselves to be unemployed, may have given their last occupation, or listed work they had previously taken. Thus John Williams from South Wales described himself as an 'ex-miner', and many other volunteers either gave multiple occupations or, like Herbert Sines from London, listed their employment as 'various'.[120] However, the number of unemployed is clearly not as high as some estimates would suggest, a fact pointed out at the time by Tom Wintringham, one of the earliest British volunteers to arrive in Spain, and a commander of the British Battalion in 1937.

> I have been assured, by the brother of a minister of the National Government, that 'all except about twenty were unemployed before they went to Spain' . . . The proportion of unemployed in our ranks when I knew the battalion varied between a quarter and an eighth, which is not so very much greater a

proportion than that 'normal' in England thanks to the wisdom of those that rule us.[121]

The level of trade union membership supports Bill Alexander's remark that '[a] high rate of trade-union membership was not untypical.'[122] This presents a clear contrast with the ambivalence towards the Republic shown by the leaders of the British labour movement such as Ernest Bevin, who were driven by a desire to 'preserve the unity of the British labour movement and by a chauvinist hostility towards its Spanish counterpart'.[123] Like the British government, their views were always coloured by a deep fear and loathing of communism.

The significant level of Communist Party membership is important, for it helps provide some understanding of why nearly 2,500 British volunteered to fight with the Spanish Republican forces. However, only a small proportion of the total membership of the CPGB fought in Spain and, as we have seen, a number of the volunteers were not communists, or waited until they arrived in Spain before joining. So, clearly some questions remain unanswered by a quantitative analysis of the socio-political background of the volunteers. What drove these individuals to travel hundreds of miles to fight in a foreign country 'of which they knew little'? Were they the same reasons that encouraged people to join radical political organisations such as the CPGB or the ILP? The next chapter examines closely the motivations of the volunteers for the Spanish Republic in order to come up with some answers to these questions.

# 2   Why did they go?

The chance to strike back at fascism.[1]

The very air we were breathing was different then.[2]

No study of the British volunteers for the Spanish Republic would be complete without attempting to explain why nearly 2,500 men and women left their homes and families in Britain to volunteer to fight in a war in 'a far away country'. This issue seems to be particularly baffling to contemporary students, who find it difficult to understand why anyone – particularly anyone to whom foreign travel would have been considered extraordinary – would undertake a hazardous journey across Europe and an exhausting climb over the Pyrenees, all to risk death fighting in a foreign civil war. To a great extent, this puzzlement is founded on a contemporary belief that there is no longer 'a great cause' worth fighting for, a view perhaps fostered by the difficulty many have found establishing 'good from evil' in bitter European conflicts, such as the civil war in Bosnia. The view of the Spanish war as one between two equally abhorrent factions was widely prevalent amongst those elements of the British establishment who were not actively hostile to the Spanish Republic.[3] The remark attributed to Stanley Baldwin, the British prime minister at the outbreak of the war, is somewhat revealing: 'We English hate fascism, but we loathe bolshevism as much. So, if there is somewhere where fascists and bolsheviks can kill each other off, so much the better.'[4] The alien nature of the conflict, and a desire to 'keep out of it' and limit the war to Spain, lay behind support for the policy of non-intervention in the war, or so the somewhat charitable interpretation would have it. In fact, as many commentators have demonstrated, certain parts of the British government, much of the British establishment, and the higher echelons of the labour movement were all driven by a fear and loathing of communism, which meant that the Republic was actively discriminated against.[5] As E. H. Carr points out, 'the non-intervention declaration was tainted with hypocrisy from the outset.'[6] The complaint that 'the treacherous non-intervention pact'[7] ensured that the rebels were better armed was a constant refrain amongst the British volunteers in Spain.[8] As Jack Jones pointed out,

Since the Governments of the world, Governments like Britain and France were not prepared to go to their aid and were standing on the side-lines, many of us felt that it was right to give whatever help we could in supporting them.[9]

Roderick MacFarquar, who served as an ambulance driver and first-aider in Spain from January 1937 to October 1938, went further and argued that 'the so-called Non-intervention agreement organised by Chamberlain and Eden throttled the Republic.'[10] This throttling of the Republic spurred many to volunteer, such as Louis Hearst, who arrived from London in September 1936, soon after the implementation of the agreement.

When England took the reins of 'Non-intervention' I could hold back no longer. I put everything else aside, and decided that I could not identify myself even passively (being a Socialist both by personal conviction and by family tradition) with this political farce; I decided to go to Spain to defend democracy with deeds.[11]

For many observers the Spanish struggle was seen in a wider European context. For those supporting the rebels, the war was a crusade against communism, which many on the right believed had been fermenting a revolution that had been pre-empted by the rising.[12] For those who were 'neutral' or considered the war of little relevance to British interests, it was important to limit the struggle between the two alien philosophies of fascism and communism to Spain and prevent the conflagration spreading. And for those supporting the Republic, the war was seen within the wider context of the struggle of democracy against international fascism, which had been taking place across Europe from Germany to London's east end. In the words of one British volunteer, they were volunteering to help defend 'a duly and properly elected government, it wasn't even a socialist government, more like a Labour one',[13] from the foreign aggression of international fascism. Thus, as we shall see, many volunteers believed passionately that the Spanish Republic's fight was their fight.

If the war in Spain was not a 'foreign' war to the volunteers, neither was the idea of volunteering for a war in 'a far away country' a new one. As other works on British involvement in the Spanish Civil War have recognised, there was a tradition of 'volunteering for liberty' stretching back to the poet Lord Byron.[14] 'There had, indeed, been a romantic and libertarian British tradition of volunteering in the nineteenth century which had made going to fight in other people's wars a right – even a duty – of free-born Britons.'[15] Indeed, Lord Byron is cited in a memorial pamphlet to the British volunteers that was issued after the war:

Out of the proud traditions of Britain's past they came. Part of the long struggle for freedom, carried forward from Wat Tyler through men like Byron and movements like the Chartists, through Keir Hardie to the present day. Our modern bearers of Britain's great traditions came forward in answer to the call, ready to give their lives that freedom might live.[16]

To many, this 'Byronesque' and heroic image of the volunteers is epitomised by a picture of the poet John Cornford, his head sheathed in a white bandage: the young brave intellectual dying for liberty.[17] But, as the previous chapter has shown, this image is not, and never has been, typical of British volunteers for the International Brigades. In the wealth of memoirs and oral accounts, references to this 'great historical tradition' do not appear very frequently, if at all. This does not mean that the volunteers were not following in the steps of Wat Tyler, Byron and the Chartists, but that this tradition was not a conscious factor in the motives of most of the British volunteers for joining the International Brigades. In fact, there are several inaccuracies, myths and generalisations that surround explanations for the motivations of the men who fought in the International Brigades in Spain. These take three main forms: that the volunteers were adventurers; that they were either paid mercenaries or tricked into volunteering; and that most of them were unemployed (the implication being that they only volunteered out of a desperate wish to get 'off the dole').

The belief that many volunteers joined the International Brigades more for adventure than for conviction reappeared recently. It was claimed that 'Undoubtedly a group of men, often unemployed, volunteered because they sought adventure and may have been misled about what they were letting themselves in for.'[18] Bill Rust, in his deeply sympathetic account of the British volunteers, perhaps contributed, no doubt accidentally, towards the portrayal of them as adventurers: 'A spirit of adventure? Yes, and may our youth never lose that spirit.'[19] The impression of the volunteers as adventurers might also be gained from Hugh Thomas's study of the civil war. This quotes Nick Gillain, a Belgian, who gave his reason for joining as: 'spirit of adventure, lassitude, and this rainy Autumn of 1936'.[20]

Understandably, few volunteers accept this view, and many are at pains to point out that they themselves certainly were not adventurers.[21] Tom Wintringham, commander of the British Battalion at Jarama, who had a large involvement in the formation of the British Battalion, was quick to stand up for one of his British comrades, George Nathan, when the latter was accused of being an adventurer:

> It was not so much his political views that had brought him to Spain as a certain alertness, an aliveness that could not be crushed out by the Labour Exchange and the hopeless monotony of odd jobs. An adventurer? No: he was not 'on the make.'[22]

Though Tom Buchanan may be right to argue that adventure may have played a part in motivating a small number of the volunteers, there seems little evidence to suggest it was a major factor, and it was certainly not representative of the majority. Indeed, one of the few to admit he volunteered for adventure and gain was singularly disappointed as Jimmy Jump, a volunteer from Cheshire, who served as an interpreter, paymaster, clerk and machine-gunner with the Machine-Gun Company during his time in Spain remembers:

> I met a number of people, like the Blackburn waiter, whose political awareness

was nil at the time of going. I remember another man, John Smith . . . he was a Glasgow shipyard worker I think, and he told me that he went to Spain for three things: 'Loot, women and wine.' And then he added, with a touch of sadness in his voice, 'And I've never come across much of any of them.'[23]

The second accusation, that the British volunteers were duped or 'hoodwinked' by communist recruiters into joining the International Brigades should be given little credence.[24] The claim first appeared in the right-wing press, particularly the *Daily Mail* and *Morning Post*,[25] which carried numerous unfounded stories about the Spanish Republic and its supporters.[26] This accusation in particular has infuriated British members of the International Brigade. Bill Alexander argued vehemently that 'there is not a scrap of evidence that anyone went to Spain without being told that they were going to fight as a soldier.'[27] And, in James Hopkins's study of the British volunteers, Alexander's claim is supported:

> It was a choice freely made, based on their experience of life, their reading of books and newspapers, and the kind of open exchange of ideas that they had known on street corners, in great public places, and in their educational classes.[28]

In fact, volunteers were fully informed of the seriousness of the situation into which they were placing themselves. Several opportunities were offered to them to change their minds, not just in London, but also in Paris and in Spain itself. John Longstaff, a runner with the British Battalion, describes in detail the lecture he was given by 'Robbie' when, in August 1937, he volunteered to join the International Brigades:

> They told me that if I went out there, that if I got killed there'd be no pension for my family. That was the first thing. They told me that if I got badly wounded and lost a limb or became blind or something, that again there'd be no pension. And neither could they, who'd be agreeing that I could go out, be able to pay me any pension, they had no money.
>   They told me that the food I'd be eating would be Spanish food and I might not like it but you can't eat any more because that was the only food that they can provide. They told me that the clothing I'd be wearing would be poor quality clothing. They told me that I wouldn't be issued with boots, that I'd have to wear an item called alpagartas which is a straw based sandal. They told me that my rate of pay would be the rate of pay of the Spanish Army which if I think correctly, was round about five pesetas a day which worked out about three halfpence for each peseta, something of that nature.
>   They told me that if I went into hospital, that I might not have the drugs necessary to get me better from suffering from an illness. And that if I lost a limb – they came back to these points time and time again – so I was under no illusion as to what it meant. They told me that I would be joining the British Battalion of the International Brigade, they told me that I would not get leave until the war was over unless I was so disabled I was of no further use to the peoples of Spain.[29]

On arrival in Paris, many volunteers were advised that, if they wished to change their minds and return to Britain, it was still possible for them to do so.[30] Jimmy Jump recounts how:

> We were given a medical examination and we were given a final opportunity to change our minds if we wanted to, they said, 'If you want to change your minds do so now, they'll give you a ticket back and that will be the end of it.' But none of my group did.[31]

Jan Kurzke, a German volunteer who fought in the British section of the Commune de Paris Battalion in Madrid in 1936, remembers clearly one of André Marty's subordinates at the brigade base in Albacete briefing the volunteers on the war, and what was expected of them, before advising them that they were not yet in the Spanish Army and that any who wished to change their minds would be returned to France.[32] Perhaps as many as 80 volunteers[33] who left London for Spain either changed their minds, or were refused admission into the brigades on their arrival in Spain on medical or age grounds, or because their behaviour (usually drunkenness) on the journey to Spain had suggested that they might be trouble-makers.[34] Chris Smith from Glasgow, who volunteered in the spring of 1937, was at first refused by Peter Kerrigan, an experienced Communist Party member who had attended the Seventh World Congress of the Comintern in 1935 and later became the base commissar at the International Brigade headquarters in Albacete. Kerrigan didn't believe Smith understood the seriousness of the situation in Spain and told him to come back in two weeks if he was determined to volunteer, and if not, 'I'll forget all about it.' In the event, Chris Smith did return, and served in the Anti-Tank Battery in Spain from May 1937 until he was repatriated in October 1938.[35] Whilst Fred Copeman, one of the commanders of the battalion in Spain during 1937, hinted that young single members of the Communist Party were encouraged to volunteer, he states categorically that, 'They really honestly didn't just pick up people. In any case I wouldn't have taken them out.'[36]

Although it may be true that not all the volunteers had as detailed an understanding of the full horrors of warfare as Edwin Greening, a canvasser from Wales who had read widely on warfare before he volunteered,[37] the portrayal of the volunteers as dupes or, in the words of a senior member of the British Foreign Office staff in Spain, as 'misguided stiffs'[38] is clearly not accurate. Hugh MacKay, a Scot who is unusual in that he admits volunteering on the spur of the moment, is, nevertheless, determined to demonstrate that there was no element of coercion.

> Oh, I just decided to go to Spain, spontaneously I suppose. No hassle. I didn't even think about what I could do or what I shouldn't do, I just decided to go to Spain, and that was it . . . Anyone begging me to go or influencing me in any way? No, no. I went of my own accord.[39]

That the volunteers were paid mercenaries, seduced off their life on the dole – another accusation to appear regularly in the *Daily Mail*[40] – is also somewhat implausible. As Tom Buchanan points out, 'pay was minimal and erratic' in the International Brigades and rather unlikely to have been sufficient to tempt men into risking their lives.[41] Any volunteers who were thus tempted would have been sorely disappointed, for, where they were paid at all, International Brigaders were not always paid as much as Spaniards; in February 1938 the payment for a Spanish soldier in the 15th International Brigade was 100 pesetas, whilst that of an International was 70 pesetas.[42] An interesting twist on the 'financial incentive' accusation appeared in an anonymous contemporary account penned by a disillusioned ex-member of the British Battalion. He asked: 'How widely is it known that the local branches of the Communist Party were receiving a bonus for every recruit they sent out to the International Brigades?'[43] Whilst the author may have been a member of the British Battalion (and by his own admission was hardly an exemplary recruit), there is no evidence to support this accusation. That this account was published by Burns, Oates and Washborne, whose other titles on the civil war are all extremely pro-Nationalist, does not add any reason to trust the anonymous author's objectivity. Certainly, the volunteers resent this accusation deeply and are vociferous in their denials.[44]

The last of the accusations, that a number of the recruits were or had recently been unemployed, appears, on first sight, to be not unreasonable. However, the implicit suggestion here is that, as they were unemployed, there was little for them in Britain, making the offer of paid service in the Spanish Republican Army an attractive proposition. When Tom Buchanan recently outlined what he considered to be a motive for volunteering, he remarked how one recruit had stated that he wanted 'to get the hell out of the dole',[45] and this interpretation resurfaced in Ken Loach's film *Land and Freedom*. However, though it is clear that many volunteers, such as Tommy Kerr from Aidrie,[46] had been through or were experiencing unemployment, the evidence suggests that most were not unemployed. K. W. Watkins's assertion that 'somewhere between an eighth and a quarter were unemployed, the rest relinquished their jobs, often secure ones, in order to go'[47] is supported by several other studies.[48]

In fact, though there are several generalisations that may be drawn,[49] the reasons lying behind the decisions to volunteer for Spain are as wide and as diverse as the volunteers themselves. And indeed, as one volunteer noted, individuals often had many reasons for electing to fight in Spain.[50] Miles Tomalin, who served with the Anti-Tank Battery in Spain between May 1937 and December 1938, pointed out that 'undoubtedly the great majority are here for an ideal, no matter what motive prompted them to seek one.'[51]

What becomes clear from interviews with volunteers is that, as Tom Buchanan noted, 'It is easier to define what the volunteers were fighting against than what they were fighting for.'[52] The constantly recurring theme in their interviews and memoirs is that most felt that they were fighting not so much for something they all believed in, but against something to which they were all opposed: the spread of fascism. Thus, the supporters of the Republic, like those of the rebels, saw the war as a struggle for national liberty.[53] As Jud Colman, one of many Jewish volunteers from

Manchester, explained, 'The first thing was to defeat Franco, to defeat the fascists'.[54] Bill Alexander, in what might be seen as the 'official' history of the battalion, not surprisingly stresses this rather pointedly:

> The dynamic force which drove volunteers from Britain to Spain and welded them into an effective fighting unit was a deep hatred of fascism . . . The British volunteers went to Spain because they understood that fascism must be checked before it brought wider repression and war.[55]

When Esmond Romilly, nephew of Winston Churchill and author of one of the best memoirs of the British volunteers, was asked, 'Why have you come to Spain?', he knew it was a simple question to answer. 'This was an easy one, the poster on the barracks wall proclaimed the answer: "To smash fascism."'[56] However, this explanation is rather simplistic and begs many questions. As Romilly stated, 'I am assuming it will be taken for granted that everybody who joined the International Brigade had "political convictions"; but these were not necessarily the only reasons why they joined.'[57]

The statement raises the issue of the volunteers' perceptions of the war in Spain. After all, though Franco may have draped himself in fascist ideological window dressing when it suited him, this was more to outmanoeuvre any rivals in the Nationalist camp than a result of any ideological leaning. But, to the British volunteers for the International Brigades, Franco was backed by the fascist powers of Italy and Germany and was thus clearly a fascist, at least by association.[58] Thus the volunteers saw this not as a civil war within Spain, but as one more episode in the European war against fascist aggression, 'a world war in embryo', in the words of the liberal newspaper the *News Chronicle*.[59] And to many of the British volunteers this was the latest episode in an international struggle in which many of them had already participated at home.[60]

In Britain the battle was with Oswald Mosley and his supporters in the British Union of Fascists (BUF), who had been combated with some degree of success. Several volunteers witnessed how grass-roots protests had made many areas of the country no-go areas for the Blackshirts, and the size of the demonstration in Cable Street in London in October 1936 had sent a clear message. And whilst Mosley and his Blackshirts may have been seen as the British representation of this European fascist phenomenon, by 1936 they were no longer a powerful political movement in Britain, more 'an irritant than a threat'. From a membership of around 50,000 in 1934, the BUF had slumped to around 5,000 in 1935. Even though, after 1935, numbers were increasing, back up to 10,000 by March 1936, the BUF only ever 'challenged, not threatened the British body politic'.[61] But the volunteers from Britain did not see it in these terms, as Bill Alexander explains:

> It was not only from abroad that the menace came. Oswald Mosley was actively trying to build a fascist movement in Britain, and sent disciplined, uniformed groups of Blackshirts to beat up Jewish people in London's East End. British

fascists also attacked unemployed workers in Merthyr Tydfil, Aberdeen and elsewhere; any hecklers or interrupters at Mosley's rallies were treated with extreme brutality. It was clear that British fascism had the same ugly face as its German counterpart.[62]

The views expressed by Sam Wild, leader of the British Battalion during the latter part of 1938, are typical of many of the volunteers:

> Well, to me it was elementary. Here was fascism spreading all over the world, the rape of Abyssinia, the rise of fascism in Germany and the persecution of the Jews there, and the rise of the Blackshirts in Britain with their anti-Semitism, and especially their anti-Irishism. I felt that somebody had to do something to try and stop it.[63]

Wild makes no distinction between fascism in Germany, Italy, Britain or, crucially, Spain; indeed, it is clearly perceived as various manifestations of the same evil. Italy, Germany, Portugal, Austria and now Spain were all 'going fascist'. As the Labour councillor (and later general secretary of the Transport and General Workers' Union) Jack Jones, who served in Spain between March and August 1938, explained:

> The awful realisation that black fascism was on the march right across Europe created a strong desire to act. The march had started with Mussolini and had gained terrible momentum with Hitler and was being carried forward by Franco. For most young people there was a feeling of frustration, but some determined to do anything that seemed possible, even if it meant death, to try to stop the spread of fascism . . . This was Fascist progression. It was real and it had to be stopped.[64]

And drawing parallels between the regimes was perhaps not that unreasonable; fascism is, after all, a somewhat fluid ideology.[65] As an article in *The Times* remarked in 1936, '"Fascism" is a very comprehensive term nowadays.'[66] The rapid and determined support for the Spanish rebels by Germany and Italy provided convincing evidence for a connection between the regimes. And parallels could also be drawn between continental and British fascism: David Goodman, a volunteer from Middlesbrough, cites the anti-Semitism of Hitler in Germany, and of the BUF in Britain, as a major factor in his decision to volunteer:

> Influences during that period were the rise of Hitler and the threat of fascist aggression spreading around the world in the 1930s. There was the humiliation and degradation of the Jewish communities and the confiscation of their property, so you had this feeling of kinship with the victims of Hitler in Germany. Then, over the years, there was the external aggression of the Nazi regime when Hitlerism was able to extend those same policies to other territories and new Jewish communities were the victims.[67]

Charles Hutchinson, a lorry driver from London, felt with the Jewish volunteers that fascism was a very real threat to his existence, beyond any theoretical abstraction. As he later stated, 'I am half black. I grew up in the National Children's Home and Orphanage. Fascism meant hunger and war.'[68]

For these volunteers, this was a struggle that went beyond national boundaries, a perspective expressed lucidly by the sculptor Jason Gurney, from London:

> The Spanish Civil War seemed to provide the chance for a single individual to take a positive and effective stand on an issue which appeared to be absolutely clear. Either you were opposed to the growth of Fascism and you went out to fight it, or you acquiesced in its crimes and were guilty of permitting its growth ... for myself and many others like me it was a war of principle, and principles do not have a national boundary.[69]

And in Spain, for the first time in continental Europe, the 'fascists' were not having it all their own way. At the outset of the war the two sides were relatively balanced and there seemed a genuine chance that, at last, the hitherto seemingly irrevocable advance of fascism might be held back.[70] To political exiles from countries such as Italy and Germany this, of course, was the moment they had been waiting for – their chance to strike back against the cause of their exile. But the British were hardly political exiles, even if many had been jailed for subversion or anti-fascist activities.[71]

Many of the British volunteers for Spain had been involved in fighting the BUF at their meetings, such as Olympia in 1934 and Victoria Park in Hackney in July 1936, and at the biggest and most infamous of all confrontations in Cable Street in the Jewish neighbourhood of London's east end in October 1936. As Noreen Branson has shown, these were important moments in the growing realization that direct action against Mosley's Blackshirts was a highly effective strategy. It was also realised that it was a strategy the official labour movement was not prepared to countenance.

> To some on the left, the lessons were clear. So long as there was no opposition, Mosley's movement went from strength to strength. In contrast, the challenge at Olympia, though it had involved relatively small numbers, had achieved an important result. It had led the BUF to reveal itself in its true colours. It had brought home the ugly truth about fascism to many who had hitherto been barely conscious of the menace.[72]

Wally Togwell, a waiter from St Pancras, is a typical example of this type of seasoned anti-fascist campaigner:

> Wherever the fascists were, our group of the YCL was there also. I was thrown out of the Albert Hall, I took part in anti-Mosley demos at Olympia and Hyde Park, I was at Cable Street helping to erect barricades.[73]

Joseph Garber, a cabinet-maker's apprentice from Bethnal Green in London, had been an anti-fascist activist with the Young Communist League (YCL) and had been involved in clashes with Blackshirts at Olympia. He felt that his involvement in fighting against fascism in Britain was a major factor in his volunteering for Spain: 'I decided to go to Spain especially after the Cable Street battles when we stopped the Blackshirts getting through.'[74]

Charles Goodman, a Communist Party member from Whitechapel, had also been involved in anti-fascist activities. He had been a part of all the major demonstrations against Mosley in London – at both Olympia and the Albert Hall, in the St George's area of East London, and in Cable Street.[75] And one of the well-known intellectual volunteers, the poet and writer Christopher St John Sprigg (also known as Christopher Caudwell), was arrested along with seven others on 7 June 1936 for protesting against Mosley in Victoria Park in London.[76] Bob Cooney, an office-worker from Aberdeen who later gained the reputation as probably the best political commissar in the British Battalion in Spain,[77] had a long history of anti-fascist activity: 'I felt we had to smash them off the streets', he remarked later.[78]

The view was widely held that elements of the British establishment, particularly the police, did not treat anti-fascists as leniently as Mosley's Blackshirts.[79] So whilst the volunteers were not political exiles as such, the communist volunteers in particular had more in common with anti-fascists from other European countries than with British mainstream political culture. Volunteering to fight in Spain was a natural extension of the struggle against Mosley and what were believed to be his powerful backers. Just as the opposition to Mosley and his supporters was against the British exponent of international fascism, so the fight against Franco's forces was the Spanish equivalent. Thus to the British who volunteered for the war in Spain, and indeed to many foreign observers, the conflict was seen not so much as a domestic war between Spanish Republicans and Nationalists, but as part of the international struggle between fascism and communism. Walter Gregory, who arrived in Spain in December 1936, is typical when he states that, 'although the war was fought exclusively on Spanish soil, I never saw it as a domestic conflict.'[80]

As A. J. P. Taylor shrewdly observed, 'What men believed at the time was more important than what was actually happening.'[81] Those explaining their motives for volunteering for the war in Spain were much more likely to state that they were opposing Hitler and fascism than defending the Spanish Republic against Franco, though this is not to say that they would have disagreed with this interpretation. Time and time again the refrain 'We went to Spain so that we could defeat Hitler'[82] is repeated in interviews with volunteers. John Henderson, a woodworker from Gateshead who arrived in Spain in early 1937, puts across this view of Spain as a country under an invasion from Mussolini and Hitler very cogently:

> When the Spanish war got under way, the issues were perfectly clear to me. Franco was being used by Hitler to form part of an international fascist conquest and unless this was stopped there'd eventually be another world war. This was quite apart from the domestic issue of here was an army general who'd attacked a duly and properly elected government.[83]

Some of the volunteers saw Franco as no more than a puppet whose masters were Mussolini and Hitler, whilst others saw him as the Spanish equivalent. This perception of the internationalism rather than the nationalism of Franco's movement was what the volunteers constantly remarked upon, just as supporters for the rebels accused the Republicans of being pawns of Moscow.

For the British volunteers, perceptions of the war in Spain came via two main channels. For those who were members of political organisations such as the Communist Party or the Labour Party (at least the grass-roots members), or involved in trade union activities, there was regular contact with the multifarious aid-Spain organisations.[84] As Tom Buchanan states, 'It was through campaigns of this nature that British people came most directly into contact with the conflict.'[85] Meetings were often addressed by ex-members of the British Battalion who had either been repatriated following injury or extended service or, in some cases, sent back to Britain especially for this task.[86]

But for those not actively involved in the 'aid-Spain movement'[87] the most influential source of information was likely to be the British national press.[88] There was a larger number of national newspapers published in the 1930s than there is today, and there was, likewise, a considerably larger readership. Only three national British newspapers' coverage of the civil war was strongly pro-Republican – the *News Chronicle*, the *Daily Herald* and the *Daily Worker* – though the *Manchester Guardian*, whose influence rather belied its small regional circulation, was also pro-loyalist. The coverage of the Spanish Civil War in the British press has come under considerable, and justifiable, criticism for the extent of its flagrant bias.[89] George Orwell's oft-quoted remark is perhaps the most well known:

> No event is ever correctly reported in a newspaper, but in Spain, for the first time, I saw newspaper reports which did not bear any relation to the facts, not even the relationship which is implied in an ordinary lie.[90]

His criticism could be applied to a number of newspapers, both Nationalist and Republican in sympathy.[91]

The *Daily Herald* was the national newspaper of the trade union and labour movement and acted as their official voice, with around 2,000,000 sales every day. Though pro-Republican, the *Daily Herald* supported the government's policy of non-intervention in the war and closely followed what one commentator has described as a media consensus, that Britain should 'keep out of it'.[92] Thus it came in for bitter criticism from the Communist *Daily Worker*, and the paper's influence on the volunteers must be seen, therefore, as negligible. Likewise, the *Manchester Guardian*, though clearly pro-Republican, was more politically independent than many of its rivals, and its reporting of the conflict was much more measured than that of the *News Chronicle* or the *Daily Worker*.[93]

The *News Chronicle* was the best selling liberal newspaper in Britain,[94] and the paper remained determinedly pro-Republican throughout the war.[95] *News Chronicle* correspondents in Spain included Arthur Koestler and John Langdon-Davies, both members of the Communist Party who penned avidly pro-Republican books on

*Table 2.1* British pro-Republican national daily newspaper circulation figures, 1936–1939

|                    | 1936      | 1937      | 1938      | 1939      |
|--------------------|-----------|-----------|-----------|-----------|
| Daily Herald       | 2,000,000 | 2,000,000 | 2,000,000 | 2,000,000 |
| Daily Worker       | n/a       | 60,000    | n/a       | n/a       |
| News Chronicle     | 1,360,000 | 1,324,000 | 1,273,436 | 1,298,757 |
| Manchester Guardian| n/a       | 50,000    | n/a       | n/a       |

Sources: *The Newspaper Press Directory* (London: Mitchell, 1936), pp. 312–313; (1937), pp. 313–314; Curtis, *The Press*, pp. 56–67; *Audit Bureau of Circulations*, vol. 6, April 1937, vol. 7, September 1937, vol. 9, November 1937, vol. 10, March 1938, vol. 11, September 1938; Gannon, *The British Press and Germany 1936–1939*, pp. 34–74.

their experiences in Spain.[96] The *News Chronicle* repeatedly stressed the importance of the international context of the war of Spain[97] and that Britain would soon be fighting the fascists itself.[98] The paper always gave the International Brigades extremely positive coverage, and its reporting of meetings in aid of Spain played a significant part in the decision of Leslie Preger, another of the large number from Manchester to volunteer:

> I saw an account in the *News Chronicle* of a trade union meeting which set up a Medical Aid Committee and appealed for lorry drivers and Spanish speaking people. So I hared off to London to volunteer and I was accepted.[99]

Other volunteers, such as Dougal Eggar, an ex-metropolitan policeman from London, also cite the *News Chronicle*'s reporting as influential.[100] The newspaper's argument that 'On it [the International Brigade] hangs the fate of democracy in Spain and, it may be, of Europe' was one that would be repeated by many of those who volunteered to fight to defend the Spanish Republic, and its statement that, 'If they [the Spanish Republic] should fail, not they alone, but all of us would be the losers'[101] could have come from one of the volunteers themselves.

The *Daily Worker*, Britain's Communist daily newspaper, was aimed squarely at members, and potential members, of the British Communist Party. The *Daily Worker*'s role in disseminating the Communist Party's interpretation of the nature of the conflict in Spain played an essential part in the recruitment of volunteers for the Spanish Republic. As Bill Alexander noted, many would-be volunteers heard about recruiting through the paper.[102] One volunteer described how he saw the newspaper as 'the Bible' and that he read it avidly to make sure that he was following 'the line' correctly.[103] Many others remark upon their readership of the newspaper,[104] whose influence on members, and potential members, of the Communist Party was unrivalled.

As one would expect, the paper unequivocally supported the Republicans during the civil war, though this was always achieved within the context of the official Communist Party line, whether it be the sectarian attacks on the POUM in Spain that so outraged George Orwell, or support for affiliation of the Communist Party to the Labour Party in Britain that so outraged the labour establishment. The Spanish

Civil War was the major issue for the paper in the second half of 1936; on only one occasion did the conflict not receive coverage on the front page.[105] The constitutional crisis surrounding the abdication of Edward VIII in December 1936 which so dominated other British newspapers had to share the *Daily Worker*'s front page.[106] In fact, the *Daily Worker* had played close attention to the events in Spain throughout 1936, following the Popular Front's victory in the February election. The paper was quick to point out the relevance of the events in Spain for Britain: that the success of the Spanish 'Peoples Front' provided an object lesson for the British working class.[107]

A number of party figures who were to have a bearing on Spain were regular contributors to the newspaper. Ralph Fox, who was killed in Spain and received several glowing obituaries in the paper,[108] wrote a regular feature entitled 'A Worker's Notebook'. Tom Wintringham, who, with Fox, founded the *Left Review*, and was later commander of the British Battalion, wrote regular articles on the war in Abyssinia.[109] Wintringham also reported on the early stages of the war in Spain, and wrote an article claiming that the rebels were cheating their Moorish troops by paying them in worthless foreign currency.[110] R. W. Robson, in charge of vetting new recruits for the International Brigades, penned an article encouraging readers to join the Communist Party.[111] A half-page article written by Will Paynter, who would later be base political commissar at the International Brigade headquarters at Albacete, urged support for his election campaign for a seat on the executive of the South Wales Miners' Federation.[112]

The war in Spain was covered by Claude Cockburn (writing under the pseudonym Frank Pitcairn), who had been in Barcelona in July 1936 to cover the Workers' Olympiad for the *Daily Worker* and had briefly fought for the Republic in the Sierra de Guadarrama, and by William Rust, a senior figure in the British Communist Party and its representative in Spain. When the uprising began in July 1936, the *Daily Worker* carried reports confidently predicting that the 'unity' of the Spanish working class would triumph: 'The fascists have suffered a crushing blow and it is only a matter of days before they are finally beaten.'[113] Accounts criticising the reporting of the conflict in other newspapers were not long in coming, and it was the voice of the Labour Party, the *Daily Herald*, which was first censored.[114] Other articles complained of the biased coverage in other pro-rebel newspapers, particularly Lord Rothermere's *Daily Mail*.[115]

Pitcairn stressed that the communists were playing the central role in the defence of the Republic,[116] likewise that the British volunteers were playing a similar part in the International Brigades.[117] At the same time, articles demonstrated the Communist Party's support for the Republican government, following the position outlined by Georgi Dimitrov, the Bulgarian secretary-general of the Comintern, at the Seventh Congress in 1935. This replaced the policy of 'class against class', which had portrayed bourgeois Republican parties as 'social fascists', with the policy of 'Popular Frontism', aligning all parties from Social Democrats to Communists in a People's Front against fascism. For example, an article penned by André Marty, the future leader of the International Brigades, stressed that the party's task was to 'defend, consolidate and develop the bourgeois democratic revolution', and argued that, 'the present struggle in Spain is not between capitalism and socialism, but between fascism and democracy.'[118] This was essential if the Communist Party was to have any success in pursuing two major aims: first, embroiling the British labour movement in a 'united front' in the defence of the Republic and, second, persuading the Western democracies that their major foe was fascism, not communism, and that an alliance with Russia was essential if fascism was to be contained. The *Daily Worker* was thus quick to pounce on reports of intervention on the side of the rebels, which would display the international – rather than national – aspects of the struggle in Spain, such as 'Italian Arms for Fascists'.[119]

However, at least until mid-November 1936, the *Daily Worker* was extremely cautious in requesting direct military help for the Republic. At first it limited itself to criticisms of the British government's policy of non-intervention in the conflict on one hand, and pointing out the significance of the war for Britain (the threat of fascism) and the British working class (the need for unity) on the other. However, the paper did regularly suggest ways in which the Republic could be assisted without actually mentioning volunteering, such as making bandages.[120] In October 1936 the *Daily Worker* printed a request for letters and deputations to be sent to Transport House, the headquarters of the Trades Union Congress, pressing them to drop their support for non-intervention.[121] Regular advertisements for the 'Relief Committee for the Victims of Fascism' pressed home that this was the chance to contribute to the great cause from Britain. And, indeed, many did,[122] some of whom later went to Spain, such as the Manchester furniture reupholsterer Josh Davidson.[123] However, following the success of foreign medical units in Spain in August and September 1936, Frank Pitcairn's article requesting medically trained volunteers appeared on the front page. It stated that 'there is urgent and vital need for stretcher-bearers, sanitary and medical orderlies, lorry drivers, mechanics, nurses, surgeons, Red Cross workers of all kinds, with experience if possible.'[124] The request stopped short of asking for trained military volunteers, but clearly showed that the Communist Party had now decided to be actively, rather than passively, involved in the war in Spain. The situation was similar in France, where the communist press was at first reluctant explicitly to put out a request for military volunteers for the Spanish Republican forces.[125]

Whilst there were mentions of British individuals in Spain, such as the death of the artist Felicia Browne,[126] it was not until mid-November that any reports of an organised international contingent of volunteers appeared, and even then it was in somewhat coded terms. Under the headline, 'The Big News Yesterday', the *Daily Worker* described how: 'The Government forces have received powerful and well-trained reinforcements, which British eye-witnesses have admired for their military precision and martial bearing.'[127] Whilst there is no explicit mention of an international column, the meaning is clear. The article described how the 3,000 reinforcements marched down the Calle de Alcalá to the west of Madrid. Two days later the report was no longer ambiguous and reported how 'Spaniards, Germans, Hungarians and Yugoslavs, belonging to the International Brigade' had stemmed the rebel advance on Madrid.[128] However, there was, again, no mention of a British contingent. The eulogistic portrayal of the volunteers was continued a week later, when Harry Pollitt described how:

Men Are Flocking From All Over Europe . . . To Help Save Europe . . . Have you read of the magnificent part of the International Legion is playing in Spain? We are proud of the fact that a number of our comrades are playing a leading part in the work of this legion.[129]

If there was any doubt that Pollitt was referring to British rather than international comrades, it was resolved three days later when he described how 'the British section of this International Legion is carrying out a great fight'.[130] The appeal continued in December 1936 with a warning to the 'forces of democracy' and what is virtually a call to arms:

> The International Column and the Spanish Militia are fighting for the democracy not only of Spain, but also of Britain and all of Europe. Never was there a greater need for all the forces of democracy in this and other countries to support and strengthen a band of men who have now to defy not only Franco's men, but all the weight of German militarism.[131]

Stories of the intervention of Italian,[132] German and Moorish forces on the side of the rebels were essential in fostering the picture of a nation and its legitimate government under siege. Again, articles portrayed the struggle as the Spanish people fighting against foreign invaders, an image which appears in many of the volunteers' memoirs: 'We are witnessing the fascist invasion of a peaceful democratic country.'[133]

In December 1936 the *Daily Worker* carried several, at the very least, highly exaggerated reports,[134] describing the role of thousands of German troops in the attack on Madrid.[137] Several men remember this German attack on Madrid having played an important part in their decision to volunteer. Frank Graham from Sunderland believed that:

> The full significance of what was going on wasn't realised until you had the Germans in the fight for Madrid. The early battles for Madrid where the German fascists played a very important part I think brought the whole thing up to the front.[136]

This theme was regularly referred to by other British volunteers, such as Albert Charlesworth, a metal polisher from Oldham:

> I was, and still am, inclined to side with any little party where I think an injustice is being done, and this, I think, is what took me to Spain . . . There was the German and the Italian involvement. I knew of it before I went and that's what made it so unjust.[137]

As James Brown from Paddington in London phrased it,

> You can over-simplify it in terms of goodies and baddies but in essence it was

very clear cut. After the Spanish people appealed for help when Hitler and Mussolini had invaded and they were ferrying Moroccan troops over, I decided to go.[138]

The *Daily Worker* constantly stressed the vital role the British were playing in the defence of the Republic, though remarking how much more could be achieved with more volunteers. On 5 December 1936, the *Daily Worker* described in glowing terms how the 100 British volunteers in the International Legion were a 'fine, cool, brave' response to the German intervention.[139] By 12 December, it was reported that the British contingent numbered 300, but demanded that 'We Must Make the British Unit Stronger and Mightier Yet.'[140] Frank Pitcairn reported how, by the middle of December, 'The fourth all-British company has arrived . . . Soon, it is to be hoped, we shall have our own British Battalion.'[141]

Having lost its earlier caution, the *Daily Worker* sang the praises of the British contribution to the Republican war effort.[142] Harry Pollitt continued to claim that the British volunteers were extremely highly regarded (and thus vital) and, on 19 December, made a clear plea for British volunteers for Spain. Under the headline 'Spain Has a Job for You to Do', Pollitt claimed that 'The British section of the International Brigade continues to earn high praise. There are now over 400 of our best and bravest in it.'[143] Two days later the British contingent numbered 'over 450', and was 'growing every day'. Pollitt described how 150 men, led by Peter Kerrigan, who had been closely involved in organising the Scottish part of the march on London by the National Unemployed Workers' Movement (NUWM) in 1936, were departing for Spain.[144] By 23 December, Frank Pitcairn believed there were now sufficient British volunteers 'to form two companies'.[145] The following day, the paper proudly proclaimed the naming of the British volunteers as the Saklatvala Battalion,[146] after the Indian communist MP for Battersea (though this name never actually caught on with the volunteers themselves). This was followed by a more circumspect, but just as passionate, appeal from Charlotte Haldane, whose son and husband were both in Spain, to 'talk, talk, talk of the Brigade', for 'a lot more can be done'.[147] The *Daily Worker*'s appeals for volunteers from their mainly CP and YCL readership continued throughout 1937 and into 1938. Despite the real danger of being killed in Spain, it is clear that many, the majority of whom were communists, continued to respond to the call.

The organisation and recruitment of the volunteers for the International Brigades probably represents the outstanding success for the British Communist Party, for, though extremely vocal, the party was singularly unsuccessful in its attempts to break into the mainstream body politic. Hugo Dewar has shown how 'the general effects of the economic crisis, the shock of the destruction of the German working-class movement, and the outbreak of the Spanish Civil War, induced a leftward mood both of organised labour and among intellectuals.'[148] This led to a rise in the support for direct action during the 1930s, particularly in the demonstrations against the BUF. However, attempts to succeed through the ballot box met with only one success, the election of Willie Gallagher in the West Fife by-election, where he gained 29.2 per cent of the vote. Harry Pollitt, standing in Rhondda East, an area that generated many recruits for the International Brigades,[149] was unsuccessful even though he polled 30.6 per cent of the vote. The membership of the party tells its own story, peaking at nearly 11,000 in 1926 at the time of the General Strike, then slipping into decline until 1931, after which the membership starts to increase once more. Between 1935 and 1942, Communist Party membership rose from 7,700 to 56,000, mainly as a response to the rise in European fascism.[150]

The membership of the British party numbered less than a quarter of the American Communist Party (which had 41,000 members in 1936, rising to 82,000 in 1938), yet the total number of British volunteers was approximately 2,400, only 200 fewer than the American total.[151] Whilst, clearly, travelling the vast distance from the USA to Spain presented a major obstacle to the American volunteers, it still suggests that the number that volunteered from Britain (of whom, as we have seen, around 60 per cent were CP members) represents a remarkable achievement.

Other, more subtle, forces also played a part, if not in directly influencing people to volunteer, then certainly in forming the cultural and political milieu in which many of the volunteers were steeped. The most influential of these was undoubtedly the Left Book Club (LBC), established in early 1936 by the publisher Victor Gollancz, a member of the Labour Party, but with sympathies for the further left. The editorial panel consisted of Gollancz, together with John Strachey and Harold Laski from the London School of Economics, the latter two both being regular contributors to the *Daily Worker* and supporters of affiliation of the CP to the Labour Party.[152] The rapid rise in membership of the Left Book Club was astonishing and exceeded all expectations: 9,000 members by May 1936, 28,000 by October, almost 40,000 in March 1937, and 57,000 by the spring of 1939.[153] The LBC produced a journal, the *Left News*, which was distributed free to members, and there were many

*Table 2.2* British Communist Party membership

| Date | Membership |
| --- | --- |
| 1922 | 5,116 |
| 1926 | 10,800 |
| 1927 | 7,377 |
| January 1929 | 3,500 |
| December 1929 | 3,200 |
| May 1930 | 2,850 |
| November 1930 | 2,555 |
| November 1931 | 6,279 |
| 1932 | 9,000 |
| December 1934 | 5,800 |
| February 1935 | 6,500 |
| October 1936 | 11,500 |
| May 1937 | 12,250 |
| September 1938 | 15,750 |
| July 1939 | 17,750 |

Sources: Dewar, *Communist Politics in Britain*, p. 94; Branson, *History of the Communist Party*, p. 188; Stevenson and Cook, *Britain in the Depression*, p. 315.

powerful affiliated university organisations, plus hundreds of local discussion groups, many of whom became involved in Spanish aid organisations.[154]

The Left Book Club published many works by communists or sympathisers, including *Soviet Communism* by Sidney and Beatrice Webb, and had a close relationship with the Communist Party; regular advertisements for the LBC appeared in the *Daily Worker*. The club published several works on the war in Spain, of which *Spain in Revolt*, published in 1936, was perhaps the most widely read and most influential.[155] Several volunteers, such as Len Crome, the commander of the 35th Medical Division, cited the influence of the LBC on their political development,[156] and, within Spain, members of the British Battalion often participated in political discussions focusing on the LBC's monthly selection.[157] Nearly half of the books commissioned were written by communists, and roughly one-sixth of the membership were party members. As Ronald Blythe stated: 'No small national Communist Party ever had so respectable, brilliantly organised and popular a vehicle for its propaganda as that provided by the Left Book Club in the Britain of the late thirties.'[158]

Many of the volunteers had also been involved in the hunger marches organised by the NUWM, one of the many communist-dominated organisations, 'the most important organisation of the unemployed during the depression'.[159] A number of studies have commented on the strong link between participating in the hunger marches and later volunteering for the Spanish war. As Hynes explains, 'If one is to seek a major factor in the motivation of a significant proportion of the British Battalion, one could well begin with the hunger marches and the conditions which provoked them.'[160] Likewise, Lance Rogers, one of the large number of Welsh communist volunteers, explained that 'It was a continuing process. Here we were in Myrthyr Tydfil in a continuing struggle night and day. The Hunger March over, we left for the Spanish war. It was a fulfilment and a most natural step to take.'[161] And, as James Hopkins has pointed out, for many of the recruits who were members of the CP or the YCL, or otherwise politically active in left-wing political organisations, volunteering for Spain appeared to be a logical development in their political activities:

> There was a logical, sequential development of issues in the lives of many British militants: first, looking for explanations for the unemployment and repression they experienced; second, seeing the rise of fascism on the continent as an issue that concerned them; and third, seizing the opportunity to strike back at oppression, if not in Great Britain, then in Spain.[162]

John Lochore, who fought in Spain between 1936 and 1937, was a youth leader on the Scottish hunger march in 1936.[163] Peter O'Connor, a volunteer from Ireland, who served from Christmas 1936 until July 1937, when he was 'repatriated for political reasons with an excellent record',[164] claimed that, 'being politically conscious and having participated in a couple of hunger marches, I felt fascism was hell-bent on war'.[165] British Battalion commanders Sam Wild and Fred Copeman, political commissar Peter Kerrigan and the Labour councillor Jack Jones had all been involved in the NUWM. So too had many others who are less well known, such as Frank Graham from Sunderland,[166] Sidney Quinn,[167] and John Henderson:

A number of my comrades from the Party and the NUWM around the Tyne had volunteered and it was on my conscience that me, who'd been shouting his bloody mouth off about fascism and Spain and how we had to do something, well, I felt I had to go.[168]

Another volunteer, Tommy Kerr from Airdrie, remembered: 'I was out of work and became active in the National Unemployed Workers Movement and the Young Communist League; I went on their marches in Glasgow.'[169] Sidney Quinn, from Scotland, who was unemployed at the age of 21, went on a hunger march to London before joining the army. After he was sent home from Aden in 1936, he returned to unemployment and became involved in anti-Mosley protests before volunteering for Spain in November 1936.[170] Hugh Sloan (who fought in Spain under the name Hugh Smith), a miner from Fife, explained how 'My participation in political activities and the conditions which I saw around me at home gave me a growing understanding of what was happening.'[171]

As the previous chapter demonstrated, geographical considerations also played a part, for there were certain areas in Britain that sent large contingents of volunteers – in particular large conurbations such as London, Manchester and Liverpool. These were areas of high Communist Party membership, with large Jewish communities and, frequently, a combination of both. London's east end provides perhaps the best example; Whitechapel, Bethnal Green, Hackney and Stamford Hill sent a large contingent of volunteers. London's east end was historically an area of high Jewish residency, the population there soaring between 1880 and 1914, following the pogroms in Eastern Europe.[172] It also had a strong, militant Communist Party, many of the members of which were Jewish, motivated by stories of the persecution abroad, particularly in Germany, and by personal experiences of intimidation by Blackshirts in their own neighbourhood.[173]

South Wales too had a particularly militant character, led by the South Wales Miners' Federation (SWMF), and was another area targeted by the BUF.[174] A large anti-fascist demonstration in Tonypandy in the Rhondda in May 1936 successfully prevented the BUF from meeting: 31 men and 5 women were summonsed for incitement to riot and several communists were jailed, including Harry Dobson, who was later a political commissar in Spain and was killed in 1938.[175] Upon his release from prison, Dobson, who had served six months' hard labour, is supposed to have asked, 'How do I get to Spain?'[176] The Rhondda was a particularly fertile area for the CP, especially the 'Little Moscows' of Maerdy and Bedlinog.[177] As Hywel Francis has noted,

> The oral history evidence collected in the area has suggested that there was something of a revolutionary syndrome with the same men being involved in strikes, hunger marches, victimisation and the International Brigades.[178]

Welsh miners, aware of the severe repression that miners in the Asturias had suffered after the abortive rising of October 1934, would have seen from the front page of the *Daily Worker* how their Spanish comrades were once again in the thick of the action.[179] Welsh miners' requests for aid for the Spanish Republic were also given front-page coverage in the *Daily Worker*.[180] Though Francis argues that the means test was always a more important issue for the South Wales miners,[181] their militancy generated by the hard conditions of their employment lay behind the motivations of the Welsh volunteers who fought in Spain.

The large Irish contingent within the British Battalion, from both the Free State and Northern Ireland, both Catholics and Protestants, had their own particular reasons to volunteer. Bob Doyle, a cook from Dublin, stated:

> I joined the Republican movement because of Kit Conway and I was in the youth section of the 1st Battalion of the Dublin IRA . . . From the beginning of 1936 I was hearing more of Spain in the news and from the propaganda of the Catholic Church. The official press was one hundred per cent in support of Franco . . . I thought there was a danger that Ireland would go fascist and that was one of the motivating factors making my mind up to go. I didn't know much about Spain but my thoughts on the way to Spain were that every bullet I fired would be a bullet against a Dublin landlord and capitalist.[182]

Likewise, Peter O'Connor from Waterford later stated that he felt that Spain 'offered a chance to reverse the decision of the war of 1922–23, to vindicate a cause which had then been tragically overthrown by traitors who were . . . little less than agents of British imperialism.'[183]

For some volunteers the decision to go was influenced by friends, or comrades from the local party branch, who had themselves decided to go. Harry Addley was a friend of Arthur 'Babs' Ovenden, and both volunteered together.[184] Phil Gillan from Glasgow, for whom 'politics became a way of life', joined the Gorbals branch of the Young Communist League, which used to take him hiking. He remembered that half a dozen others from the branch went to Spain and were killed, including John Connolly, Jimmy Rae, Jimmy Hyndman and Martin Messer.[185] Maurice Levine, one of the many volunteers from Manchester, stated:

> One of the prime factors in me making an application to go to Spain was that Eddie Swindell, a glass worker friend of mine, was very friendly with Arnold Jeans who had already gone to Spain with Clem Beckett.[186]

Levine also worked for the Manchester clothing manufacturers Marshall and Crosslands with Julius 'Jud' Colman. Levine and Colman, with Ralph Cantor(ovitch), George Westfield, Bill Benson and Eddie Swindells, travelled to Spain together.[187]

Several of the volunteers in the early stage of the war were already in Spain, or nearby.[188] George Hardy was a member of British Workers' Sports Federation in Barcelona at the outbreak of the war and later returned as a volunteer.[189] Bill Scott, an ex-IRA member, was at the Workers' Olympiad in Barcelona, 'the socialist riposte to the Berlin Olympics',[190] when war broke out, as was a friend of Leslie Preger from Manchester: 'He came back towards the end of July full of stories about the uprising and brought back cartridge cases, flags and all the rest of it.'[191]

Sam Masters was on a cycling holiday with Nat Cohen around Spain and was in Barcelona in July 1936 when the fighting started,[192] whilst Ralph Bates was walking in the Pyrenees with his wife, Winnifred. They both served in Spain: he in the Republican government's propaganda and information service and she as a liaison officer.[193] Many others joined because of the influence of their family, friends or work colleagues. Tommy Kerr felt that his uncle, who had been a member of the Communist Party, was a great influence on him:

> With him I read books, talked things over and saw the general lie of the land, you might say . . . When I said I was interested in going to Spain Uncle Bill said, 'If you want to go, go right ahead.'[194]

In a number of cases, members of the same family volunteered. Ronald Burgess served in the International Brigades, whilst his mother, Charlotte Haldane, worked in Paris in the recruitment office and his step-father, the illustrious world-famous scientist J. B. S. Haldane, visited the Republican front and worked on measures to counter potential gas attacks.[195] Thomas Gibbons, who died at Brunete, was one of three brothers to volunteer.[196] Mick Brown, who deserted in December 1936, declaring, 'this isn't war, this is bloody madness. I've had enough',[197] was the brother of George, company commissar at Brunete, who was killed at Villanueva de la Cañada in July 1937.[198]

Thomas Murray, a farm-worker from Edinburgh, explained that he volunteered because 'My interest in the Spanish Civil War, of course, was aroused by the circumstances in which a democratically elected government was attacked by a junta of military officers.'[199] In this, of course, he was hardly alone. However, he was unusual in that he had met *La Pasionaria* previously, at the International Peace Congress in Brussels, where she had made a great impression on him.[200] In addition, his sister Anne was a nurse in Spain and his brother George was in the British Anti-Tank Battery of the 15th International Brigade.[201]

Other volunteers had been involved in a variety of protests. Joseph Norman's political teeth were cut on an action to gain access to open spaces in what is now the Peak District National Park, where he met other individuals who would later fight in Spain:

> My first real experience of political activity was the mass trespass on Kinder-scout in Derbyshire which eventually led to the designation of the area as a National Park. Dozens of those that fought the police and landowners on that mass trespass were later to fight and die in Spain – men like Clem Beckett and George Brown. Some received up to six months hard labour for that trespass.[202]

Thus for many of the men it was not just their political association that pushed them into volunteering; other things acted as a catalyst. John Cornford, who was one of the first British volunteers to be in Spain, claimed that he simply wanted 'to find out what was happening'.[203] John Angus, later to be a political commissar at a Republican 're-education' camp, expressed the oft-stated view that, 'Like many young men of the time I was oppressed by the gathering menace of Hitler in Europe and frustrated and almost in despair at the passive, indeed cooperative, attitude of our National Government towards this fascist advance.'[204] However, he went on to explain: 'On the personal side I had nothing very much to inhibit me from going away. A rather uninteresting and unrewarding job, no particular girlfriend, friendly but not very close relations with my father.'[205]

One volunteer, a clerk from Middlesbrough, admitted he had 'No real recollection of Blackshirts, or class conflict, or Spain to any degree, apart from Spanish and Latin-American music', and that he hated his work.[206] After he had been working for 18 months, the revolt broke out in Spain:

> One day I bought *The Times* . . . I remember reading a paragraph saying, 'There is no doubt that if the Spanish Republican government wins the war a socialist state will be set up'. Really that was the trigger. I thought, Christ, here's a way out.[207]

Likewise, the veteran activist Fred Copeman, who had been involved in numerous hunger marches and demonstrations, felt 'it would make my girl proud of me.'[208] John Peet, a teacher from London, was unusual in that he had travelled extensively through Europe and had experienced personally what Hitlerism and fascism represented:

> I think I had a much more immediate reason than many of the people who went from Britain for more theoretical reasons, because I had been through central Europe, I had seen Nazi Germany, I had seen a clerical fascist dictatorship which had already been established in Austria. I could see, as everybody could practically see, that the Nazis were going to take over Austria and Czechoslovakia in the near future and that another world war was on its way and it seemed fairly obvious that the war in Spain was only a precursor of that war.[209]

Similarly, the Labour councillor Jack Jones had been involved in campaigns to free political prisoners in Germany after meeting some young German sailors: 'I'd talked with young German seamen some of whom were later put in concentration camps, I think in one case was executed. So I knew something about what was going on in Germany.'[210]

Nevertheless, whilst there might have been as many reasons for volunteering as there were volunteers, and whatever their individual reasons for volunteering happened to be, there were factors that all of them had in common: they shared a hatred of fascism, which they combined with the willingness and determination to do something about it. The war in Spain brought together those who had been sympathetic to particular causes, whether it was the right to ramble in the Peak District or protesting against BUF marches. For opponents of fascism, and its advocation of intolerance and injustice, the Spanish war was the defining moment. As one American volunteer put it eloquently, 'I saw in the invaders of Spain the same people I've been fighting all my life.'[211]

# 3 Madrid, 1936

## Manning the Spanish barricades

We realized perfectly that if Madrid fell the war would go on. It was only one front of many.[1]

Following the crucial airlift of Franco's Army of Africa across the strait into southern Spain in early August 1936, the rebel army advanced swiftly northwards towards Madrid. By 10 August they had reached the old Roman town of Mérida and linked up Franco's southern zone with the northern zone under General Mola. The rebels then turned on the town of Badajoz, the capital of Extremadura, which lay near the Portuguese border and remained in Republican hands. Despite a desperate defence, the town was captured by Franco's African columns and a brutal repression followed, during which nearly 2,000 people were shot. Stories and rumours of this savagery inflicted on the defenders preceded the advance of the rebel army on Madrid, and worked considerably to the rebels' advantage. Militiamen, terrified at the prospect of being outflanked, retreated headlong, often dropping their weapons and ammunition, back along the main roads to Madrid, where they could be picked off with ease by the advancing rebel forces.[2]

At the end of September, the rebel army made another detour to lift the siege of the city of Toledo, which, crucially, allowed the defending Republicans time to prepare the defences in Madrid. After another massacre of militiamen – Moorish soldiers killed 200 Republican wounded in the hospital in Toledo by throwing grenades into the wards – the march towards Madrid resumed. By 1 November, the rebels had reached the south-west of Madrid adjacent to the Casa de Campo and the University City. Here, at last, the advance was slowed by a defence established by militia units and Madrileños, who had no illusions of what defeat would mean for them. On 10 November, the desperate last-ditch defence was joined by a new force, an international column of volunteers: the first of the International Brigades, determined to help ensure that Madrid would not fall, that the rebel army would not pass.

In fact, foreign volunteers, including a number from Britain, had been drifting into Spain right from the outset of the civil war. However, until the creation of the British (16th) Battalion of the 15th International Brigade just after Christmas 1936, there was no single group of British volunteers. Instead, volunteers joined the various militia units that had sprung up as early as July to defend the Republic

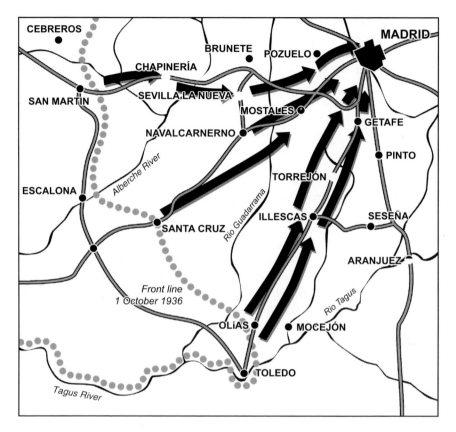

*Map 3.1* The rebels' advance on Madrid, October–November 1936.

against the military uprising or were attached to battalions of French or German volunteers.

Though the majority of the British volunteers for Spain came from a working-class background, the 'first few' did not entirely conform to this picture. The first British volunteers to arrive in Spain comprised a much higher proportion from middle-class or 'intellectual' backgrounds than those who arrived from 1937 onwards, when the Communist Party had established a firmer hold on recruitment.[3] For example, amongst the small number of British that fought in the battles of Madrid at the same time as Romilly in November and December 1936 was a scientist, Lorimer Birch, the restaurant owners Harry Addley and Arthur 'Babs' Ovenden,[4] and, in particular, the literary intellectuals Christopher Caudwell (whose real name was Christopher St John Sprigg) and John Cornford. The presence of Caudwell and Cornford in the battles in Madrid in 1936 did much to help create the myth that the brigades were made up of large numbers of intellectuals, the 'vague notion that every-one in the brigades was a poet or writer.'[5] In addition to being more 'middle class' than the later volunteers, the first few were also younger than the later arrivals.[6]

Amongst the first British volunteers to arrive in Spain were the sculptor and artist Felicia Browne, who was painting in Barcelona when the rising began, and the Marxist intellectual John Cornford, who entered the country on 8 August 1936. Felicia Browne was eventually allowed to volunteer for a militia unit in Barcelona after attempts to dissuade her by both the Communist Party and the leader of the unit, and she was killed on 28 August 1936 in a mission to blow up a munitions train near Tardienta in Aragon.[7] John Cornford arrived with a friend and fellow Trinity College student, Richard Bennett,[8] a week before Britain's decision to ban the selling of arms to Spain. Cornford briefly fought with the POUM militia units in Huesca in August on the Aragon front, before returning to Britain to help raise more recruits for the Republic.[9]

Other volunteers from Britain also became involved almost immediately following the military rising. Two clothing workers from London, Nat Cohen and Sam Masters, were cycling around the Pyrenees on holiday.[10] Both Communist Party members, they made their way to Barcelona to volunteer and, with three other British volunteers,[11] participated in a raid on Mallorca in August 1936, which was, unfortunately, widely expected by the rebel forces defending the island.[12] Led by two Spanish captains from the air force and civil guard, the raid failed to penetrate more than a few miles inland of the landing-point at Porto Cristo, on the east of the island, before being forced to retreat to the mainland.[13] Richard Kisch, a young British volunteer, was injured in the abortive attack and repatriated to Britain in October after only a month in Spain.[14] Nat Cohen, who distinguished himself in the action, was elected leader of the group, which on its return to Barcelona became the Tom Mann Centuria. The names of the British members of the centuria appear in Table 3.1.

David Marshall, who arrived from Britain in August 1936, also joined the Tom Mann Centuria. Marshall could not have been less the hardened political activist; he is highly unusual amongst the British volunteers in Spain in admitting that he lived 'totally outside' the world of politics before his time in Spain.[15] Marshall paints a vivid picture of Barcelona at the end of the summer of 1936, 'seething with enthusiasm'. His descriptions of several of his comrades are just as vivid, though in the case of Keith Scott Watson, who left the centuria to work as a journalist with Sefton Delmer of the *Daily Express*, not always so enthusiastic.[16] Watson did not endear himself to the communists by later sabotaging their attempt to explain to a Labour delegation in Spain that [Republican] Spain was a democratic country.[17]

On 6 September 1936, another member of the centuria, Tom Wintringham – who would later become commander of the British Battalion – wrote to Harry Pollitt in London urging the party to support the centuria officially and turn it into a British column.[18] He wrote again a week later, explaining what type of volunteers he thought were needed: 'A respectable number of English comrades, CP, LP or TU, to make a Centuria.' Wintringham's criteria for potential recruits were straightforward, and laid no great weight on military experience: 'Send ten per cent trained men if you can to act as corporals, and the rest kids and enthusiasts. Most of them will come back with very valuable experience.'[19] At this stage, the emphasis seems to have been more on the political dimension than the military. Wintringham also

*Table 3.1* 'British' members of the Tom Mann Centuria

| Surname | First name | Comments |
|---------|-----------|----------|
| Avner | Sid | Killed at Boadilla del Monte in December 1936 |
| Barry | Jack | aka 'Blue'; Australian; killed at Boadilla in December 1936 |
| Birch | Lorimer | Killed at Boadilla in December 1936 |
| Cohen | Nat | Leader of Tom Mann Centuria; repatriated in April 1937 |
| Cox | Ray | Killed at Boadilla in December 1936 |
| Donovan | John | aka Paddy; deserted to Barcelona and later fought with Lenin Division; returned to UK 1937 |
| Gillan | Phil | Wounded at Boadilla; repatriated to UK in February 1937 |
| Kisch | Richard | Wounded in Mallorca, September 1936; repatriated to UK in October 1936 |
| Marshall | David | Wounded at Cerro de los Angeles, November 1936; repatriated to UK in November–December 1936 |
| Masters | Sam | Killed at Brunete in July 1937 |
| Scott | Bill | Hospitalised with kidney problems, December 1936; later joined British Battalion; repatriated to Ireland in 1937 |
| Sheller | Alex | Returned to UK in August 1936 without joining the front line |
| Watson | Keith | Left the Thaelmann Battalion to work as a *Daily Express* journalist in November 1936 |
| Wintringham | Tom | Later commander of British Battalion; repatriated in November 1937 |

Source: computerised database of the British volunteers.

wrote expressing his concerns that the British Communist Party needed urgently to establish 'effective representation and control of the work of the C.P.G.B., present and future, in Barcelona.'[20]

By the end of October, after a stay of six or seven weeks during which time the centuria took part in no fighting, the volunteers were becoming bored and desperate to get involved.[21] Phil Gillan, a lorry driver from Glasgow,[23] who also arrived in September, remarked on their disappointment following unfulfilled expectations of being sent to the Aragon front.[23] Thus the British volunteers welcomed the decision to group foreign volunteers together, which led to their transfer to Albacete and their official attachment to the mainly German Thaelmann Battalion.

On 2 October 1936 a new contingent of British volunteers arrived. James Albrighton, a student from Salisbury, came with six other British volunteers[24] and was joined two days later by another half-dozen from Britain.[25] Albrighton is unusual in that he kept a diary of his experiences in Spain[26] and that his role in the war has received little attention.[27] His story deserves consideration for, according to Albrighton, the Muerte es Maestro group was involved in 'special duties', including executions.[28] Albrighton's group was charged with 'searching out and destroying the fascist spies in Madrid' and acting as a firing squad. As recompense for these special duties the men received extra pay, leave and privileges. Albrighton is unusually candid about the use of executions in the Republican Army and claims that at the end of January 1937 two Spanish members of his Muerte es Maestro Centuria were charged with desertion at an open court martial, after having been discovered by a patrol behind enemy lines. The two Spaniards eventually admitted they were trying to return to their families. According to Albrighton, André Marty, infamous for his rigid discipline, was determined to make an example of them, *pour encourager les autres*. Albrighton claims that they were both executed by a firing squad made up of members of their own unit.

According to Albrighton, his group fought in one of the three sections of the Spanish Muerte es Maestro Centuria, which was involved in the desperate attempts to halt the rebels' drive on Madrid in early October 1936 from Toledo, which had fallen on 27 September. On 14 October several of the British contingent, including their leader, Sidney Lloyd Jones, were killed in a counter-attack on rebel Moorish troops at Chapinería, roughly 30 miles to the west of Madrid.[29]

Albrighton's unit, together with other militia columns, was forced backwards as the Nationalist Army swept towards Madrid. On 30 October, Albrighton witnessed the bombing of Getafe, site of a Republican airfield just to the south of Madrid. He describes in harrowing detail the heavy bombing of the town, during which a school was hit.[30]

> I consider this scene as one of wholesale carnage that exceeds any other act of barbarism that history has recorded over the past several centuries . . . This is indeed the modern version of the slaughtering of the innocents . . . I find it very distressing to even try and describe the picture that I saw . . . The remnants of limbs, the particles of flesh and blood splattered against white washed walls, fragments of all that remained of what only a few minutes before had been innocent, carefree, joyful toddlers playing in the morning's sun.[31]

On 9 November, Albrighton and the Muerte es Maestro Centuria were transferred to the Casa de Campo, in a last-ditch attempt to prevent the rebels from entering the

*Table 3.2* British members of the Muerte es Maestro Centuria

| Surname | First name |
| --- | --- |
| Albrighton | James |
| Beale | John |
| Bentley | Albert |
| Campbell | Bruce |
| Garland | Frank |
| Harris | Michael |
| Henderson | John |
| Hudson | William |
| Lloyd Jones | Sidney |
| Mackenzie | David |
| Middleton | George |
| Morton | Sidney |
| O'Connor | Frank |
| O'Malley | Patrick |
| Zanettou | Benitzelos |

Spanish capital. Here the centuria was to fight alongside the newly formed 11th International Brigade, which also included several British volunteers. Like many Madrileños, Albrighton at first believed that the International Brigade was a Russian force that had come to the Republic's aid.[32]

> About ten minutes ago we had a messenger with fresh orders . . . He tells that the Russians are driving the Fascists back . . . He has also seen the Russians, they are all in a different uniform from ours . . . They have steel helmets and new rifles . . . They even have tanks standing by ready for their big offensive.[33]

The following day the members of the centuria discovered that the forces were, in fact, 'Internationals', and Albrighton later met several of the British members of the brigades. On 14 November, in the Hall of Philosophy in the University City, Albrighton met Bernard Knox and John Cornford, who were fighting there as part of the 11th International Brigade. Two days later he also ran into three British members of the Thaelmann Battalion fighting with the 12th International Brigade: Bill Scott, Lorimer Birch and the young Esmond Romilly. There, 'someone tried to kid me he is related to Churchill', Albrighton declared unbelievingly (which, indeed, Romilly was, much to the disgust of his uncle). He also met Jock Cunningham, who suggested Albrighton transfer to their section, but he instead elected to stay with the Muerte es Maestro Centuria where, shortly afterwards, he was elected a political commissar.

Albrighton's unit suffered similar casualties to other units involved in the desperate defence of Madrid. By 14 November the centuria was reduced to only 40 men out of the original 128. Albrighton's diary describes how, since 10 October, 42 men had been killed (including two Britons, Albert Bentley and George Middleton, on 12 November), 27 were seriously wounded and another 10 were missing, presumed dead. After Albrighton was put in charge of a section of 16 men in the Casa de Campo, eight of them were killed by a single salvo of shells. Albrighton remained with Spanish units and later served alongside the British No. 1 Company led by Captain George Nathan, as part of the 14th International Brigade under the Polish General 'Walter'.[34] He worked as a medic at Jarama, where he witnessed the decimation of the British Battalion, and in several other major conflicts before being repatriated following a serious injury in the spring of 1938.

Whilst many foreign volunteers, like James Albrighton, were fighting with various militia units in which they had ended up almost by chance, the Spanish government had, in October, started taking steps to formalise integration of the *extranjaneros* into the Spanish Republican Army. On 12 October 1936, Largo Caballero, the Spanish prime minister, agreed to the formation of International Brigades, and the town of Albacete, which lay on the main railway between Valencia and Madrid, was chosen as their base.[35] By 14 October, there were already 650 recruits from overseas, and by the end of October there were over 2,000.[36] On 25 October the first of the International Brigades was formed (the 11th), which went into battle in Madrid on 9 November.

Following the government's evacuation to Valencia on 6 November, the defence of the Spanish capital was officially conducted by General José Miaja, later to be heralded as 'the hero of Madrid', though, in reality, Miaja's chief of staff, General Vincente Rojo, was the true director of operations.[37] The International Brigades made up a small but significant part of the force defending Madrid, approximately 1,900 in the 11th International Brigade, with another 1,550 joining in the following week. Disciplined, determined and many with military experience, they took their place alongside 35,000 Spanish militiamen, with a further 75,000 armed men able to be called upon.[38] The 11th International Brigade was commanded by General 'Kleber',[39] and consisted of the Hans Kahle, later to be called the André Marty, Battalion, the Dombrowski Battalion, and the Commune de Paris Battalion, which included amongst their number several British volunteers (see Table 3.3). Bill Rust estimates that there were 12 British members in the Machine-Gun (No. 4) Section,[40] though there were, in fact, slightly more. No. 4 Section was part of a company commanded by a Parisian building worker, Alfredo Brougère,[41] and, according to one of the British members of the unit, Bernard Knox:

> There was a core of convinced Communists all right (who did not, of course, need to be recruited) but the rest were a heady mixture of ex-Legionnaires, unemployed workers, kids just out of the Lycée, and the inevitable contingent, in a French unit, of semi-alcoholics.[42]

Several of the British, including H. Fred Jones and Jock Cunningham, had previous military experience and were generally fairly scathing about the whole 'set-up'.[43] Jan Kurzke, a German volunteer who arrived in Spain with John Cornford's group, described the suspicion with which the contingent of militarily experienced British volunteers viewed the concept of political commissars, who operated alongside the traditional military hierarchy (such as it was in 1936) and who were charged with maintaining the morale and political will of the volunteers:

> They scorned the ideas of political commissars, 'They [Cunningham and the others] were soldiers first', they said. We had a great many arguments about it. They thought that the political commissars would meddle with tactical and military matters and said it was impossible to have two commands. They did not understand that the job of political commissar was as important as that of any other army officer.[44]

Sam Russell[45] described the military calibre of the British contingent in the Commune de Paris Battalion as 'just a collection of odds and sods',[46] though the 'Oxbridge contingent' (three from Cambridge and one from Oxford) had all been to schools with cadet corps.[47] What little ammunition was available was, according to Russell, bad and 'quite dangerous'; bullets were loose in the casing so every clip of cartridges had to be checked individually.[48] There were few weapons available and drill was conducted in whichever style the nationality of the instructor determined. As another British member of the battalion, John Sommerfield, noted, 'We saw the Spanish and the Poles, the Italians and the Germans, the French and the Hungarians,

*Table 3.3* 'British' members of No. 4 Section, Commune de Paris Battalion,
11th International Brigade

| Surname | First name | Comments |
| --- | --- | --- |
| Barry | Jack | 'Blue'; Australian; killed at Boadilla, December 1936 |
| Burke | Edward | Also known as Edward Cooper; wounded at Cordoba, December 1936, died in hospital, Madrid, 12 February 1937 |
| Clarke | Jock | Probably from Glasgow |
| Cornford | John | Killed at Cordoba, December 1936 |
| Cunningham | Jock | Later commander of the British Battalion; repatriated August 1937 |
| Hinks | Joe | Later commander of the British Battalion; repatriated August 1937 |
| Jones | H. | 'Freddie'; leader of No.4 Section; killed at Madrid, November 1936 |
| Knox | Bernard | Political leader of battalion; repatriated around January 1937 |
| Lesser | Sam | aka Sam Russell; repatriated January 1937; later returned to Spain to work for the CP as broadcaster and replaced Peter Kerrigan as correspondent with the *Daily Worker* |
| Mackenzie | David | Incorrectly reported killed, December 1936. Actually repatriated December 1936 |
| McLaurin | Griffin | 'Mac'; born in New Zealand; killed Madrid, November 1936 |
| Patton | Thomas | Irish; killed at Boadilla, December 1936 |
| Sawyers | Robert | Scottish; wounded at Boadilla, December 1936; repatriated February 1937 |
| Sommerfield | John | Incorrectly reported killed December 1936; returned to Britain in January 1937 |
| Sowersby | George | From Edinburgh; arrived October 1936, repatriated January 1937 |
| Stevens | Joseph | Australian; killed at Brunete, July 1937 |
| Symes | Robert | Killed at Madrid, November 1936 |
| Thorneycroft | Chris | Later joined the Thaelmann Battalion |
| Yates | Steve | Born in New Zealand; killed at Madrid, November 1936 |

and they each had their own way of doing things.'[49] The multi-national nature of the brigade caused misunderstandings and confusion. The drilling was all in French, the movements as well as the commands, which many of the British found baffling. Knox was also highly critical of the training at the International Brigade base: 'One thing is certain: the training we were given at Albacete, the Brigade base, was a farce.'[50]

Nevertheless, on 7 November the newly formed 11th International Brigade marched along the Gran Via in Madrid on their way to the front.[51] Two days later the British volunteers in the 11th Brigade found themselves occupying a ridge in the Casa de Campo, the park to Madrid's west, bounded by the Manzanares River, where they took up defensive positions overlooking the park, waiting for the Moroccan *Regulares* to advance.[52] On the morning of 9 November 1936, the battalion positions were shelled, and once it had ended the Commune de Paris Battalion moved forward to meet an expected assault by the rebel forces facing them in the Casa de Campo. It came as predicted, but was directed at the German positions, where the line was held.[53] Later the same day, the 11th Brigade launched an assault on the rebel soldiers, and, though initially successful, the Republican force was counter-attacked by a rebel force made up of greatly superior numbers. Two New Zealanders, Steve Yates and Griffin McLaurin (who had travelled to Spain from Britain), accompanied by a British volunteer, Robert Symes, left the main group to set up a forward machine-gun position.[54] The following day the cost of the battle was counted; over 100 from the French battalion were dead, including McLaurin and Yates, who had been killed whilst covering a Republican infantry retreat in the Casa de Campo with a Lewis machine-gun. Robert Symes was badly injured and died shortly afterwards of his wounds.[55] Despite this setback, by the morning of 10 November 1936, the defenders had recaptured the entire park with the exception of Mount Garabitas, and the rebels were forced to abandon the direct attack through the Casa de Campo.[56]

The following day, 11 November, the volunteers were, with the rest of the Commune de Paris Battalion, part of an unsuccessful flank attack near Aravaca, just north of the Casa de Campo to the west of Madrid, where they were involved in a freak accident. One of the British volunteers was injured and the leader of the group (John Sommerfield's 'Freddie') was killed when an ambulance broke through a

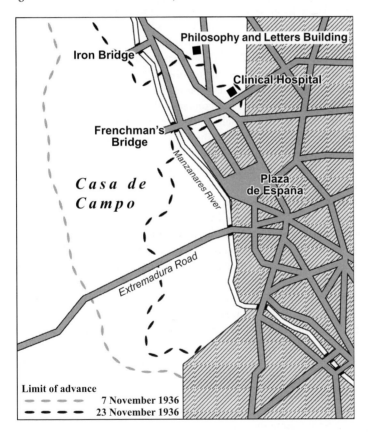

*Map 3.2* The rebels' direct assault on Madrid, via Casa de Campo, November 1936.

roadblock formed by a steel cable, which snapped and hit the group.[57] Following the death of Jones, Joe Hinks, who had fought with both the British Army and the Chinese Red Army (and another future commander of the British Battalion), was elected commander.[58]

Several days later, Hinks's group advanced into the University City near the Philosophy and Letters building, which was occupied by Spanish Moroccan soldiers on 15 November.[59] They attacked the rebel communication lines and moved into the Philosophy and Letters building, where they fought alongside some of Durruti's anarchists and a number of Asturian miners. The Commune de Paris Battalion defended the building successfully for a week, with the literary figures John Cornford, John Sommerfield and Bernard Knox all resorting to using books as barricades against rebel small-arms fire.[60] However, the defending force was hit by an artillery shell (probably Republican), and in the explosion John Cornford received a head injury that required his head to be bandaged. By 23 November, General Mola's rebel forces controlled two-thirds of the area of the University City, yet it had become clear to the Nationalists that the Republican forces were now well established and organised and that the direct frontal attack on Madrid had failed. Consequently, the rebel generals reluctantly called off their attack. With the front line reduced to a stalemate, on 7 December Joe Hinks's British contingent was withdrawn with the rest of the Commune de Paris Battalion to Albacete for a short rest.[61]

Meanwhile, another group of British had also been fighting in Madrid, as part of the 12th International Brigade. This group numbered more than a dozen, and included members of the Tom Mann Centuria and some later arrivals, such as Esmond Romilly, with whom they had been united at Albacete. Bill Rust states that there were 18 British attached to the Thaelmann Battalion,[62] though, again, this total probably includes volunteers from outside the UK (such as the American Ettore Fontana – known as Jerry – and Richard Whateley from Australia). Esmond Romilly counted only 10 when he joined the group at Albacete in October following their machine-gun training in Barcelona[63] (see Table 3.4).

The Thaelmann Battalion was divided into companies, which were themselves divided into *Zugs* (sections) of 30 men; the British contingent was No. 3 *Zug* of No. 1 Company. At both company and *Zug* level the commanders were Germans, though the *Zug* was divided into two smaller groups of 10 men which were both British led: one by Arnold Jeans from Manchester, who, fluent in six languages, also acted as interpreter; the other by Lorimer Birch, a scientist from Cambridge University and one of Esmond Romilly's 'Real Communists'.[64]

At the village of Villafranca, near Madrid, the volunteers were split into machine-gun groups of five and taught how to advance in 'little triangles', in which Lorimer Birch fired the machine-gun, Ray Cox loaded and David Marshall ran backwards and forwards with ammunition, whilst Esmond Romilly and 'Chris' (Thornycroft, who rapidly decided he wasn't cut out to be an infantryman)[65] positioned themselves 20 metres in front protecting the machine-gunners with rifle fire.[66] However, when the tactic was actually tried later in earnest, Romilly's first two attempts at firing were thwarted by defective ammunition.[67]

The British group was involved in a number of small skirmishes to the south of

*Table 3.4* 'British' members of the English section of the Thaelmann Battalion, 12th International Brigade

| Surname | First name | Comments |
|---|---|---|
| Addley | Harry | 'Tich'; killed at Boadilla, December 1936 |
| Avner | Sid | Killed at Boadilla |
| Birch | Lorimer | Killed at Boadilla |
| Cox | Ray | Killed at Boadilla |
| Donovan | John | 'Paddy'; left battalion before battle of Boadilla and joined POUM militia; repatriated July 1937 |
| Fontana | Ettore | 'Jerry'; American; deserted from battalion before battle of Boadilla |
| Gillan | Phil | 'Jock'; wounded in the neck at Boadilla; repatriated 1937 |
| Gough | William | 'Joe'; killed at Boadilla |
| Hutchinson | | Wounded in October 1936 and later fought with the British Battalion |
| Jeans | Arnold | Killed at Boadilla |
| Marshall | David | Wounded in November 1936; repatriated to England December 1936 |
| Messer | Martin | Killed at Boadilla |
| Norman | Philip | Deserted to UK before battle of Boadilla |
| Ovenden | Arthur | 'Babs'; repatriated December 1936 |
| Paester | Samuel | From Stepney; fought on the Aragon front in 1936 |
| Romilly | Esmond | Repatriated December 1936 |
| Scott | Bill | Repatriated to Ireland in 1937 |
| Sollenberger | Randall | American doctor who briefly fought with the Thaelmann Centuria |
| Thornycroft | Chris | Battalion armourer; later with 35th Division Medical Services; repatriated to England April 1938 |
| Watson | Keith | Left before battle of Boadilla to work as a journalist with the *Daily Express* |
| Whateley | Richard | 'Aussie'; seaman from Melbourne; repatriated 1937 |

Madrid as the rebels continued their advance on the Spanish capital.[68] The first occurred on 12 November, when they launched a badly planned, ill-executed and disastrous attack on Cerro de los Angeles, a hill to the south of Madrid.[69] As David Marshall describes, the military preparations for the attack were hopeless and the volunteers' level of military proficiency was appalling: 'We hadn't even fired the rifles before we went into action.'[70] Chris Thornycroft, who was operating as the No. 2 on a Lewis machine-gun, believed for some time that the operation was a training exercise.[71] As Phil Gillan described,

> We were engaged in our first action, at a place called the Hill of the Angels. On top of the hill was what we called a fort, but I think it was a monastery. The Moorish forces were in there and our job was to attack it and put them out. Anyway it didn't work out that way and the losses on our side were fairly heavy, fairly substantial.[72]

During the débâcle Marshall was wounded in the foot by a sniper's bullet, and he was repatriated soon afterwards.[73]

The remainder of the group was soon withdrawn to Chinchón, just south of Madrid, for reorganisation, before being moved to a new billet at Fuencarral, directly to the north of the city, where they took up reserve positions and made occasional attempts to retake positions held by the rebels. Hans Beimler, the German communist and leader of the Thaelmann Battalion, was killed in one of these abortive raids.[74] The stalemate was broken two weeks before Christmas, when the Thaelmann Battalion was transferred to the village of Boadilla del Monte, west of the capital, which had come under a very heavy rebel artillery barrage.

The Thaelmann Battalion was ordered to advance, though, as Romilly recognised, the Republican forces were already in a disorganised retreat. Unbeknown to the members of the Thaelmann Battalion, the other British group, fighting with the Commune de Paris Battalion, was amongst the Republican forces forced out of Boadilla by the rebel advance.[75] During the retreat Bernard Knox was injured by a bullet in the throat, but it passed right through and he survived.[76] He later described his feelings as he lay, believing himself to be dying:

> I have since then read many accounts by people who, like me, were sure that they were dying, but survived. Many of them speak of a feeling of heavenly peace, others of visions of angels welcoming them to Heaven. I had no such feelings or visions; I was consumed with rage – furious, violent rage. Why me? I was just 21 and had barely begun living my life. Why should I have to die? It was unjust. And, as I felt my whole being sliding into nothingness, I cursed. I cursed God and the world and everyone in it as the darkness fell.[77]

In the confusion the English section advancing with the Thaelmann Battalion became separated from their Spanish comrades and came under intense machine-gun fire from a ridge, which only moments before had been occupied by the Spanish Republican soldiers. As they in turn tried desperately to retreat they were caught in a murderous crossfire, with bullets also coming from their own trenches.[78] Only 17 of approximately 40 managed to retreat successfully. Richard Whateley later recounted to Esmond Romilly what had happened to the others: the rebel soldiers pretended to be Republicans and called out '*Camaradas!*' as they moved into the trenches and then 'finished off' any wounded.[79] News of the loss of 6 British volunteers (Lorimer Birch, Ray Cox, Harry Addley, Sid Avner, Joe Gough, Arnold Jeans and Martin Messer) appeared in the *Daily Worker* on 28 December, which claimed that German, rather than Spanish, soldiers had killed them.[80] With most of the contingent dead, this saw the end of the involvement of a British group in the Thaelmann Battalion. Of the surviving British, Phil Gillan returned to Britain after spending two or three weeks in hospital in Castellón de la Plana, north of Valencia.[81] Romilly, accompanied by 'Babs' Ovenden, also returned safely to Britain, just as Romilly's brother Giles was arriving in Spain.[82]

It has been suggested that the arrival of the first international volunteers made the crucial difference – that they 'saved Madrid'. Geoffrey Cox, writing in the *News Chronicle*, described the International Brigades as 'the first truly international army since the crusades', and was in no doubt that their arrival prevented the fall of

*Plate 3.1*  Survivors of the Thaelmann Battalion, Arthur 'Babs' Ovenden and Winston
Churchill's nephew Esmond Romilly (right) on their return to London in
December 1936.

*Plate 3.2*  The Tom Mann Centuria in September 1936, left to right: Sid Avner, Nat Cohen
(the leader of the group), Ramona, Tom Wintringham, later to command the
British Battalion (kneeling at the front in white), Georio Tioli (Italian), Jack Barry
(the Australian 'Blue') and David Marshall.

Madrid: 'Whatever happens, their name will go down to [*sic*] history as one of the finest and most courageous bodies of men ever in arms.'[83] As several historians have pointed out, it is certainly beyond doubt that the arrival in the first week of November 1936 of a well-disciplined group of soldiers provided an important psychological boost to the population of Madrid.[84]

> The military efficiency exhibited by the Internationals, which by Spanish military standards was phenomenal, was seen by many as one of the most important contributions to the defence of the city.[85]

However, as Hugh Thomas points out, it is hardly conceivable that they 'saved Madrid', for they comprised less than 5 per cent of the defending forces.[86] Phil Gillan, an ex-territorial who fought in the battles in the University City, also feels that, though the foreign volunteers played an important role, it was the Spanish who actually saved Madrid: 'The International Brigades played a big, big part but it was the Spanish troops themselves that held them out because the front was a big long front.'[87] Bernard Knox agrees:

> Obviously the Eleventh Brigade did not 'save' Madrid; the city had saved itself on the seventh, but the arrival of the Eleventh on the eighth and of the Twelfth some three or four days later, maybe an important and possibly decisive contribution to the continued success of the defence in the bloody weeks to come.[88]

Likewise, the 'English captain' Tom Wintringham, who took over command of the British Battalion from Wilf McCartney on 6 February 1937 and, as an ex-captain in the British Army, had some experience of military strategy, admitted: 'Don't let us exaggerate: our brigade did not save Madrid. Madrid would have saved itself without us.'[89] However, this does not mean that he believes the International Brigades' role was negligible, and Wintringham stresses that,

> Without us Franco would have got further into Madrid; he would have crossed the Casa de Campo and forced his way into the streets of the city itself. There street-fighting would have stopped him; but he would have had a foothold in the city. That he has not is thanks to the fighting quality, the skill in action, the digging powers of our first International Brigade.[90]

Following the reorganisation of the Republican Army that had created formal International Brigades of foreign volunteers in November, new arrivals were incorporated into these units, rather than in the plethora of volunteers' militias that had sprung up in the summer. By the end of 1936, volunteers were arriving from Britain in such numbers that Tom Wintringham's dream of uniting the British volunteers in a battalion, rather than attaching small groups to a German or French unit, was becoming a realistic possibility. During December 1936, Ralph Bates, a senior party official who worked in the Republican government's propaganda and information services, wrote back to Britain that,

What is wanted is a body of military volunteers. Not ones and two's [*sic*] of who usually have the poorest of reasons for coming out, but definitely organised and controlled by the party. The sending of a few comrades out in small groups does not lead to good results. They are put into predominantly Spanish, or at least foreign-speaking regiments, and get into difficulties as a result.[91]

The first step towards the creation of a British Battalion came in December with the formation of an English-speaking company as part of the 14th International Brigade commanded by 'General Walter'. The 145-strong British contingent[92] comprised the No. 1 Company of the French 14th (La Marseillaise) Battalion, which was commanded by a Frenchman, Lieutenant-Colonel Delasalle. The company itself was placed under the command of Captain George Nathan, an experienced officer who presented the very image of the British army officer, dressed impeccably and carrying a cane.[93] A number of the English-speaking company had seen action before: in addition to Nathan and the section commanders, Jock Cunningham and Joe Hinks, there were a number of others, including Sam Russell and John Cornford, who had seen action in Madrid in the 11th International Brigade.[94] There were also a number of IRA veterans, such as Kit Conway, who commanded another section, and the first of several Cypriot volunteers to arrive via London, Mike Economides, who would later become political commissar of the British Battalion.[95]

The English-speaking company was based in the small town of Madrigueras and was sent to the Córdoba front in southern Spain on Christmas Eve 1936, where they were involved in an attempt to capture the town of Lopera, about 30 miles to the west of Córdoba.[96] Many recruits had not handled a weapon before their arrival at Andújar railway station, near Lopera, when they were presented with Austrian Steyr rifles, constructed at the turn of the century.[97] On 28 December, the poorly armed and trained British company advanced up the hill towards the town, to find it heavily defended by rebel forces. For John Tunnah, a postman from Edinburgh who had arrived the previous November, his first experience of action in Spain was terrifying:

> We were moving against a town called Lopera. And the resistance stiffened . . . at times I could see parts of the town just coming out of the trees and little else. And it seemed as if every point of it was spouting fire – mainly at me.[98]

Faced with a superior enemy force – in particular from enemy aeroplanes, which machine-gunned the British lines causing considerable panic and confusion[99] – the British had little alternative than to make what Bill Alexander later described as an 'orderly and controlled' retreat, during which heavy casualties were inflicted.[100] The company commissar, Ralph Fox, a talented author who wrote a regular column for the *Daily Worker*, and the 'poet-intellectual' John Cornford were both killed. Without the experience of George Nathan, who managed to organise the withdrawal under a heavy rebel artillery barrage, the number of casualties would probably have been much higher.[101] Nathan was an experienced officer, of whom other volunteers spoke highly, 'resourceful, brave as a Lion and respected by all'.[102] The battalion moved backwards and forwards over the next three days, repeatedly reoccupying positions as the rebels launched their own powerful counter-offensives.[103] However, any hope of capturing Lopera had long since passed.

Senior figures at the International Brigade base saw the operation at Lopera as a catastrophe, and efforts were made to discover why the battalion had been so disorganised and ineffective. André Marty, commander of the International Brigades at Albacete, and Peter Kerrigan, a senior party figure from Scotland and political commissar for all English-speaking volunteers at Albacete, launched an investigation.[104] Marty accused the French commander of the Marseillaise Battalion, Delasalle, of cowardice and treason and claimed that the latter was spying for the rebels.[105] Whether Marty had any hard evidence to support the accusations is still a matter of some contention – Marty neither liked nor trusted Delasalle and is often cited as the personification of Stalinist paranoia in Spain; however, George Nathan, who was at the trial, was fully convinced of his guilt, as was Maurice Levine, who, with Sid Quinn, was Delasalle's escort from his prison cell to the court-room.[106] Further remarks on the matter come from James Albrighton, who claims that he was actually present at the trial when four French witnesses gave evidence against Delasalle. Albrighton states that two wounded French volunteers claimed to have witnessed Delasalle going in the direction of Lopera, which was under rebel control at the time. He also said that Delasalle was found guilty after admitting working for French intelligence, though 'acting more as an unofficial observer and reporter than a spy'. Albrighton further claimed to have spoken to both Tom Wintringham and George Nathan about Delasalle, who stated to him that a search ordered by Marty had discovered papers linking him to a French fascist movement. According to Albrighton, Delasalle died cursing Marty for being 'a maniac, [and] a homicidal neurotic'.[107]

However, Walter Greenhalgh, who also fought with the No. 1 Company at Lopera, is less convinced. He believes that Delasalle was made a scapegoat, and that 'we much preferred to believe that there was treachery rather than incompetence.'[108] Greenhalgh's account came from his friend, a Dutchman called Piet Jansen, who acted as interpreter at the trial, even though another of Jansen's friends, Maurice Levine, claims that Jansen confirmed to him that Delasalle had confessed to spying against the Russians in Bucharest.[109] Like Greenhalgh, Joe Monks believed that the military disaster that led to Delasalle's execution was also a result of a very disorganised command structure. Monks argued that Lopera was too big a sector for an officer with the rank of only colonel, and really needed an officer with the rank of general or higher.[110] Likewise, in a recent conversation with the author, Sam Russell stated that, contrary to his opinion at the time, he now believed that Delasalle was guilty of nothing worse than incompetence.[111]

Overall, the balance of probability seems to suggest that the evidence of the four Frenchmen, which was little more than hearsay, was not reliable. Though Delasalle may well have had connections with French military intelligence, he was unlikely to have been a rebel spy, and thus became a scapegoat for the disaster at Lopera. Nevertheless, as James Brown, a volunteer from London who had arrived in November, recounts, whether he was guilty of espionage or not, many of the British blamed Delasalle for the heavy casualties at Lopera and were not unhappy to see the back of him.[112] Despite the failure of the battalion as a whole, No. 1 Company was seen as having operated effectively (despite their inexperience and poor weaponry). George Nathan was promoted to replace Delasalle as battalion commander, and Jock Cunningham, who had fought with the Commune de Paris Battalion in the 11th International Brigade, replaced him as company commander.

The company remained at Lopera for about ten days before being transferred back to Madrid to help contain a major rebel offensive that had been launched to the north-west of the city, at Las Rozas. Following the failure of his frontal assault on Madrid through the Casa de Campo, Franco attempted instead to close the circle around the north of the capital. By 3 January, the rebel offensive had captured Majadahonda and Las Rozas and cut the road between Madrid and Corunna in several places.[113] The battalion attempted to retake the Madrid–Corunna Road, but by 15 January, amid rapidly deteriorating weather conditions, their attempts had ground to a halt. Again, there were a number of casualties: Walter Greenhalgh was hit in the neck by a bullet,[114] but was lucky enough to make it to Benicasim hospital, where he was operated on by the American Dr Sollenberger.[115] Seven of Walter Greenhalgh's comrades were not so fortunate and were killed at Las Rozas.[116] Only 67 volunteers of the 150 in No. 1 Company who had left for Lopera on Christmas Eve still remained to be transferred back to Albacete and united with the other English-speaking volunteers.[117]

However, within a fortnight, numbers had climbed back to 450, enough for them to refer to themselves as the 'English speaking Battalion'.[118] The battalion, including the remainder of the volunteers from No. 1 Company, was sent to Madrigueras, a small village about 20 miles from Albacete, which would become the British volunteers' base.[119] Bill Rust described the village as 'not very lively . . . like all Spanish villages it also had a church – a very big one; and a school – a very small one.'[120] Arrivals to the village were told a familiar story,

> That the local priest had been a Franco supporter and when he . . . got wind of Franco's revolt that he got up into the bell tower of the church with a machine-gun and fired on anyone who went to the local fountain for water.[121]

It was during this time, whilst the English-speaking volunteers were based at Madrigueras in January 1937, that the Irish volunteers controversially elected to leave the British Battalion and fight instead with the American volunteers in the Lincoln Battalion. Clearly this decision rankled with many of the British, and it was claimed, pointedly, 'that distinctions must be made between anti-fascist working-class comrades from Britain and British imperialism.'[122] However, establishing this distinction was not helped by the widely held belief that two senior British officers in the battalion, Wilf McCartney and George Nathan, had played a part in British Army covert activities in Ireland.[123]

That divisions arose between the English and Irish is not surprising; James Hopkins suggests that 'most, if not all, of the Irish volunteers were members of the Irish Republican Army.'[124] Certainly a number had been, and both the leading figures amongst the Irish contingent, Frank Ryan and Chris 'Kit' Conway, were experienced IRA fighters.[125] Not surprisingly, the ex-IRA activists and supporters found fighting alongside their old adversaries extremely difficult, no matter the international rhetoric of the political commissars.[126] Likewise, many of the English seemed to find it difficult to overcome an ignorant and stereotypical view of the Irish as wastrels and drunkards. Not all were as tactful as the postman from Edinburgh, John Tunnah, who stated that 'There were Irish attached to the British Battalion. And they were grand people. But ideologically they didn't hit it off.'[127]

The official history of the British Battalion, which resides in the Moscow archive, is very uncomplimentary about the Irish volunteers, and suggests that many of the British were glad to see the back of them.[128] It refers to a number of elements of very bad character amongst the Irish comrades, some of whom were habitual drunkards, others of very bad anti-fascist spirit. According to the report, on several occasions a number of Irish volunteers were carried into the battalion barracks late at night by the local peasants, so drunk they could not stand or walk.[129] It also claims that some of the Irish volunteers were not welcomed; one sailor, who had been living in London before he went to Spain, was described as an 'absolute drunkard and undisciplined', and Fred Copeman refused to allow him back into the British Battalion at Brunete.[130] Whilst Bill Alexander later claimed that 'English, Scots, Welsh and all other nationalities mixed, with some chaffing and jokes, and without thought to their label "British"',[131] he later admitted that there was a degree of tension between the Irish and English volunteers. His claim that 'These tensions, inevitable against the background of Irish oppression, vanished in action',[132] seems rather too upbeat. However, it is true that the surviving Irish volunteers returned to the British Battalion after the battle of Brunete.

According to Bill Alexander, the military contribution of the early British volunteers, who arrived before the Communist Party had gained control of recruitment, was not as significant as from those who arrived after Christmas 1936. As this chapter has shown, it is true that the first few volunteers from Britain differed from those who arrived after the end of 1936, in that they were generally younger and more middle class. The youthful enthusiasm of those like Esmond Romilly, one of the few British volunteers to survive at Boadilla, earned them a grudging respect from some of the older, more experienced volunteers. Phil Gillan was in no doubt that Romilly was courageous: '[He] was a very brave little lad who volunteered for most things, but in other ways as a soldier, you know, a big question mark . . . how he wasn't killed, really I don't know.'[133] Unfortunately, Gillan's main recollection of Romilly as a soldier was that he could never put his ammunition pouches on properly, and that, as he tied up his trousers with string, they were constantly falling down.[134] Romilly, candid as ever, makes no secret of this, and also suggests that his lack of military professionalism was hardly a rarity: 'I never managed to keep any of my stuff together. Fortunately, losable objects like belts and bayonets and plates could be found anywhere – abandoned by someone else.'[135]

Likewise, John Cornford, the communist intellectual and the very epitome of the Byronic figure, died precisely because of a result of this image – his white bandage acting as a perfect target for the Moorish snipers in the rebel army, who, as Phil

Gillan remembers, were expert shots.[136] Walter Greenhalgh, who claimed to have seen Cornford killed at Lopera, describes how the latter climbed up to the brow of the hill to reconnoitre and the sun caught his 'lovely white bandage'. Cornford, who had refused to wear a hat, was shot through the head.[137]

Hugh O'Donnell, who was in charge of the English volunteers in Barcelona, was also ambivalent about the overall quality of the early volunteers, claiming at the beginning of 1937 that 'the poor organisation . . . makes it impossible at the base to sort out the wheat from the chaff.'[138] The battalion would be given little chance to overcome these problems, for the following month would provide these British volunteers with a terrifying ordeal through which few would pass unscathed. In February 1937 the volunteers, both wheat and chaff, would find themselves facing Franco's crack troops, the Moorish *Regulares*, in a desperate battle at the Jarama Valley.

# 4   Cerca de Madrid, 1937

## The battle of Jarama and 'the furnace of Brunete'

It wasnae a battle at a', it wis a bloody slaughter as far as we were concerned.[1]

Following the return of No. 1 Company to Albacete at the beginning of 1937, the British Battalion was considered to be of sufficient strength and readiness for front-line action. With the Yugoslav Dimitrov Battalion, the Franco-Belge Battalion[2] and the American Abraham Lincoln Battalion, they comprised the 15th International Brigade, which was commanded by the 'incompetent, bad-tempered and hated' Russian, Colonel Gal.[3] Gal's chief of staff was the Englishman George Nathan, who had shown himself at Lopera to be a rather different proposition. The 15th Brigade commissar was a Yugoslavian called Čopić, rather more popular than Gal, whom he would later replace as brigade commander;[4] Čopić was assisted by the French communist Jean Chaintron, known in Spain as 'Barthel'.[5]

The British Battalion was commanded by a Scottish journalist, Wilf McCartney, who had impeccable revolutionary credentials, having served ten years in Parkhurst prison for spying for Russia.[6] The battalion political commissar, working alongside McCartney, was Dave Springhall, the secretary of the London district of the Communist Party and a member of the party's political bureau, who had studied at the Lenin School in Moscow, the finishing school for the party's elite.[7]

The battalion itself was divided up into four companies, one machine-gun company plus three of infantry. No. 1 Company was led by Jock Cunningham, ex-Argyll and Sutherland Highlanders, and veteran of the battles in the University City in Madrid and Lopera. No. 2, the Machine-Gun Company, was led by Tom Wintringham, who after his time in the Tom Mann Centuria had become an instructor at the officer training school in Pozorrubio. Wintringham also acted as second-in-command of the British Battalion. No. 3 was led by Bill Briskey, an experienced trade union activist from London, and No. 4 by Bert Overton, who had served in the Welsh Guards regiment in the British Army. There were now approximately 750 British in Spain, including 500 in the British Battalion,[8] 60 in other units of the 15th International Brigade (such as mapping and catering), 75 new arrivals and 25 still at the base at Madrigueras[9] and in hospital, plus another 20 in the cavalry.[10] So, at the end of January 1937, despite the loss of most of the Irish contingent, the British Battalion was in relatively good health, with all but one of its commanders from company level upwards having military experience, and with most of them having already gained some experience in Spain.

However, in early February 1937 came several changes, of which the most significant was the replacement of Wilf McCartney as commander of the battalion in somewhat suspicious, or at the very least bizarre, circumstances. As part of his parole requirements following his release from Parkhurst, McCartney had regularly to report to the authorities, and he was due temporarily to return to England. Prior to his departure, a farewell supper was held in his honour at the International Brigade base at Albacete. At the end of the evening, Peter Kerrigan, the political commissar at the base, was exchanging pistols with McCartney when the pistol went off, wounding McCartney in the arm[11] and ensuring his period of leave became rather more permanent.

James Hopkins's study of the British Battalion raises the old controversy of whether or not the shooting was an accident. Bill Alexander states that 'Kerrigan was deeply upset, offering his resignation', and is categorical that the shooting was an accident. Many other volunteers agree with him.[12] And, as Alexander argues, 'Accidents with weapons were not uncommon among so many untrained men.'[13] However, as Hopkins points out, this explanation is somewhat disingenuous, for neither McCartney nor Kerrigan were 'untrained men' inexperienced in the use of firearms,[14] both having served in the First World War. Furthermore, though originally believed to be the only man in Spain capable of leading the British Battalion,[15] by the end of January McCartney had lost the confidence of Peter Kerrigan and Tom Wintringham and was suffering from a lack of self-confidence. He was also, according to Kerrigan, becoming increasingly critical of the party.[16]

One person who believed that the shooting was not an accident was Fred Copeman, who later commanded the battalion himself. As Copeman remarked pointedly, 'What would a bloke be doing cleaning a bloody revolver in a taxi and [*sic*] he's got all day and all night?'[17] Copeman is not the only one to level the accusation. George Leeson, who fought with the Machine-Gun Company at Jarama, had nothing good to say about McCartney. Describing him as 'a complete poseur', Leeson is in no doubt that Kerrigan shot McCartney deliberately.[18] John Tunnah, who served as a runner in the British Battalion, is also convinced that it was no accident.[19] Nevertheless, though the shooting conveniently ensured the removal of McCartney from his position, it is unlikely that it was anything more than an accident, despite Copeman's protestations.[20] McCartney was already returning to Britain, and, had Peter Kerrigan and Harry Pollitt decided that the British Battalion would be better served in Spain without McCartney, they could easily have prevented him from returning to Spain, as they would later demonstrate when three senior British figures in Spain (the brigade commissar George Aitken, the former battalion commander, and now a brigade staff officer, Jock Cunningham, and battalion commissar Bert Williams) were recalled to Britain following heated arguments after the battle of Brunete.[21]

McCartney was replaced as battalion commander by Tom Wintringham, with Harold Fry, the ex-sergeant from the British Army who had served in India and China, taking command of the Machine-Gun Company.[22] At the same time, the battalion commissar, Dave Springhall, was promoted to brigade commissar and replaced by George Aitken, the full-time Communist Party organiser for the North-East of England. The new commanders took up their posts on 6 February 1937, but were not given much time to settle in, for the same day the rebels launched an offensive to the south-east of Madrid, in an attempt to cut the vital road linking the capital city of Madrid with Valencia, the seat of the Republican government.[23] By the evening the Republicans, including advance elements of 15th International Brigade, had been pushed back to the Jarama River, and rebel troops were within shelling distance of the road.[24]

The following day General Miaja, in charge of the defence of Madrid, sent General Lister's 11th Division from Madrid to reinforce the defending Republican force, and on 9 February, the Republican defences were reorganised along the heights to the east of the Jarama River. Meanwhile, the 500 British in the battalion left their base at Madrigueras and were taken by train to the International Brigade base at Albacete, and then by lorry to Chinchón, about 15 miles from Madrid and 10 miles south-east of the site of the rebel advance.

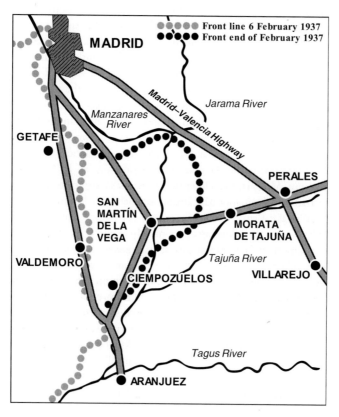

*Map 4.1* The rebels' attempt to encircle Madrid, February 1937.

Despite the Republicans' defensive efforts, a small number of Nationalist troops managed to move stealthily across the railway bridge on the small dirt road which ran towards the Madrid–Valencia Road (between San Martín de la Vega and Morata de Tajuña) after knifing the sentries, members of the French André Marty Battalion of the 14th International Brigade. The rest of the rebel column crossed immediately after them, then moved forward into the Tajuña Valley, in an attempt to cut the road.[25] During the evening of 11 February, another rebel unit also managed to get across the Jarama, using the same strategy employed at dawn. During the night they consolidated their position, in preparation for an assault on the ridge which overlooked them, the Pingarrón Heights.

The newly formed 15th International Brigade was now thrown into the defence. The British were transferred from Chinchón early in the morning of 12 February to the junction of the Morata to San Martín de la Vega and Chinchón to Madrid roads, where they arrived at 5.30 a.m.[26] The battalion was ordered to move forward towards the Jarama River, which lay beyond the next ridge. They moved off, fuelled with 'copious quantities of coffee'[27] and encouraged by a speech from their political commissar, urging them to make whatever sacrifices were necessary to stem the rebel advance.

> We are prepared to sacrifice our lives, because this sacrifice is not only for the peace and freedom of the Spanish people, but also for the peace and freedom of the French people, the Germans, the English, the Italians, the Czechs, the Croats, and for all the peoples of the world.[28]

The volunteers moved up the hill in single file to a plateau overlooking the Jarama River, near a farmhouse where the cookhouse was established.[29] The three British companies then continued to advance, having little idea when they would meet the enemy.

> We dropped down into the first gulley and there we were told to leave all the packs, large packs and the belongings and like, which we did . . . We continued to advance up the hill and on to the top and into the olive groves . . . There was still no fighting going on – at least not with us. We could hear the artillery and the like but there was no fire of any kind coming to us and we weren't firing.[30]

The British had no maps and thus had no knowledge of the position of the Nationalist forces. Jason Gurney, the London sculptor, was one of the volunteers who helped to draw sketch maps of the area but, as he stated, 'Under these circumstances I think it must have been quite impossible for Gal [the 15th International Brigade commander] to have had any precise idea of the state of affairs at the front from his position at brigade headquarters.'[31]

The volunteers moved forward over the ridge, then, after crossing a narrow sunken road, began to descend into the valley of the Jarama River, which lay in front of them. At this point, the British volunteers began to come under fire from the rebel force, which the Republican command did not realise had already crossed the river.

For Albert Charlesworth, a metal-polisher from Oldham, it seemed like a beautiful day. It was a dream from which he would shortly be very rudely awakened:

> I thought it was a glorious day actually. It was a nice day, beautiful day. There was the sun got up, it got really warm and the birds seemed to be singing very nicely to me. We weren't being fired on although firing seemed to be taking place – I thought so anyway. But it wasn't until eleven o'clock in the morning that I realised that the birds that were singing were bullets whistling past and there was a fierce battle going on.[32]

Charlesworth was not the only volunteer not to realise the lethal situation they were marching into. James Maley, who had served in the British Territorial Army, was one of the volunteers in No. 2 Company advancing towards the river. He later described the confusion as they moved forwards through retreating Republican soldiers:

> After two hundred yards going forward the retreat was coming back and going down past us and we were going through. There were soldiers running past us and we were going up. And there were soldiers of the British Battalion dropping as we were going up. Without firing a shot they were getting killed.[33]

When they realised that the rebels had already crossed the river, the British rapidly pulled back to the top of the ridge, later to be named 'Suicide Hill' by the surviving British volunteers, and took up defensive positions, with No. 3 Company to the left, No. 4 Company to the right, and the Machine-Gun Company just behind them. They then prepared to engage with the advancing rebel forces.[34]

For many of the British volunteers, it was their first experience of action, and they were facing the battle-hardened, elite regulars of Franco's Army of Africa. The Moorish troops, 'the most ferocious enemy in the world', were highly skilled soldiers, in their element when advancing across the open terrain of the Jarama Valley.[35] Jason Gurney described the absolute horror the advance of the North African troops had on the poorly trained volunteers and effectively summarised the inequality between the two opposing factions:

> Nobody at Madrigueras had said anything about artillery fire or the genius of Moorish infantry to move across country without presenting a target for anyone but a highly-trained marksman – a category that included no one in our outfit . . . [The Moors] were professionals, backed by a mass of artillery and heavy machine-gun fire supplied by the German Condor legion. It was a formidable opposition to be faced by a collection of city-bred young men with no experience of war, no idea how to find cover on an open hillside, and no competence as marksmen.[36]

The volunteers rapidly discovered that the minimal training they had received at Madrigueras in no way readied them for taking on Franco's elite soldiers, despite their initial confidence.[37] What training there had been, as one would expect, owed

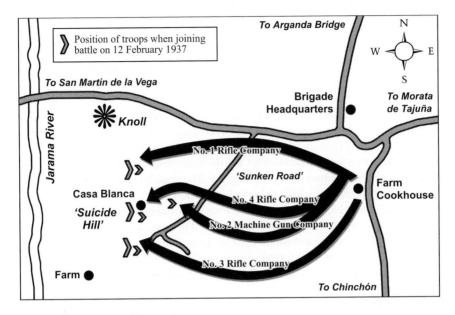

*Map 4.2* The British positions at Jarama.

much to the British Army.[38] James Maley described his experiences of military training: 'Well it really wasn't much. It was really marching and we didn't really get time to train because we were only there five weeks before we were moved up to the front.'[39] Likewise, Harry Stratton, a Swansea taxi driver, described how '[We] were issued with rifles (Russian made) and ammo on the way. I hadn't handled a rifle until then, but Jock McCrae had taught me rifle drill with a walking stick on the way up.'[40] And John Tunnah, who at least had served in the Royal Navy Volunteer Reserve, put it very succinctly, 'I can't even remember my training. I can remember one miserable day, only about a morning, running about a field. And I think that was my training.'[41] Of course, many of the problems with training were a result of the well-documented limitations of quantity and quality of Republican arms.[42] Guns and ammunition were scarce in the extreme, as Eddie Brown, an experienced anti-fascist activist from Scotland, wryly pointed out, 'Ye couldnae waste ammunition. We had none to waste.'[43]

In fact, the ammunition situation was critical, for the members of the Machine-Gun Company discovered that their Maxim machine-guns had been given cartridge belts filled with the wrong ammunition.[44] Worse still, a lorry driven by a British sergeant which was carrying the correct ammunition had been involved in an accident and had overturned.[45] Deprived of their machine-guns, Fry's company, only 72 men strong, was forced to resort to firing their rifles desperately at the rebel soldiers advancing expertly towards them.

Tom Wintringham had initially ordered No. 1 Company to hold in reserve, much to the disgust of its commander, the ex-IRA man Kit Conway,[46] but due to the rebel threat it was soon moved up to a small bare hill to the north, to the right of the companies on the ridge. Under the ferocious attack, the Franco-Belge Battalion further to the north of the British was forced to pull back. This brought the British companies and the battalion headquarters under lethal enfilading machine-gun fire, which swept across them from their right. The British held on desperately, but for the volunteers it was utter carnage. Tom Clarke, a labourer from Dundee, described how many of the volunteers were brave to the point of recklessness: 'Unfortunately you had fellows who, more out of bravado than anything else, when they were firing, instead of lying down and taking cover, they were standing up. It was just a slaughter.'[47] Jason Gurney, the London sculptor, could see that 'these were completely raw troops, imperfectly trained and disciplined, ordered to hold a position on an exposed hillside against heavy artillery fire. They had no entrenching equipment, nor had they received any instruction in fortification.'[48]

Both No. 3 and No. 4 Companies came under sustained artillery fire and, as the day progressed, casualties mounted up quickly. The wounded were taken out of the line under fire by stretcher-bearers such as Tom Clarke, a friend of Bob Cooney from the hunger marches of 1934, whilst, nearby in Chinchón, members of the Scottish ambulance unit, such as Roddy MacFarquar, ferried the wounded to Republican hospitals.[49]

No. 3 Company lost their commander, Bill Briskey, and his replacement, Ken Stalker, within a short time of each other. Also killed when their French Chaucot light machine-gun jammed were Christopher St John Sprigg (known as Christopher Caudwell), the 'brilliant Marxist intellectual', and his close friend Clem Beckett, the daredevil speedway rider (and the inventor of the 'wall of death' motorcycle stunt).[50] Deprived of leadership, the rapidly diminishing No. 3 Company attempted desperately to prepare itself for the assault that would follow the end of the barrage. Meanwhile, No. 4 Company was also sustaining casualties at a horrifying rate, but its terrified commander was making little preparation to defend the company against the imminent assault.[51]

By late afternoon, the desperate position of the battalion and its mounting casualties left its members with little option but to attempt an orderly retreat from Suicide Hill back to the battalion headquarters on the plateau. Where possible, they dragged their wounded comrades with them, covered by Sam Wild, the battalion armourer, and a few other volunteers.[52] But, as Albert Charlesworth noted, 'There weren't many to go back to the sunken road.'[53] As the British pulled back, Moorish soldiers rushed forward over the top of Suicide Hill to occupy the positions relinquished by the retreating men.

However, after a desperately frustrating day spent without ammunition for their machine-guns, the correct calibre ammunition had at last appeared, though it still required Harold Fry, helped by Fred Copeman,[54] to load the shells individually, by hand, into the belts. Just in time Fry and Copeman brought the machine-guns into operation and used them with devastating effect on the rebel soldiers, who, for once, were caught out in the open and totally unawares. Copeman managed to bully the frightened volunteers into holding fire until the *Regulares* were almost on top of them, much to the volunteers' alarm:

On they came. And, of course, the nearer they came the more timid the bloody crowd got. They wanted to fire. They wanted to kill them, you know. They'd heard about Moors doing awful things to prisoners. 'Never mind the effing Moors. Hold your fire.' One kid said, 'I'll fire and eff you too.' So I got stuck into him. And we held on.[55]

Joe Garber, a cabinet-maker from Whitechapel, was one of the company who was very reluctant to hold fire, but remembers things slightly differently: 'And this silly bastard comes along, Copeman, don't fire yet . . . And I thought, "Sod this" and I opened up.'[56]

The Moroccan troops retreated out of range, which brought to an end the first day of the battle of Jarama. The British Battalion had endured seven hours of heavy losses, and 'Out of the 400 men in the rifle companies, only 125 were left. Altogether less than half the battalion remained.'[57] The remnants of the battalion gathered at the battalion headquarters on the sunken road, or the cookhouse next to the farm, desperate for food and water. After dark, Jason Gurney was asked by the battalion commander, Tom Wintringham, to reconnoitre the sunken road which ran across the plateau, near its forward edge. Here Gurney made a horrifying discovery; about 50 injured men were lying on stretchers, where they had been left and forgotten in the chaotic and desperate times during the day. By the time Gurney discovered them it was too late; most were dying or already dead.[58]

During the night about 30 stragglers from No. 3 Company were found at the cookhouse by the battalion political commissar, George Aitken. Where possible, Aitken cajoled them to return to the line but, as he freely admits, on occasions he forced some volunteers back to the front under threat of his pistol.[59] However, Aitken never actually used it; like most of the other senior figures in the battalion, he was vehemently opposed to the shooting of deserters.[60] Aitken claims that he was approached at Jarama by higher officers, 'and a civilian', with the idea of trying, and possibly shooting, some of the deserters. Aitken resisted it and states that he remained totally opposed to the idea of shooting men who had volunteered. He later stated categorically that 'there was nothing of the kind while I was there.'[61] However, coerced or not, the volunteers were a desperately needed addition to the front line.

The second day of the battle was to be no less terrifying for the shocked volunteers. The battalion commander, Tom Wintringham, prepared the depleted forces as best he could. Harold Fry's (No. 2) Machine-Gun Company was kept in a forward position, overlooking the valley and river below them. No. 4 Company, under Overton, was placed to the right and No. 1 Company was facing the open left flank, now following the death of Kit Conway under the command of André Diamant (an Anglicised Egyptian, whose name appears variously as Andre Diamond and Andre Diamont). Stand-to was at 3 a.m. Dave Springhall, the assistant brigade commissar, brought orders from brigade headquarters that the battalion should prepare for an advance on the Nationalist forces, which he said would be supported by tanks and another International Brigade.

When dawn broke Fry's company was able to see a number of rebel soldiers who had moved up in the night between the ridge and Suicide Hill and drive them back with concentrated machine-gun fire.[62] But as the day progressed the Franco-Belge and Dimitrov Battalions on the right were gradually pushed back and the British Battalion found itself once again surrounded on three sides. By late afternoon Wintringham was aware that a rebel assault on Fry's position was imminent, as small groups of Nationalist troops could be seen working their way forward to Fry's right, where Bert Overton's No. 4 Company was situated. At this point the nervous Overton finally panicked and withdrew his company right back to the sunken road, as he had been begging the political commissar George Aitken to allow him to do all day.[63] This left the Machine-Gun Company's flank totally unprotected, and rebel forces quickly took advantage of the situation and surrounded them. Tom Wintringham wrote a desperate note to Fry requesting that the Machine-Gun Company hold on,[64] but before the note could be delivered they were overrun by Nationalist forces. As many as 30 members of the Machine-Gun Company, including its commander, Harold Fry, and his number two, Ted Dickenson, were captured.[65]

The exact circumstances of the capture of the Machine-Gun Company remain rather unclear. Originally it was believed that they had been tricked into surrendering by Nationalist troops who approached the British positions singing the Internationale and holding their clenched fists raised in the Popular Front salute. Several accounts describe how:

> I heard the strains of the 'International' coming from the direction of the outpost trench. As I got nearer I was surprised to see numbers of Fascists coming over the land between us and them, singing the 'International' and holding up their fists in the anti-fascist salute. Our boys were holding up their fists in welcome to the boys who were coming over. I had not the least doubt that here was a mass desertion from the Fascist lines. 'Yank' Levy seemed to be the first to realise the trick that had been played, but by this time there were swarms of Fascists in the trench.[66]

This story appears regularly, in various forms, in accounts of the battle, such as an article in *Workers Weekly* recounted by Tom Spiller[67] from New Zealand, a member of No. 4 Company, and in the book of contributions of volunteers edited by the Irish Republican leader Frank Ryan.[68] A similar version is to be found in the Moscow archives:

> At about 5.30, the men of the Machine-Gun Company, still lying in the trenches, heard during a lull in the firing the singing of the Internationale and saw a body of men advancing towards their positions, giving the anti-fascist salute and shouting: 'Vivan las Brigadas Internacionales'. At that distance and because of the similarity of dress, our comrades mistook them for the Spanish Battalion. Some thought it was a mass desertion from the fascist lines. Our comrades held up their fists in welcome to the men who were coming over. When they were about 30 metres from the Machine-Gun Company's positions,

Company Commander Fry recognised them as fascists by their Mauser rifles and the dress of their officers. So he immediately gave the order to load and fire. Hand to hand fighting took place. Many died in the fascist ranks. The Company lost 10. Comrades M. Gunners, Doran and his crew Jasper Philies and Plum were blown up by grenades while operating their machine-guns. Katscoronas, veteran of four revolutions, ammunition gone, died cracking skulls with his rifle butt.[69]

This story has become part of the legend of the battle of Jarama,[70] though doubts must remain about this version of events.[71] That even the relatively inexperienced British volunteers could confuse conspicuous Moorish troops with Republican soldiers seems unlikely, particularly as the Moors had been their main adversaries the previous day. But as Donald Renton, who was the Machine-Gun Company's political commissar and one of those captured that day, explains, the situation was very confusing with various contradictory instructions being given: 'There were different voices raised, you know, to keep firing. Others were for cease fire – "These are our own comrades."'[72]

Nevertheless, there is an alternative, and more convincing, version, which originates with George Leeson, a section commander in the Machine-Gun Company, another of the volunteers captured that day.[73] Leeson states that the troops that infiltrated Fry's Machine-Gun Company were members of the Spanish Foreign Legion who had replaced the North African troops. Leeson believed that Fry mistook the advancing Nationalist soldiers for deserters and stood up and told his company to cease fire,

And led them all in singing the Internationale and standing up and giving thanks . . . About half the men holding that line were shot as they came over. The rest of us just had our rifles knocked out of our hands and we were surrounded.[74]

John Tunnah, the Scottish volunteer acting as the battalion runner at Jarama, was watching events from the plateau overlooking the battle, and is in no doubt that the story of the Nationalist soldiers deserting with their hands raised whilst singing the Internationale is false. Tunnah rather scathingly states:

I've heard this story about the Moors coming over singing the Internationale . . . I wouldn't have this for one minute. I don't believe it . . . Moorish soldiers, almost illiterate, could understand probably some Spanish commands, who live in North Africa and talk the Arab dialect, and they've been sweeping round through the south of Spain for the past six months going pretty fast. And then somehow on the way they learnt to sing the 'Internationale' as they come over the hill at the International Brigade. And a British commander that would believe such a thing? Well![75]

Tunnah believes that Harold Fry did not dispute Bill Meredith's version of events, for he realised that his company was in the wrong position and felt responsible.[76] Tunnah argues that the machine-gun group were too far forward and should, instead, have been on the plateau to the rear with himself and Fred Copeman:

> They shouldn't have been there. They should have been up on the ridge beside us but thought that they were in a safe place, a good . . . well-placed to deal with the enemy probably and relatively safe themselves. And they sat there. And whoever the military commander was on the other side saw the opportunity and came over in force at first light in the morning and swept round both sides of them. They hadn't a chance. And if they hadn't surrendered they would have been killed.[77]

In fact, Tom Wintringham was fully aware that the placement of the Machine-Gun Company was unconventional, but he felt that the position was the only one offering a good field of fire.

> According to the text-book it was wrong to have the heavy machine-guns out in front. But their position was really a magnificent one, and the only one available with a good field of fire covering nearly a mile of front.[78]

As Wintringham rather pointedly states, 'Well dug in, with plenty of belts and ammunition, our machine-gunners could hold that terrace – if their flanks were safe.'[79] Overton's withdrawal of No. 4 Company ensured that this was not the case; realising the extent of his error, Overton tried to make amends by leading a charge of 40 men in a desperate attempt to retake the trenches recently occupied by Fry's Machine-Gun Company. The Nationalist soldiers simply mowed them down with the machine-guns they had just captured. Only 6 of the 40 men made it back to the British positions. In the mêlée Tom Wintringham sustained a leg wound, which ended his period of commander of the British Battalion, and George Aitken, the battalion political commissar, took temporary control. By nightfall only 160 still remained in the line.[80] With Wintringham injured, Fry captured, and Overton in tatters, the British Battalion was in an unenviable position. Thus the arrival of the experienced and widely respected Jock Cunningham, who took over command from Aitken during the evening, came not a moment too soon.

The third day of the battle, on 14 February, brought a new assault on the British line by a fresh rebel brigade, supported by tanks. With the British machine-guns crushed underneath the tanks, the desperately weakened British line finally broke and the volunteers retreated in small groups back down the slope towards the Chinchón road and the cookhouse. Here they were visited by Lieutenant-Colonel Gal, the commander of the 15th International Brigade, who explained to them that they were the only troops between the rebels and the Valencia Road.[81] Despite their physical and mental exhaustion, 140 volunteers marched back with Jock Cunningham and Frank Ryan to try to recapture their lost positions. Under no illusions about the situation they were walking into, the volunteers advanced, singing the Internationale to bolster their spirits, and picking up stragglers on the way.[82] Joe Garber was one of the starving and desperate British volunteers who ended up at the cookhouse and was talking to Paul Lewis, one of the brigade staff, when George Nathan marched up and persuaded him to return with him to the front.[83]

> Then we started getting together all remnants. Spaniards as well, all started singing the International and he was in front, with Jock Cunningham, and marching up, pushing, and we were singing away and then we start to scream up this hill . . . back to the sunken road.[84]

The march back into the line on the third day of Jarama has, not surprisingly, become one of the images used in sympathetic accounts of the British involvement in Spain.[85] However, there is no doubt that, as Hugh Thomas admitted, 'It was a brave performance.'[86] The volunteers' courage, and the deception that enabled them to fool the rebel forces into thinking they were faced by more than a handful of men, held the line at a critical moment for the Republic. Frank Graham was another of the volunteers who returned to the front:

> We advanced up the road and we were told whenever we could get into a position, when we met strong opposition and we couldn't go any further we should stop there and hold that ground. We went up the road to reach the top of the hill and we nearly reached the top and then we came under heavy fire and we dug in there and we held that up. One of the things we did was, we were told we had to keep on firing, no matter what happened, and we weren't to worry too much about firing accurately and we had to keep up the firing along at least two miles of the front to create the impression there was a large number of troops there and we hoped that that would stop them. We couldn't kill many, we'd kill a few by accident. We went on firing, we got spare rifles, and most of us had two or three rifles because the rifle got so hot that we couldn't use them. And we went on firing the whole of that day for about seven or eight hours without stopping.[87]

The rebel soldiers, fooled into believing them to be fresh reinforcements, retreated to their earlier positions and, during the night of 14 and 15 February, Republican units were brought up and the gap in the line was finally plugged. Both sides dug defensive fortifications and a stalemate ensued, which neither side was able to overcome. The positions remained virtually static for the rest of the war.

Celebrated as a great victory over the fascist army, the battle of Jarama was, like the earlier battles for Madrid in November and December 1936, really only successful in that it stemmed the rebels' advance on Madrid. And at great cost: the Republicans lost somewhere in the region of 25,000 soldiers to the Nationalists' 20,000. Of the 500 who had gone into battle with the British Battalion on 12 February, a conservative estimate would suggest that 136 were killed and a similar number wounded, with at least 50 quitting the front line (though some of these would return to the battalion), leaving less than half the battalion remaining.[88]

*Plate 4.1*  From left to right: the first battalion commander Wilf McCartney, who left Spain just before the battle of Jarama in February 1937, the battalion and brigade commissars Dave Springhall and Peter Kerrigan, the battalion commander Tom Wintringham, and the Irish republican Frank Ryan, who died as a prisoner of war in 1940.

*Plate 4.2*  The British Battalion at Jarama, May 1937: standing at the back, fifth from left, is battalion commander Fred Copeman; to his right (with pipe) is company commander Bill Meredith, killed at Villanueva de la Cañada two months later, and two to his left is Copeman's friend Charles Goodfellow, also killed during the battle of Brunete, with the battalion commissar Bert Williams between them.

The lack of numbers forced the command to amalgamate Nos. 3 and 4 Companies on 15 February.

On 27 February an attempt was made to break the Jarama stalemate with an offensive, involving the recently arrived American volunteers in the Lincoln Battalion. In what was later described as a 'well planned but poorly executed' attack, many volunteers refused to advance. Twelve English who did were all killed instantly.[89] Charles Morgan, one of the volunteers from Manchester, was involved in the disastrous attack.

> We were all in trenches, we were told on the morning that there would be air cover, there would be a bombardment. There was neither. We were just rushed over the top to face crossfire machine-guns. It was a slaughter. We didn't stand a cat in hell's chance! I saw lads, my comrades that I'd learnt to love, die and some of these boys never fired a bloody shot.[90]

As Jud Colman, a comrade of Morgan from the Manchester YCL, explained, 'Most of the attacks were almost suicidal, because there's no way you can send men against machine-guns without losing some. It was just physically impossible.'[91]

The high level of British casualties at Jarama came as a severe shock to Pollitt and the other party leaders, which may explain why it took until 6 March for news of the British casualties at Jarama to appear in the *Daily Worker*.[92] The article admitted that losses numbered as many as 400 but, as one might expect, stressed the 'heroic' and 'epic' nature of the British defence:

> You have never read and you never will read a story greater than this.
>
> When you have read it, you will know why there are no words in the English language capable of doing justice to this 'epic of valour unequalled in all history': – the epic of the Anglo-Irish Battalion of the International Brigade at Arganda Bridge: the epic of British and Irish men who 'endured so that they might possibly prevent such things happening in our native land'.
>
> When you have read how the Anglo-Irish Battalion saved Arganda bridge – and saving it helped to save Madrid, and Britain and all Europe from war and death, you will understand why the young general in command said that in all his career he had 'never seen such tenaciousness and bravery'.
>
> Nothing that we can do will ever fully repay our debt to these men who fought for us and died for us.[93]

The high level of casualties and, in particular, the disaster of 27 February also made a huge impact on the volunteers' morale, which was already in a bad way due to the extended period in the front line which followed the slaughter of 12 to 14 February.[94] As a report drawn up at Albacete in April 1937 described, the high levels of casualties at Jarama took their toll, with the injury of the highly popular and experienced Jock Cunningham and his replacement by the 'quick-tempered' and relatively inexperienced Fred Copeman causing particular concern amongst the company commanders.[95] The disgruntlement permeated right through to the upper ranks of the battalion; on a visit to Spain in March 1937 Harry Pollitt was forced to bring Jock Cunningham and George Aitken together with Fred Copeman and Bert Williams in an attempt to resolve differences amongst the leaders in the battalion.[96] The situation was further exacerbated by the conditions in the trenches caused by terrible weather; it rained for long periods, rendering it virtually impossible ever to get warm and dry, and making any attempt at hygiene very difficult. A spate of orders from battalion headquarters warned of the importance of the digging and using of latrines,[97] but 'there were times when, in spite of urgent need, there was a reluctance to let the pants down in the face of the icy wind, and one would try to wait for a least a momentary let-up in the rain.'[98] Waste food was also not disposed of, raising the risk of dysentery and typhoid. This issue cropped up regularly in the battalion orders, particularly as there seemed to be an unwillingness by volunteers to be inoculated.[99]

The volunteers' disgruntlement at their long period on the Jarama front line was made considerably worse by the lack of leave, especially when, on the occasions when they were relieved from front-line duties and sent to Morata de Tajuña, between 5 and 9 March, and to Alcala de Henares, at the end of April, the leave ended with their returning to their old positions on the Jarama front. In fact, apart from the two short rest periods, the British Battalion remained at Jarama until 17 June, when, after 73 days in the line, the brigade was finally withdrawn to Mondéjar, finally allowing some of the British to take a few days' rest in nearby Madrid.

On the night of 27 and 28 April, Bert Overton's actions during the battle of Jarama were raised in a battalion meeting.[100] The meeting was chaired by Bert Williams, who had replaced George Aitken as battalion commissar on 23 March, when Aitken was promoted brigade commissar. During the meeting it was also alleged that, further to his conduct on 12 and 13 February, whilst in hospital Overton had promoted himself from sergeant to captain and had since been claiming the pay.[101] Bill Alexander recounts that 'all were allowed to speak' at the meeting, though (apparently without any sense of irony) he states that Overton was not present to make his own defence.[102] At the official brigade court martial which followed shortly afterwards, Overton was charged with desertion, promoting himself to captain and drawing the pay, and sentenced to work in a labour battalion. Overton was later killed 'by a shell while carrying munitions to a forward position'.[103] As James Hopkins points out, several brigaders have hinted darkly that Overton was, if not actually murdered, certainly sent deliberately 'into harms way . . . [as] . . . an expedient means of getting rid of a soldier who had become a dangerous embarrassment'.[104]

Whilst the main British contingent making up the British Battalion remained on the Jarama front until May/June 1937, a small group of new arrivals and those recently released from hospital were formed on 15 March into No. 2 Section of an Anglo-American company in the 20th Battalion of the 86th (Mixed) Brigade.[105] On 20 March the brigade was sent to the Pozoblanco sector, about 50 miles north of Córdoba in southern Spain. A novel form of attack using a train, behind which the battalion followed on foot, was abandoned when the train came under heavy artillery fire and was forced to retreat rapidly into a tunnel.[106] The Anglo-American

*Plate 4.3* An advanced dressing station used to treat the urgent casualties at Brunete in July 1937: on the far left (in shorts) is Anthony Carritt, who was killed at Brunete; his brother, Noel, also served with the medical services after being wounded at Jarama.

*Plate 4.4* Lorry from the battalion cookhouse hit by shellfire near Jarama in February 1937: though the driver, Leon Beurton, and his passenger, Captain George Nathan, escaped injury, Nathan was killed by a shell at Brunete a few months later.

section was then transferred to the nearby Chimorra front, in the same sector, positioned high in the peaks with virtually no cover, forcing volunteers to build piles of stones to shelter behind.[107] In a disastrous error they were attacked by an anarchist battalion, and several of the volunteers were killed. Not surprisingly, many men were disheartened and there were a number of desertions before Will Paynter, the British base commissar, managed to get them transferred to the British Battalion.[108]

July 1937 saw the British Battalion thrown once more into battle in a well-planned but, ultimately, over-ambitious attack devised by the sophisticated Republican tactician General Rojo.[109] The offensive, launched 15 miles to the west of Madrid, was a diversionary attack designed to relieve the pressure on Santander in northern Spain by breaking through the Nationalist lines at their weakest point.[110] Thus, on 2 July, rested and back up to strength with new recruits from England and those recovered from their wounds, the battalion, with the other battalions comprising the 15th International Brigade, was moved out of Albacete. The brigade now comprised six battalions, plus the newly formed Anti-Tank Battery, which had been transferred from the 24th Brigade.[111] The infantry battalions were grouped into two regiments: the British, the Lincoln and the Washington in one, the Franco-Belge, the Dimitrov and the Spanish in the other. The experienced and popular George Nathan was chief of operations for the brigade, and the British Battalion was now under the command of Fred Copeman, who had taken over from Jock Cunningham on 17 March.[112] It was, believed Copeman, a very different situation to that experienced at Jarama: 'Brunete was an action where we had everything. We had the arms. The battalion was 660. Every man was trained and the commanders knew their job.'[113] The Republican offensive was well equipped, with 50,000 men, 136 pieces of artillery, 128 tanks and 150 aircraft.[114]

Orders arrived at midnight on 6 July for the launch of the offensive aimed at capturing the heights around Brunete and pushing back the rebel artillery out of range of Madrid. The British Battalion's orders were to move on the village of Villanueva de la Cañada, a few miles before Brunete. They arrived at dawn, after a 15 mile march, and were at first held in reserve, but, when the Spanish unit failed to capture the village, the 15th International Brigade was brought in to assist them. Whilst the American Washington Battalion advanced on the northern end of the village, the British and Dimitrov Battalions launched an assault on the south in an attempt to cut off the defending rebel force. However, machine-guns and snipers strategically placed in the church tower forced the attackers to take whatever cover was available and wait in mid-summer temperatures of over 100 degrees, desperate with thirst, until nightfall.[115] As darkness approached, several of the cornered rebels tried to escape by the subterfuge of hiding behind civilians and then opened fire as they approached the Republican forces. In the confusion several of the villagers were shot and killed in the crossfire, as Fred Copeman explained:

> A crowd came out of the village. It was getting dusk and the village was on fire anyway. It was still defending itself. We were going to storm it anyhow and were on our way. And then a crowd of people came out and down the road,

women and kids, be about a hundred of them. And we greeted them. I said, 'Cease fire, lads. Let these women through.' And when they got right in the middle of the battalion – it was now getting a bit dark – all hell let loose. Bloody hand grenades were being thrown. There were fascist troops behind them. And they got through. That eased off. And then somebody was calling on the road. A bloke was lying on the road calling. And by now the only light was the flames from the village. And Bill Meredith went over to help him and it was one of these fascists. And as old Bill bent over to help him he [the rebel soldier] shot him [Meredith], killed him.[116]

As other members of the battalion testify, they were left with little choice but to shoot back, knowing full well that this would cause civilian casualties.[117] Albert Charlesworth, the Oldham apprentice, had been separated from the main body of the battalion, but could hear that something significant was happening:

A terrible hullabaloo went out. Firing burst out in all directions, there was shouting, there was screaming. After a few minutes I could hear the voice of Fred Copeman crying, 'Stop firing! Stop firing!' And very shortly [*sic*] the firing did stop and everything went deadly quiet.[118]

Villanueva de la Cañada was eventually captured by midnight. Peter Harrisson, who worked as an administrator in the hospital run by Dr Alex Tudor-Hart,[119] visited the village soon after it had been captured.

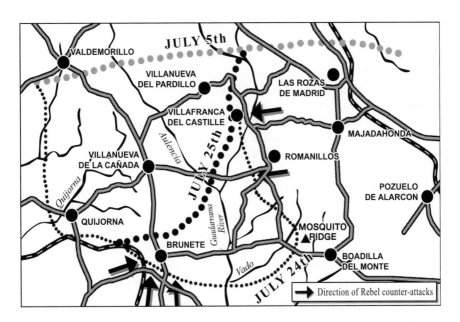

*Map 4.3* The Republican Brunete offensive, July 1937.

It was a vision of what would be only too familiar in the future. A village reduced to rubble, seen in those pictures of villages on the Somme from the First World War. It had been defended by small fortified positions on an old front line protected by barbed wire. Huge bomb craters everywhere and overall the stink of the decaying enemy dead buried beneath the rubble, and flies, flies and more flies.[120]

The following day the British Battalion advanced on Mosquito Ridge – the heights overlooking the Guadarrama River and the villages of Romanillos and Boadilla del Monte – which had been its original objective before it had been pinned down by the Nationalist defenders. As the British Battalion crossed the river, Villanueva de la Cañada was already coming under attack from rebel artillery and planes. As they moved forward they also came under air attack, which caught the relatively inexperienced Americans of the Lincoln and Washington Battalions, who were just ahead of them, unawares:

> Some aircraft – three Junkers 52s – came over. We got down, the Americans got down. The 'planes passed overhead and immediately the Americans got up. We stayed down. The Americans got up and started to advance, the 'planes circled back – had seen them – circled back and dropped bombs on them . . . We found that quite a large number of Americans had been killed by these bombs.[121]

The brigade runner, Frank Graham, was ahead of the main British contingent and discovered that Mosquito Ridge, the strategically vital heights overlooking the capital, were neither defended nor even occupied.

> Now if we'd reached the top of that hill, we might have won the battle, because below was the road. But we had no mobile, we had no trucks, we were on foot carrying all our packs and that, and the heat. It took them all the time to reach the fortifications. I knew then that as they came to the fortifications I saw two or three people [rebel soldiers] on the top of the hill and I knew it was over. We tried five days to take the hill. In fact we shouldn't have tried because it was impregnable, it was so difficult. Once we'd lost the surprise, at that point I think we should have just dug in and waited. We had terrible losses. We couldn't get water up to the troops and so on.[122]

Weakened by fatigue, thirst and constant bombardment from the air, the brigade could not advance sufficiently rapidly to capture the unoccupied heights, and rebel forces quickly took the opportunity to move into the position. Rebel artillery laid a two-hour barrage on the advancing Republicans, which allowed even more rebel reinforcements to be brought up. These forces were able to pin down the British Battalion by well-directed artillery and gunfire, combined with total air superiority. As P. D. Harrisson could see, 'existence for the soldiers was almost unbearable under the boiling heat and the flies.'[123] As Huw (Alun) Williams, a Welsh nurse and first-aider working at Villanueva, described, the situation for the wounded was diabolical. The medical unit ran out of morphia within the first hour, and water remained desperately short, leading to more than 50 per cent of the seriously wounded dying within an hour.[124]

As David Anderson, who was commanding one of the British companies, and who had seven years experience in the Gordon Highlanders, observed,

> Mosquito Hill was a position that we couldn't capture with the means that we had. It was absolutely impossible. I mean, they had domination, and as a matter of fact we could see right behind, the lights of the supplies going up to the fascist positions. It wasn't long before we realised that the position we occupied was absolutely impossible. And then of course we had to withdraw. It was the end of the offensive as far as the Republican Government was concerned.[125]

Fred Copeman is probably correct when he pointed out that the brigade shouldn't have bothered taking Villanueva de la Cañada, and should have pressed straight on to Mosquito Ridge: 'The taking of the village of Villanueva de la Cañada, it was just a whole day's slaughter where we just got casualties and couldn't hit back except to take the tower and one old tank.'[126] Frank Graham viewed the failure to capture the heights in even more serious terms.

> It was a great defeat because, firstly, we'd lost too many men. We hadn't inflicted very heavy casualties on the enemy and some of our best troops had been lost in the process. It weakened considerably the Republican Army. Of course there were many big battles took place but, in a sense, although it's difficult – looking back it's easy to say it – I think, in a sense, that a lot of us realised that the war had been lost at that point . . . After that it was only a question of prolonging it as far as possible until changes could be taking place in Europe. Well, the changes didn't take place. It was only after the war was over that the changes began to take place.[127]

Having failed to capture the ridge, the Brunete offensive was to proceed no further. Though the Republic had gained over 40 square miles of territory, the offensive could hardly be judged a success. The Romanillos Heights, the Republic's main objective, remained in Nationalist hands. Furthermore, from this time, the International Brigades would make up only 5 per cent of the Republican Army, compared to 20 per cent before Brunete.[128] The British Battalion had 331 volunteers in the ranks at the start of Brunete and only 42 remained at the end.[129]

With the offensive now at a standstill, on 11 July the British and American Battalions were moved temporarily into reserve positions but, a week later, the rebels launched a huge counter-attack, comprising at least 300 planes and 300 artillery pieces. The British Battalion – boosted by the return of some of the less seriously wounded from earlier actions and a small number of new volunteers, but still less than 100 strong – was split into two groups, one led by Joe Hinks, who had been a section leader at Lopera, and the other by Walter Tapsell, an experienced political activist who had been the circulation manager for the *Daily Worker*. Outnumbered and overwhelmed, both groups were forced to withdraw, as were other Republican forces, including the elite 5th Regiment of General Lister, which was pushed out of the town of Brunete itself. The failure of the offensive and the subsequent retreat, which incurred the loss of valuable troops and armaments, was to become a recurring scenario for the Republic. Whilst the Republic haemorrhaged men and arms, the rebels enjoyed an increasing dominance, fortified both by their allies and by the certain knowledge that the only countries which could save the Republic were determined not to do so. As 1937 moved into 1938, the main thrust of the war would move east from Madrid to the Aragon. But, for the Republic, the pattern would remain the same: in the battles at Belchite, Teruel and the Ebro, 'an initial Republican breakthrough was followed by an attritional battle due to the lack of exploitation, and, eventually, a stalemate ensued so both sides then planned new offensives to break the deadlock.'[130]

# 5   Into Aragon, 1937–1938

## Teruel, 'the great retreat' and the Ebro offensive

> It was a marvellous moment when we climbed out of the boats and scrambled up the south bank [of the River Ebro]. What exhilaration! We were on the move again, we were taking the initiative and we were on top of the world.[1]

The costly failure of the Brunete offensive left the units of the 15th International Brigade in a state of crisis.[2] A report by 'Gallo' (Luigi Longo, formerly an Italian youth leader and a senior member of the Comintern, who had been involved in the creation of the International Brigades) estimated that over half of the brigade was killed, wounded or missing after the offensive.[3] The situation was deemed so serious that a report written by the departing base commander at Albacete went as high as Stalin, who ordered Marty to report on the situation and put forward proposals to resolve the problems.[4] Of the small number of British volunteers who were still fit for front-line service following the offensive, many were low in morale, and questions were being asked regarding the discipline and commitment of their Spanish comrades. Disputes that had been simmering since Jarama between senior British figures in Spain took on an increased significance.[5] Walter Tapsell, the British Battalion's political commissar, openly criticised the Republican battle strategy[6] and accused the commander of the 15th Brigade, Gal, of gross incompetence.[7] Tapsell, perhaps somewhat rashly, declared that 'only stupidity or a deliberate disregard for life would keep men in such an exposed position [on Mosquito Ridge]. Gal isn't fit to command a troop of Brownies, let alone a People's Army.'[8] Gal wanted Tapsell shot for this insubordination, though he was persuaded to back down by Fred Copeman, the commander of the battalion, who went to the brigade headquarters to remonstrate with Gal – backed up by Joe Hinks's Machine-Gun Company. In fact Gal was already unpopular with the British, for his dislike of George Nathan had led to Nathan's transfer to the 14th International Brigade after Jarama.[9]

Blame and accusations were flying around within the battalion, and a major argument developed between Walter Tapsell on one side and George Aitken and Jock Cunningham – both on the brigade staff – on the other. The central feature of the dispute was that Tapsell believed that the promotion of Cunningham and Aitken to the brigade staff had cut them off from the battalion. Tapsell was particularly unhappy about the discussions surrounding what he termed 'the annihilation of the British Battalion', a plan to incorporate it into the American battalion. However, the argument also developed a personal dimension. Tapsell complained that George Aitken had accused him of being a bad influence in the battalion and responded by claiming that, six weeks previously, Jock Cunningham had demanded Aitken's return to Britain, on the grounds that he was 'utterly useless'.[10] Walter Tapsell claimed that 'Aitken's temperament has made him distrusted and disliked by the vast majority of the British Battalion who regard him as being personally ambitious and unmindful of the interests of the battalion and the men.'[11] He also alleged that Cunningham 'fluctuates violently between hysterical bursts of passion and is openly accused by Aitken of lazing about the brigade headquarters doing nothing.'[12]

Dave Springhall, the assistant brigade commissar at Albacete, claimed that there was a total disintegration of the battalion leadership after Brunete, and, though Aitken denied that the situation was this serious, he did admit that certain leading figures had collapsed under the incredible strain. Aitken claimed that Bert Williams, a political commissar then working with the Americans, was 'at the end of his tether', Fred Copeman 'was in a very bad state', and Walter Tapsell was 'absolutely demoralised, and not quite normal'.

> This showed itself in the statements he [Tapsell] was making to all and sundry and very loudly about the whole offensive and about the new Spanish Army. For him the whole offensive had been a ghastly failure and a severe defeat while the new Spanish forces were worse than useless – a menace. It is no exaggeration to say that he was talking as one panic-stricken. He was also loudly criticising in front of all the men the whole conduct of the operation – shouting about our lack of artillery and aviation, creating the impression that the British Battalion had had a specifically raw deal, had been *deliberately* placed in all the tough spots, a suggestion which was absolutely false and which, in the frightfully difficult circumstances then prevailing, was criminal and dangerous. (What would have happened if I had talked thus to the comrades when we put in reserve for a few days after the desperate days at Jarama?)[13]

As Aitken pointed out, it was important to recognise 'what three weeks battle such as we went through at Brunete can do to some men'.[14] Aitken's criticisms were supported by Will Paynter, the base commissar at Albacete who had arrived in May,[15] who accused Tapsell of, albeit unwittingly, encouraging anti-brigade feeling and general disaffection, just as Bill Rust later criticised Fred Copeman, Bill Alexander and Sam Wild.[16] As Bill Alexander states, both Tapsell and Copeman had what were, essentially, nervous breakdowns following Brunete. In fact, Tapsell was physically detained for some days after his outburst, as Aitken believed that 'He was not at the time fully responsible for his actions.'

The dispute was unable to be settled in Spain, so the five leading figures involved were called back to Britain in late August 1937 to try and resolve it. After an exchange of bitter accusations and counter-accusations, Harry Pollitt ordered Jock Cunningham, Bert Williams and George Aitken to stay in Britain, whilst Fred

Copeman and Walter Tapsell were to return to Spain.[17] Copeman describes how, at the meeting,

> Harry [Pollitt] got up and said, 'The only people who have expressed a point of view as to what is happening to the battalion at the moment, that they're out there and we're here, has been Fred Copeman and Wally Tapsell. And therefore my proposal is that they return to Spain and everybody else remain where they are and now start to build up political support for the dependants because there's no longer any recruitment possible.[18]

The decision infuriated George Aitken, who wrote a letter stating that he wanted 'To protest against the decision to send Comrade Tapsel[l] back to Spain. This decision, in my opinion, is monstrous and dangerous and the decision that Comrade Copeman should also return to Spain is a grave mistake.'[19]

As John Angus later remarked, the removal of several leading figures in the battalion to Britain created more bad feeling in the battalion,[20] for volunteers were now required to remain in Spain for the duration of the war as the International Brigades were reformed in line with the decree (eventually published in September 1937) that brought them under the auspices of the Republican Army.[21] The 15th International Brigade was incorporated into the 35th Division, under the command of General 'Walter', whom the British soon came to prefer to Gal.

The brigade was also reorganised internally. Malcolm Dunbar, in charge of the Anti-Tank Battery, was replaced by Hugh (Humphrey) Slater, previously a reporter for *Imprecor* (International Press Correspondence), the English-language newspaper of the Comintern, and Dunbar became chief of operations for the brigade. Tom Wintringham, now recovered from his wounds sustained at Jarama, and following a spell at the officer school at Pozorubio, joined Dunbar on the brigade staff. By August 1937, the battalion was just over 400 strong, of whom just under half were British. From now on, the British would always be in the minority in the battalion.[22]

In mid-August 1937, the 35th Division was transferred to the Aragon front, which was to be the objective of a new offensive aimed at capturing the town of Saragossa and diverting Franco's attention away from his northern campaign, which had seen the rebel forces advancing ominously towards Santander.[23] On 24 August, an assault on Quinto, a strongpoint near Saragossa, began. The British Battalion was kept in reserve, but the British Anti-Tank Battery was used to blast the numerous rebel strongholds in the village with their high-velocity Soviet guns, where 'the tenacity of the Nationalist garrisons astounded the attackers.'[24] During the street-fighting which eventually secured Quinto, Tom Wintringham, the former commander, was wounded once again.

The day after the capture of Quinto, the British Battalion was ordered to attack what they were informed by brigade staff was the 'lightly held' Purburrel Hill, a natural strongpoint overlooking the town which, on the contrary, had been expertly fortified under the guidance of German military advisors.[25] It took the British Battalion two days, and the loss of three volunteers, including its commander Peter Daly,[26] to capture the hill.[27]

*Map 5.1* The Aragon offensive of August–September 1937.

Attacks on the first day met with a fierce and determined resistance, which the British were unable to overcome. Sheltering from the machine-gun fire was as much as most volunteers could manage, and Paddy O'Daire, the new commander, withdrew the battalion to await artillery support, despite the wishes of Čopić, the brigade commander. During the night the British captured a rebel patrol, which had left the hill in a desperate search for water, who confirmed both the strength of the defences and the inadequacy of the water supply. Had the battalion the time to wait, the defenders would have been forced by their thirst to surrender, but, unfortunately for the British, the strategic importance of the hill to the offensive on Saragossa meant that they were not able to do so. Thus, 26 August saw the beginning of a new attempt by the battalion to capture the hill. However, this time the defences were first bombarded by the Anti-Tank Battery. Thanks to the accuracy of the guns – and the thirst-induced weakness of the defenders – little resistance was encountered when the frontal assault up the hill followed, and the hill subsequently fell to the British.

On 27 August, the dwindling numbers of the 15th International Brigade moved on to the nearby town of Belchite. The British Battalion was now down to just over 100 men, and, following the huge struggles entailed in capturing Quinto and Pulburrel Hill, morale was even lower than it had previously been.[28] When the battalion was ordered to move to Mediana, 6 miles north of Belchite, in order to hold off approaching rebel reinforcements, some members of the battalion refused to follow the order. The commander, Paddy O'Daire, called a meeting of all the Communist Party members in the battalion, who agreed both to obey the order and to persuade the rest of the group to do likewise. Albeit reluctantly, the battalion marched on Mediana and made a 'short and sharp' attack on the rebels, which forced them back into the town, and the battalion took up positions on the adjacent hillside.[29] Meanwhile, the Anti-Tank Battery and the other battalions of the 15th International Brigade were engaged in a desperate assault on Belchite; according to

Bill Alexander, the three guns in the Anti-Tanks fired 2,700 shells in two days.[30] Belchite was finally captured on 6 September, following some of the most desperate hand-to-hand fighting seen in Spain, which left the town reduced virtually to dust.[31]

A later assessment of the Republican Aragon offensive of 1937 by one of the British volunteers claimed that 'the list of our victories was beginning to lengthen: Purburrell [*sic*] Hill, Quinto, Mediana, Belchite. Never before had we advanced so successfully.'[32] However, the Republican offensive in Aragon must be regarded as a failure, despite the bravery and sacrifice of the Republican forces, for it did not achieve the crucial objective of capturing Saragossa, and thus relieving the pressure on the northern front. By the end of the month Santander was in Nationalist hands; two months later the entire northern Republican zone would be too.

Following the assault on Belchite, the British were pulled out of the line for desperately needed rest. On 23 September 1937, whilst they were in their reserve positions, the official decree incorporating the International Brigades into the Republican Army was published. It ruled that there must be a quota of Spanish soldiers in the International Brigades and confirmed that volunteers were required to remain in the Republican Army until the end of the war. Within the 15th International Brigade, there was also a change, with the Canadian Mackenzie–Papineau Battalion (known as the Mac–Paps) replacing the Dimitrov Battalion, which was transferred to the 129th Brigade.[33]

Just over two weeks later, on 11 October 1937, the 15th International Brigade was briefed for an operation against the Aragon town of Fuentes de Ebro, within sight of Saragossa, which had held out the previous month. The 24th Spanish Battalion was to be carried forward on tanks, whilst the other three battalions, including the British, were to launch an assault on the rebel lines before advancing on Saragossa. The Anti-Tank Battery was held back from the main battle, and Hugh Sloan, Bill Alexander's runner, was able to observe the disaster unfold. When the operation was launched in the early morning of 13 October, Sloan counted 47 Republican tanks waiting to advance.[34] As with the offensive at Brunete, the strategy was rather more sophisticated than the tactics; as Bill Williamson, a Canadian volunteer who was watching the offensive, remarked,

> I think the High Command had seen too many documentary movies of the Russian Red Army exercises. There was a very famous one which I saw myself in Spain called *Red Army Exercises* in 1936. This was the first showing of mass landing of parachute troops anywhere in the world and the army advancing with the whole battalion put on the back of tanks. Some guy in the High Command had seen this thing and thought it was appropriate for Fuentes de Ebro. Whereas it might have been quite okay on the flat plains of the Ukraine, it was completely unsuitable for the terrain we were attacking over.[35]

The plan was a disaster. The Anti-Tank Battery was forbidden to fire, the artillery barrage was inadequate and there was only one air-force bombing raid in support. The infantry got left behind the tanks and suffered very heavy casualties. At one point the panicked brigade staff ordered the Anti-Tank Battery to advance on the rebel lines. None of the guns were able to fire and the battery's second-in-command, Jeff Mildwater, was injured before the battery was wisely withdrawn. The British Battalion also lost another commander: Harold Fry, the commander of the Machine-Gun Company at Jarama, who had returned to Spain in the summer. With Paddy O'Daire away on officer training at Pozorrubio, his place had been taken temporarily by Fry, who, along with several others, was killed on 13 October in the unsuccessful attempt to capture Fuentes de Ebro.[36]

Following the disastrous Fuentes operation, the British Battalion remained in the line for ten days, before returning once again to rest at Mondéjar and Ambite. During November came another reorganisation of the Republican Army. Whilst the 15th International Brigade was in reserve, the battalions were allocated numbers: the British Battalion was to be the 57th Battalion, the Lincolns 58th, the Spanish 59th and the Mac–Paps 60th.[37] By mid-November, despite the return of volunteers who had recovered from wounds suffered during the Aragon campaign, the British members of the battalion still numbered only 150, fewer than the numbers of a standard company in the British Army.

The battalion rested until December, during which time the men received several illustrious visitors: the *Daily Worker* correspondent and member of the British Communist Party central committee Bill Rust in November, and the American singer Paul Robeson in early December, accompanied by his wife and Charlotte Haldane, the secretary of the Dependents' Aid Committee.[38] The Labour Party leader, Clement Attlee, arrived late in the evening of 6 December with two members of the Labour Party executive committee, Ellen Wilkinson and Philip Noel-Baker, and the No. 1 Company was renamed the Major Attlee Company in the Labour leader's honour.[39] On Christmas Day there was another visit from Harry Pollitt and J. B. S. Haldane and a much-welcomed feast of pork, wine and nuts, organised by the battalion's quartermaster, Lieutenant Robert 'Hooky' Walker.[40] All the volunteers also received a food parcel from Britain, and, to entertain the volunteers and raise morale, Wally Tapsell organised a sports fiesta. Whilst an Englishman won the boxing, both the British football teams, from the battalion and the Anti-Tank Battery, were soundly beaten by Spanish teams.[41] Just after Christmas, Fred Copeman, who had returned to Spain with Walter Tapsell at the end of October, was taken into hospital for an appendix operation, and later invalided home after complications set in. Bill Alexander replaced Copeman as commander of the battalion, with Sam Wild, the battalion armourer at Jarama, becoming his adjutant.

On 15 December 1937 the Republicans launched another offensive in the Aragon, which at first went well.[42] General Lister's troops had surrounded Teruel by the evening, and by Christmas Day Republican soldiers had fought their way into the town. On 8 January, the Republic scored a spectacular success when, in appalling freezing conditions, the rebels surrendered the town to the Republic. Republican supporters all over the world hailed the victory as a turning point in the war and a demonstration of the might of the new Republican Army.[43] But the victory, once again, was to be short-lived. Within days, a Nationalist offensive threatened to win back the Republicans' hard-fought gains. On 17 January, the International Brigades were thrown into the battle in a desperate attempt to stem the rebel advance.[44] The

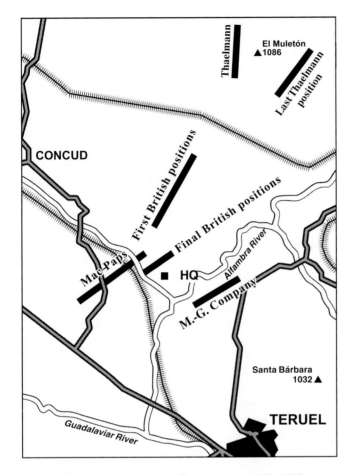

*Map 5.2* The Republican Teruel offensive, winter 1937–1938.

15th International Brigade was moved to confront the main point of the rebel offensive on the outskirts of Teruel, with the British Battalion positioned at Santa Bárbara, in 3 feet of snow.[45] The Machine-Gun Company occupied rebel emplacements on the edge of a cliff, and the Anti-Tank Battery was placed to support the battalion. On 17 January, the same day that a delegation of Labour MPs arrived at Teruel as guests of 5th Army Corps commander Juan Modesto,[46] three British rifle companies, No. 3 led by Sam Wild, with Nos. 1 and 4 following, were ordered across the Alfambra River into the valley to protect the Canadian Mac–Paps, whose position was becoming increasingly desperate due to rebel artillery fire.

On 19 January there was a huge artillery bombardment on the British positions,[47] which the battalion held onto doggedly, forcing the rebel forces to give up their direct assault on Teruel. The brigade recognised that the British Battalion had shown bravery and determination, and promoted Bill Alexander to the rank of captain and commended Walter Tapsell for his work as political commissar.[48] However, it was at some cost. The Machine-Gun Company was unable to protect the three companies in the valley, who were decimated, though they were at least able to cover their eventual retreat. Twenty-one British were killed in this action, 13 of them from the Major Attlee Company.[49] In all, the battalion lost one-third of its number at Teruel.[50] The depleted British force was withdrawn, but their period of rest and recuperation was to be short-lived, as the rebels' counter-attack gained momentum.

On 6 February the British and three other battalions of the 15th International Brigade were concentrated at Segura de los Baños, 40 miles north of Teruel. With the British Battalion desperately short of manpower, Bob Cooney, an experienced activist from Scotland, joined the battalion as a soldier.[51] Cooney was another senior party figure who had studied at the Lenin School in Moscow between 1931 and 1932 and to whom Peter Kerrigan had refused permission to go to Spain for a year. Cooney was to become a very effective political commissar with the battalion, earning high praise from his superiors.[52]

On 16 February the battalion made a night attack on Segura de los Baños, in an attempt to divert attention away from Teruel. Despite initial advances, the story was to be a familiar one.[53] Bill Alexander's time as battalion commander ended here with a wound to the shoulder, and his adjutant Sam Wild took over. With superior numbers and armaments the rebel army pressed the Republicans back, and on 21 February the Republican Army retreated from Teruel. The British Battalion was withdrawn from Segura de los Baños to Lecera, where it remained in reserve for a fortnight. For the Republic, Teruel was to be the first of a number of retreats during the first half of 1938 which would end with the Republic split into two parts, and rebel soldiers dancing triumphantly in the Mediterranean at Vinaroz.

On 7 March 1938, Franco launched a massive and well-prepared attack on the Republican forces in Aragon. What began as a series of break-throughs for the Nationalists swiftly became outright retreat for the Republicans, as their lines virtually collapsed.[54] As Hugh Thomas noted, 'the best troops of the Republic were weary after Teruel. Their material was exhausted: half the men even lacked rifles.'[55] The 15th International Brigade, led by Bob Merriman, the American chief of staff, was ordered to move up from Lecera and set up headquarters at Belchite, which had fallen to the brigade the previous autumn. The British Battalion, under the command of the newly promoted Sam Wild, was sent north on the road towards Mediana and Fuentes de Ebro, where it met retreating Republicans coming in the opposite direction. The battalion was attacked by a heavy machine-gun, artillery and air barrage as the rebels advanced in large numbers, forcing the British back into Belchite, which came under increasing pressure from the rebel forces.[56] Bombarded with anti-tank and anti-aircraft shells, the British Battalion and the members of the Anti-Tank Battery were virtually surrounded and forced to retreat swiftly from Belchite to avoid being cut off.[57] The Spanish Battalion adjutant, Jose Calatayud Mayguez, the No. 1 Company commander, and 30 other men were killed or wounded in the desperate attempt to escape from Belchite.[58] The Anti-Tank Battery was forced to destroy one of its guns that couldn't be moved; low-flying Nationalist aircraft destroyed another. With the battery no longer in existence, the men were incorporated into the British Battalion.[59] The defence of Belchite delayed the rebels' capture of the town, but only by one day. It fell to rebel soldiers from Navarre on 10 March.[60] Together with a Spanish and American battalion of the 15th International Brigade and 50 Spaniards from the 135th Brigade, the British Battalion made a fighting retreat.

What was to follow was nearly a week of a desperate struggle to retreat and evade being cut off by the rapid advance of the huge Nationalist force, which was constantly infiltrating the Republican lines or punching holes with lightning motorised attacks, thus repeatedly making the Republican positions untenable. The battalion retreated past Lecera and Vinaceite, where it was briefly reunited with the other battalions of the 15th International Brigade, before marching desperately for 30 miles through Hijar and Alcañiz, as these too fell to the seemingly unstoppable rebel push.[61] Frank Graham, the Newcastle volunteer who had briefly occupied Mosquito Ridge at Brunete the previous July, remembered the retreat into Caspe with horror:

> Over the mountains, to Caspe, the only way there, no roads at all, just over the mountains. We had to work by more or less guessing the direction to get there. We arrived in Caspe, terrible journey, never stopped walking . . . no food, no water.[62]

David Stirrat, an unemployed driver from Glasgow, had arrived in Spain the previous November, and the retreats through Aragon were his first experiences of action. Driven from Teruel, where he had arrived too late to join the British Battalion, he was sitting, unarmed, in the back of the lorry.

> The lorries made a sudden about-turn and there was an outbreak of fighting in olive-groves on either side of the road and men were running and climbing onto the lorries. We were going like the clappers back down the road again. We almost got captured. This was at Caspe . . . There was a big retreat really. We were maybe stopping in fields and they'd issue arms and take them back in again. There were all sorts of problems.[63]

On 15 March, six days after the battalion had begun its defence of Belchite, the remnants of the British Battalion arrived at Caspe, where they were forced to fight a heavy rearguard action, much of it hand-to-hand, in what Sam Wild considered to be an untenable position.[64] Unbeknownst to them, the British members of the 15th International Brigade were fighting the 14th Bandera of the Spanish Foreign Legion, which included one of the few British volunteers for the rebels, the right-wing Tory Peter Kemp. The battle was just as bitter and hard-fought for Kemp's unit:

> On the 17th March, at Caspe on the borders of Aragon and Catalonia, I fought my bitterest engagement of the war – ironically enough, though I did not know it then, against British units of the XIV [*sic*] International Brigade; in twenty four hours of fighting – often at hand to hand – my company suffered seventy-five per cent casualties, and I myself was wounded three times.[65]

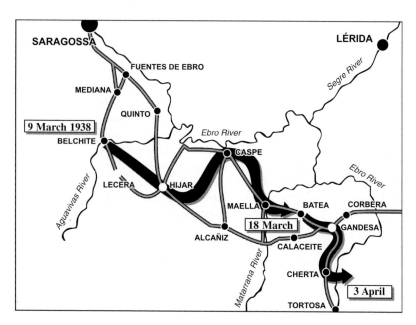

*Map 5.3* The retreat through Aragon of March–April 1938.

Sam Wild, the British Battalion commander, Joe Norman, the Communist Party organiser with the battalion, Robert 'Hooky' Walker, the quartermaster, and Harry Dobson, another Communist Party representative within the battalion, were all captured, but managed to escape.[66] Despite a desperate attempt organised by Sam Wild and Malcolm Dunbar to defend Caspe, by the end of 15 March it too had to be abandoned, when it was encircled, despite 'prodigies of valour' by the defending units of the 15th International Brigade.[67] It was only two days later, when the exhausted volunteers arrived at Batea, that Republican reinforcements arrived and the Nationalist advance was – temporarily – halted.[68] In a written report of the retreats, Sam Wild wrote, 'I complained to brigade after the Caspe action on the lack of written orders, stating at the time that the lack of written orders was responsible for a lot of the confusion.'[69]

The retreats were a time of great disorder for the British volunteers, and for many a time of panic and near-exhaustion.[70] Bill Alexander's description of the march from Vinaceite towards Alcañiz provides a graphic picture of the desperate position in which the battalion found itself:

> This march was hell for the battalion. The heat was intense, there was no water. Even at Vinaceite boots and feet were in a sorry condition. The moving columns were strafed by low-flying planes for mile after mile, each strafing run breaking the line of march. The remnants of other units were on the move, and it was almost impossible to keep together as an organised unit. Some of the battalion got left behind or mixed up with other units.[71]

*Plate 5.1*  Bill Alexander, the 'strict but fearless' political commissar and battalion commander.

*Plate 5.2*  Bob Cooney, 'the best battalion commissar in the brigade'.

*Plate 5.3*  Walter 'Wally' Tapsell, the 'personally courageous' battalion commissar who had a nervous breakdown after Brunete and was killed at Calaceite in April 1938.

*Plate 5.4*  Sam Wild, perhaps the best of the battalion commanders.

On 19 March the International Brigade base at Albacete was closed and transferred to Catalonia. Remnants of the 15th International Brigade regrouped in Batea, and the battalion found itself with yet another commander, George Fletcher, when Sam Wild was sent to Barcelona for medical treatment. The emergency encouraged a number of sick and injured volunteers to return to the battalion, which soon numbered 650, its highest number ever.[72] They would soon be called upon.

Just over a week later, on 30 March 1938, the rebels launched another offensive in Aragon, south of the Ebro River. Retreating from Belchite towards Calaceite, the British awoke the following day to very heavy rain and poor visibility.[73] The battalion was ordered to take up defensive positions, so just before daylight broke it was marching alongside both sides of the road leading out of Calaceite, with No. 1 Company in front and Nos. 3 and 4 and the Machine-Gun Company following behind. As it turned daylight the battalion was ordered to dig in beside the road, before the order was rescinded shortly afterwards and the men were ordered to return to the road and move forward as quickly as possible.[74] As they approached a bend in the road they were met by a number of tanks, which were at first believed to be their own, but were quickly discovered to be Italian when the tanks drove between the two British columns and opened fire on the volunteers.[75] Several members of the Machine-Gun Company managed to set up two of their heavy machine-guns, set one of the tanks on fire, and force the tanks to retreat temporarily, but the battalion was heavily outnumbered.[76] A large number of the Major Attlee Company were forced to surrender, with at least 50 others hit by Italian gunfire.[77] In frantic attempts by the other companies to withdraw, a machine-gun crew was also captured. David Stirrat from Glasgow was part of one of the machine-gun teams firing on the Italian tanks:

> We were getting attacked from the right flank. When I looked round the other machine-gun had completely disappeared. Groups of prisoners were beginning to appear in front of us under the guard of Fascists. They obviously had us surrounded.[78]

The full extent of the predicament that the British Battalion was in became clear when more Italian tanks were observed approaching from Calaceite, which had been in Republican hands only that morning. The loss of senior experienced members of the battalion, including the political commissar, Walter Tapsell, who was killed, and the battalion commander, George Fletcher, who was wounded in the early stages of the ambush, 'naturally added to the confusion'.[79] Tapsell had mistaken the Italian tanks for Republicans from the Communist Fifth Regiment under the command of Enrique Lister, and was gunned down as he approached them to convince the driver that they were on the same side.[80]

> 'Tappy' was marching at the head of the Battalion when the surprise attack came. 'He had that grim, determined look on his face which couldn't help but inspire us all', remarked one British comrade, recalling the scene. He challenged the tank commander, but was shot down with a bullet through his

shoulder. A Spanish lieutenant rushed to his aid, and drove off the Fascists, thus giving 'Tappy' time to crawl out of the line of fire; but he was never seen again.[81]

Other members of the battalion, such as David Gilbert,[82] the battalion runner, and Frank Ryan, the Irish Republican leader, were amongst those captured.[83] Those who managed to evade capture were mainly either on patrol or in the Machine-Gun Company, which was bringing up the rear.[84]

Those members of the battalion who managed to evade capture retreated away from the road to avoid both the advancing ground force and also air attacks from Nationalist aircraft. Their retreat allowed the Italian tanks and armoured vehicles to sweep forward along the road. It was a sobering lesson on the size and strength of the rebel force that the volunteers were attempting to contain.[85] With the leaders of the battalion captured or killed, the volunteers split into small groups and, finding Calaceite already in rebel hands, attempted to make their own way past the rebel forces to the front line, which was moving further and further away from them by the hour.[86] Only around 80 made it back to Gandesa to meet up with the remainder of the battalion under Malcolm Dunbar.

This was the first experience of action for George Drever, a research chemist from Leith. Separated from the main force, he hid in a ditch with two comrades whilst Italian tanks passed over them. After three days of trying to find their way back to the front line they were captured early in the morning by a Spanish cavalry unit.[87] For many of the other volunteers attempting to return to the battalion, the situation was not much better. With no food supplies, two Scottish volunteers, David Stirrat and his companion Donald Weston, were forced to ask locals for help, even though this entailed the risk of being turned over to the Nationalists. They attempted to live off the land, but this was no easy task for industrial workers brought up in an urban environment.[88] John Angus, the former commissar at the St Lucas 're-education' camp, managed to evade capture at Calaceite, and marched through the night with a group of Internationals in an attempt to get back to his unit. After travelling across country, they unexpectedly bumped into a group of Italian Nationalist soldiers resting on the main road. Quick thinking by an American comrade saved them when, on a challenge to identify themselves, he answered in Italian, 'Telecommunications'. The ruse worked and they were able to escape across to the other side of the road shortly afterwards. John Angus eventually made it back to Mora del Ebro, where he crossed the bridge over the River Ebro only hours before it was blown up by the Republicans.[89]

On 2 April, the surviving members of the battalion took up positions a mile south-west of Gandesa on the road to Tortosa. Still under the command of Dunbar, they were in a holding position on a steep-sided ridge, which was both easy to defend and difficult to outflank, and were reinforced with a group of 50 Spanish soldiers and a small tank. They managed to hold off rebel attacks all day, then pulled back at night, covered by a dozen volunteers from No. 4 Company under the command of Walter Gregory, who had served with the battalion since the first day of Jarama and had been promoted temporarily to the post of *teniente*.[90] Dunbar's group made a forced march of 20 miles towards Tortosa and met Sam Wild, just out of hospital, on the way and were caught up by Walter Gregory's group just as they waited to cross the River Ebro by boat at Cherta.[91]

Many of those who survived and managed to return to join the battalion were forced to swim across the River Ebro, a wide and fast-moving river. David Stirrat and Donald Weston lost their American companion to the current on their first attempt and were forced to turn around. Their second attempt was successful, though they were shot at and almost killed by a Republican patrol before they could identify themselves.[92] In all, it took three weeks from the disaster at Calaceite and a journey of nearly 45 miles behind enemy lines to return to the safety of what, by mid-April 1938, had become the southern Republican zone, separated from the northern zone in Catalonia following the rebels' capture of Vinaroz on the Mediterranean on 3 April, and another 40 miles of coastland shortly afterwards.[93] But to the surprise of everyone – not least the rebels – the Republican forces were soon to launch their own assault through Aragon, and return across the Ebro in what was probably the most audacious move of the war.

For the 15th International Brigade, the end of spring and the start of the summer of 1938 was to be a another period of reorganisation and rebuilding of morale. The commander of the brigade, Čopić, left Spain, and was replaced by a Spaniard, Major Valledor, a veteran of the Asturias uprising of October 1934.[94] The British Battalion was now back under the command of Sam Wild, who had gained considerable respect during his time in Spain,[95] and the battalion's numbers were boosted by a number of new arrivals[96] and by the men of the Anti-Tank Battery, who had been unable to find replacement guns for those lost in the retreats.[97] On 14 April, as part of the rebuilding, Harry Pollitt visited the battalion and the sick and injured in Republican hospitals. The battalion once more received important visitors: Pandit Nehru, the future prime minister of India, on 17 May and in mid-July, just before the Ebro offensive, a deputation of students, including Edward Heath, met with a group from the battalion. The rebuilding process was also helped considerably by the temporary opening of Spain's border with France between March and May 1938, which allowed new arms to reach the Republican Army, and by the new recruits who brought its strength back up to 650, of whom roughly a third were British.[98] By the end of the month, according to an official report by the head of the International Brigade base, 'Comrade Gómez', there had been 1,806 'English' volunteers, of whom 460 had been sent home and 124 killed.[99]

The battalion was kept busy training on the procedures for crossing rivers, and, as most of the volunteers guessed, these were part of the preparations for the Republican forces to launch a spectacular offensive into Aragon by crossing the River Ebro.[100] The plan aimed to divert a possible rebel attack on Valencia by capturing the town of Gandesa and, if all went to plan, reunite the two Republican zones.[101] In a battalion meeting on 21 July 1938, the rumours of an impending Republican offensive were confirmed to all the members of the battalion.[102]

Led by Juan Modesto, the Republican forces moved up to the River Ebro during the nights of 23 and 24 July and, during the following night, began the river crossing at 16 separate points along a 50 mile front. Just as the British press sympathetic to the Republic had hailed the capture of Teruel as a moment of great significance, so too

*Plate 5.5* The battalion officers: battalion commissar Bob Cooney is sitting in front, and behind him are Paddy O'Daire, the battalion commander in August–September 1937 (second from left in cap), 'Ted' Edwards, the battalion secretary (left hand resting on the ground) and (wearing cap to Edwards's left) Robert 'Hooky' Walker, the battalion quartermaster; Sam Wild (in beret) is kneeling on the right of the picture.

*Plate 5.6* Bill Rust, the British Communist Party's representative in Spain, battalion commissar Bob Cooney and battalion commander Sam Wild address the battalion, 1 May 1938.

was the crossing of the Ebro, which the *News Chronicle* argued had 'enormous psychological significance' for the Republic.[103] The *Daily Worker* carried an article by Peter Kerrigan on its front page, announcing triumphantly how the swift advance had captured considerable territory, weaponry and prisoners.[104] The newspaper declared that the offensive was a huge morale boost for the Republicans, particularly after the retreats of the previous spring, and, in this instance, the paper's hyperbole seems well founded.[105] As one volunteer recounted,

> In the Spring our forces had been thrown back across the Ebro in the last big offensive by the fascists when they had driven a wedge to the Mediterranean on April 14th. The right wing press was then jubilant and had prophesied the imminent fall of Barcelona. Valencia was threatened and indeed the end seemed near for democracy in Spain.
>
> Then three months later the world suddenly gasped. Our forces advanced on a 90 mile front to a depth of 18 miles. Over 5,000 prisoners were taken, large quantities of Italian equipment, and the fascists were well and truly on the run.[106]

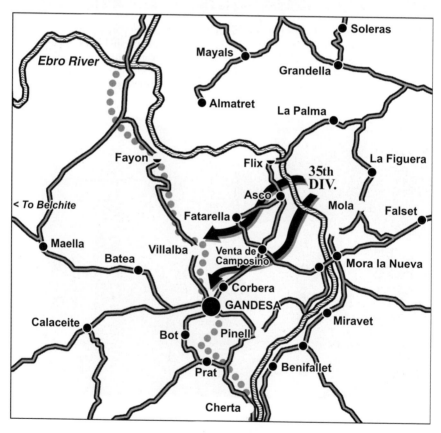

*Map 5.4* The Republican Ebro offensive, July 1938.

The British Battalion followed the Canadian Mac–Paps across the river to the north-east of Gandesa in a number of small boats and on a rope suspension bridge about a metre wide, whilst pontoon bridges upstream allowed tanks and other vehicles to cross.[107] Within two hours of the first troops crossing, rebel aeroplanes were attacking the temporary bridges across the river, but, nevertheless, the offensive

*Plate 5.7* Members of the battalion 'responding to a story in the *Daily Mail* that they had all been killed'.

*Plate 5.8* A battalion meeting just before the Ebro offensive, held under cover as a precaution against air-attacks.

once again caught the rebels by surprise.[108] Despite constant attention from rebel aircraft, by the afternoon of 25 July the British Battalion was within a mile of Corbera, a small town on the road to Gandesa, which, with the support of the British Battalion, the Spanish 13th Brigade successfully captured during the night, as rebel forces pulled back to defend Gandesa.[109]

On the following day, the British Battalion continued its advance towards the town of Gandesa, its major objective, and a major key to the Ebro offensive.[110] However, the Republicans were woefully short of motorised equipment,[111] and by now the element of surprise was no longer with them, so they were met by increasingly fierce resistance from rebel forces, particularly aircraft and artillery fire, as Franco rushed up reinforcements.[112] Nationalist reconnaissance the previous day had established how and where the Republicans were crossing the river and allowed the German and Italian units of the Nationalist air force to begin bombing the advancing troops. The battle increasingly became a struggle between Republican engineers attempting to construct river crossings and aircraft hampering their efforts. The rebels also opened the lock upstream at the reservoir at Barasona, which raised the level and increased the flow of the already powerful River Ebro, further hindering the crossing.[113] As the British Battalion approached the town it was ordered to attack a hill just under a mile to the east. This was Hill 481 – later known by the British as 'the Pimple' – which overlooked Gandesa, and needed to be captured before the town could be attacked with any chance of success.

The British No. 1 Company began its attempts to capture Hill 481 on the following day. However, in a repeat of its experiences at Pulburrel Hill the previous August, the battalion discovered the hill to have been expertly fortified and extremely robustly defended. One of No. 1 Company, a young Scottish volunteer called Steve Fullarton, later recalled how they were able to hear the defenders working on the defences during the night, further fortifying the machine-gun emplacements.[114] The natural defences were as impregnable as those constructed by the rebels; 'it was practically a sheer rise in front of us.'[115] To add further to the battalion's woes, the attacks were made during daylight and had negligible support from tanks and aircraft and, critically, artillery.[116] Fred Thomas from the Anti-Tank Battery remembered it as one of his toughest times in Spain: 'My blanket choked me, my packstrap cut into my shoulder, the night was stifling hot – in short, I never felt less like a revolutionary in my life.'[117]

As Matthew Hughes and Enriqueta Garrido have pointed out, 'The courage of the Army of the Ebro, fighting in stifling summer heat, could not overcome entrenched, properly supported and equally determined opposition.'[118] 'The Pimple' proved too much for No. 1 Company and, despite several costly attempts in which many volunteers, including the mathematician David Guest and Lewis Clive,[119] a rowing gold medallist in the 1932 Los Angeles Olympics, were killed, they were unable to capture it.[120] The following day, a desperate charge by No. 3 Company saw them get within 15 metres of the crest of the hill and attack the defences with grenades, yet still not capture the positions. Another attack that night, assisted by the Listers and the Spanish 13th Brigade, was similarly repulsed.

On 30 July, No. 2 Company joined the attack on Hill 481, but with no more success. The company commander, Lieutenant John Angus, and three replacements, Walter Gregory, Bill Harrington and Joe Harkins, were all wounded within hours of each other, Harkins mortally.[121] On 3 August the British Battalion's final desperate, and ultimately unsuccessful, assault on Hill 481 took place before the Republican forces gave up on their attempts to capture Gandesa and took up defensive positions. The battalion was moved into reserve. As George Wheeler observed, 'the offensive so brilliantly planned and executed by Colonel Modesto and the Spaniards under Lister was virtually brought to a halt in our sector at Hill 481.'[122] The battalion was withdrawn from the sector on 6 August.

With the Republicans now on the defensive, August saw the beginning of a new rebel push in Aragon as, on 11 August, the Nationalists counter-attacked in the mountains to the south of the Sierra Pandols. The 15th International Brigade was called upon to defend Hill 666, which had been occupied by the 11th Republican Division. On 24 August the British Battalion took over the exhausted Lincoln's positions on the main height of the Sierra Pandols,[123] which the British barely managed to hold after suffering a massive artillery bombardment and an attack by two rebel battalions.[124] Placed in a highly precarious position, with little defensive cover and with the hard rock making the digging of trenches impossible, the British could do little other than maintain as low a profile as possible and attempt to avoid the attentions of the accurate Nationalist artillery. Their nights were little better, as the Nationalists kept up a constant stream of rifle fire which the defenders feared could be the precursor to an attack.[125]

Two weeks later, on 8 September, the British were fighting on another strategic hill, this time attempting to recapture Hill 356 near Sandesco, in the nearby range of Sierra Caballs. The British Battalion captured the hill despite what appeared to be overwhelming numbers of Nationalist soldiers and unrelenting artillery and aircraft bombardments, as Walter Gregory, now back with the battalion, remembered: 'How we came to hate planes and cannon and how different would have been our sentiments if they had been ours and not those of the fascists; but they never were.'[126]

September 1938 was to be the last month of action for the British volunteers fighting in the 57th Battalion of the 15th International Brigade, and they were to be called on for one final action. On 21 September, the day that the Spanish premier, Juan Negrín, announced the Republic's intention to repatriate all foreign volunteers,[127] the 15th Brigade was recalled to the front late at night to replace the 13th (Dombrowski) Brigade, which had suffered heavy losses at Sierra de Lavall de la Torre.[128] On 23 September the British Battalion – under the command of George Fletcher, following Sam Wild's injury in the hand by a shell at Hill 666, and now numbering only 337 men (of whom fewer than a third were British)[129] moved up to the front for its last action on Spanish soil. After sustaining an immense five-hour Nationalist artillery barrage, under which the American Lincoln Battalion was forced to retire, the men were, in Peter Kerrigan's words, 'subjected to intense enfilading fire' from the positions previously occupied by the Lincolns. Those in No. 1 Company in particular bore the brunt of the attack, but they remained in their positions until their trenches were overrun.[130]

*Plate 5.9* The British volunteers training for the Ebro offensive of July 1938.

*Plate 5.10* 15th Brigade officers on Hill 481, near Gandesa, in July 1938: battalion
　　　　　commander Sam Wild is to the right leaning against a tree; sitting in front of
　　　　　Wild is the brigade commissar Peter Kerrigan, with George Fletcher, who also
　　　　　served as battalion commander for a time, in front of him.

The battalion was withdrawn in the evening. Two hundred members had been killed or wounded or were missing over the last three days.[131] At 1 a.m. the order finally arrived which withdrew the 15th International Brigade from the front line. For some, it was a tragic and heartbreaking end to their role in Spain. Peter Kerrigan described his shock at this terrible outcome of their last action:

> I could give dozens of individual acts of heroism but what is the use. The list of citations which I enclose, tells in brief official terms of the acts of deathless glory which were played out against a background of the cutting to pieces of our very bravest. I saw what No. 1 Coy. came through at Córdoba and I will never forget when I was told what our casualties were in those first 3 days at Jarama. But nothing can compare with the end of our battalion.[132]

As Peter Carroll observed, raw courage and a belief in the essential 'rightness' of their cause 'could not overcome inexperience, poor coordination and superior military force'.[133] But the depleted ranks of British volunteers were not to leave Spain immediately. Two events would formally mark the withdrawal of the International Brigaders from Spain. On 17 October all the foreign volunteers in the 35th Division were paraded and reviewed, and several of their number received promotions and commendations. Both Malcolm Dunbar, chief of operations for the 15th International Brigade, and Sam Wild, the battalion commander, were promoted to major, and John Power, the Irish political commissar who had tried – vainly – to persuade the Irish contingent to remain with the British Battalion in early 1937, was promoted to captain.[134]

The final appearance of the battalion was at a farewell parade in Barcelona at the end of October,[135] at which important Republican figures, including President Azaña and Prime Minister Negrín, expressed their thanks to the Internationals. The description of the parade, written the following day by Fred Thomas, not normally one for hyperbole or exaggeration, captured the full emotion of the occasion:

> Yesterday was a day I shall never forget. The Parade was, I am sure, an emotional feast for us all. It was no simple march through the streets, but a glorious demonstration of the enthusiasm and affection of the people of Catalonia for the Internationals.
>
> Trucks took us through crowded streets, with flags and bunting everywhere, the people cheering and throwing flowers, crowding every window and balcony. We dismounted finally at the Sarria Road, starting point of the procession.
>
> There the Brigades of many different nationalities were drawn up nine abreast. Spanish troops lined the route as, led by military bands, we set off. Everywhere thousands packed the broad streets, time after time men and women broke through the cordon to hug and kiss us, holding up small children and babies to be kissed in return, smothering us with affection as they cheered and cheered.
>
> For an hour and a half we made our slow way through some of the principle [*sic*] streets in one long glut of emotional excess. I was not the only Brigader

sometimes reduced to tears: we, who were leaving the fight, were yet receiving the heartfelt homage of the Spanish people.

In the street of the 14th April the March ended, and then came the speeches. From a platform full of important people from many countries as well as of the Republic, Dr. Negrin, Prime Minister, addressed us and the vast crowds. Then came President Azaña followed by the chief of the Army of the Ebro. Finally we recognised the spare figure of the indomitable 'La Pasionaria' who quickly had the crowd roaring their approval of her every word. But we British were not near enough to hear much, so I have to wait until to-day to read her stirring speech: one sentence stands out – 'Come back, as honoured sons of Spain.'[136]

As Fred Thomas states, the speech by Dolores Ibarruri, the communist deputy from the Asturias forever known as *La Pasionaria*, delivered to the more than 13,000 watching Internationals, was the highlight of an extremely emotional occasion. Describing the volunteers as 'history' and 'legend', she invited them to return to Spain 'when the olive tree of peace puts forth its leaves again'. It was to be a long wait.

For the volunteers it was to be departure that left them with mixed feelings. Though of course they wanted to get home, it is also clear that many felt that 'they were leaving unfinished the task they had undertaken.'[137] The war was by no means over, and the Republic's precarious situation was progressively worsening. The departure was, in any event, not immediate. Bureaucracy held up the repatriation, but following pressure from sympathetic MPs in Britain, and from a delegation of volunteers lobbying the British Consul in Barcelona, most of the British volunteers, 305 in total, left Spain by train at the beginning of December 1938.[138] The group arrived on the evening of 7 December 1938 at Victoria Station, where, to their surprise and delight, they were welcomed home by a huge crowd.[139] In addition to families and friends were a number of senior members of the British Labour movement, including Clement Attlee, the maverick Labour MP Stafford Cripps, the Communist MP Willie Gallagher and Will Lawther from the British Miners' Federation.

Over the next few weeks several other groups returned to Britain, including some of those who had been wounded. But not all the British volunteers were able to return, for there were a number held in prisoner-of-war camps in the Nationalist zone. For some of them, it would be several months before they would see home again; others, notably Frank Ryan, the Irish veteran captured at Calaceite, would never return.

# 6    Prisoners of war

Somebody spoke and I heard a voice say, 'Don't shoot'. They thought we were Russians with the uniforms at first. Somebody shouted, 'Ingles?' If it hadn't been for that . . . we would have been shot one at a time. They were going to shoot us. We were all lined up.[1]

As has been stated, large groups of British volunteers were taken prisoner on two occasions during the battalion's involvement in the civil war: the first during the battle of Jarama in February 1937, and the second at Calaceite, during the retreats of March 1938. In addition, individual British volunteers were captured at various stages of the war: Lieutenant Walter Gregory and several others were unfortunate enough to be captured on the British Battalion's very last day of action in Spain.[2]

The first group to be taken prisoner consisted of up to 30 volunteers from the Machine-Gun Company captured on the second day of Jarama, 13 February 1937.[3] As two members of the company, Maurice Goldberg and James Maley, later recounted, the volunteers expected to be executed, for the belief was widespread that captured Internationals were shot on sight. Indeed, the British government was aware as early as November 1936 that British volunteers captured by Franco were likely to be executed. A telegram from the British Embassy in Madrid, sent to London on 9 November 1936, stated:

It is possible that we will have a rush of some fifty British combatants who would otherwise be murdered, for protection in the Embassy. If so I would take them in and if insurgents demand their surrender I would refuse pending your instructions.[4]

The British government's reluctant acquiescence to this request is evident from the reply two days later.

I presume you have carefully considered the possibility that the lives of the 190 persons now in the Embassy would be seriously endangered by admission of these candidates who by their own actions have put themselves in a different category from refugees whose plight is no fault of their own . . . If you are in touch with any of the combatants they should be advised to make their way to territory which is not likely to fall into insurgent hands, or better still to leave Spain.

In event of emergency, however, I give you authority to act as suggested in your telegram under reference on the assumption that such persons would be admitted only as a last resort and in face of grave risk that they would lose their lives if they are captured or surrender. They should also be required to give an undertaking to take no further part in hostilities.[5]

On 9 March 1937 Franco issued a proclamation declaring that any foreigners captured under arms would be shot.[6] Despite official antipathy to the volunteers, the British government nevertheless issued a 'stiff note' to Franco threatening 'the strongest possible reaction on the part of H. M. Government if the clauses relating to the Geneva Convention were not rigorously adhered to'. However, the order was not suspended until early April 1938, following pressure on Franco from Mussolini, who was keen to use the Internationals in exchange for Italian soldiers captured by the Republicans. In general the Italians anyway took prisoners alive, even before April 1938, though amongst Spanish units the situation was somewhat different, as Peter Kemp recounts in his description of his time fighting with the rebels:

> Beyond were several half-ruined shepherds' huts; against their walls about a dozen prisoners were slumped together, while some of our tank crews stood in front of them, loading rifles. As I approached there was a series of shots, and the prisoners slumped to the ground.
>
> 'My God!' I said to Cancela, feeling slightly sick. 'What do they think they're doing, shooting those prisoners?'
>
> Cancela looked at me. 'They're from the International Brigades', he said grimly.[7]

There is no doubt that the Nationalists often shot prisoners, particularly if they were International Brigaders.[8] Internationals certainly believed they might well be shot if captured, particularly if they were political commissars, officers or machine-gunners,[9] and the prospect of being taken by Moors was especially feared.[10] A confidential report on the British volunteers in the International Brigades in Spain, compiled by a member of the British consular staff at the end of the civil war, was sent to the Foreign Office, which admitted: 'I am informed confidentially that any International Brigadier taken in the Ebro offensive was asked one question, "When did you come to Spain?" If he replied after the 19th July 1936 he was shot *sin formacion de causa.*'[11]

But it was not just the rebels who shot prisoners; it occurred on both sides during the Spanish Civil War, and it is also beyond doubt that members of the International Brigades were themselves involved. Carl Geiser, who was a political commissar in the American battalion (and thus hardly a hostile witness), testifies that during 1937 a number of Spanish Nationalist officers and NCOs were executed at Quinto in Aragon by American International Brigaders and Spanish Republican troops on the orders of General 'Walter'.[12] It has also been alleged that a number of prisoners were executed after the capture of Villanueva de la Cañada in July 1937.[13]

However, this was not to be the fate of the British Machine-Gun Company, who were extremely fortunate to be saved by the intervention of a Spanish officer.[14] Nevertheless, several individuals were still killed outright. Phil Elias, of Leeds, was shot when reaching for tobacco from his pockets:

> Another prisoner asked permission to smoke, which was granted. As he reached in his tunic-pocket for a cigarette, the guard who had given permission riddled his stomach with bullets from a sub-machine-gun. The hand shot out of the tunic-pocket, holding a cigarette.[15]

John Stevens, an engineer from Islington in London, was also killed by the same burst of machine-gun fire. The other British volunteers were understandably terrified and appalled; Edward Dickenson, the company second-in-command, protested vigorously over the shooting, and was promptly picked out as a suspected leader and shot through the head with a pistol.[16] The commander of the Machine-Gun Company, Harold Fry, escaped, Dickenson having deliberately ripped off the officer's insignia from his uniform.[17]

The remainder of the prisoners were protected by Civil Guards and marched to temporary holding areas at nearby San Martín de la Vega, where they were kept for two days before being taken to a jail in Navalcarnero, about 20 miles south of Madrid, to be fingerprinted and have their heads shaved. The prisoners were held for a week here, nine to a cell,[18] before being interrogated individually by Alfonso Merry del Val (the son of the former Spanish Ambassador in London) and photographed standing on the back of a truck by a *Daily Mail* reporter.[19] The accompanying caption is rather typical of the *Daily Mail*'s coverage of the war:

> These are the first pictures – exclusive to 'The Daily Mail' – of some of the misguided and hapless British prisoners who were captured by General Franco's forces on the Jarama front. They were sent out to Spain by Communists with promises of work at £6 a week, but the first most of them knew of their real fate was when they were given arms and drafted to the Reds' front line.[20]

Ironically, the taking of this photograph by the *Daily Mail* photographer proved to be fortunate for the prisoners, for it provided evidence to those in Britain that the captives were still alive, which the rebels might otherwise have been able to deny.

The prisoners were then moved to an old factory in Talavera de la Reina where Spanish Republican prisoners were being held, and were joined by two volunteers from Liverpool, Jack Flynn and Fred Jones, at the end of February.[21] At Talavera the British prisoners were worked hard for three months repairing roads and burying the bodies of executed Republican prisoners, with little food and the most basic living and sanitary facilities. Several prisoners were still carrying the wounds they had sustained at Jarama; many of the others fell ill from stomach and lung diseases.[22]

On 18 May 1937, after three months at Talavera, the prisoners were moved on to

Salamanca, where they were all tried by a military court for 'aiding a military rebellion'. They were tried as a collective group and no interpreter was provided, so the prisoners agreed amongst themselves not to speak in court.[23] Five were sentenced to death: the commander Harold Fry, plus George Leeson, Maurice Goldberg, Jimmy Rutherford and Charles West.[24] The remainder of the British were sentenced to 20 years' imprisonment, with James Pugh and George Watters to serve the entire period in solitary confinement.[25] In fact, none of the British prisoners were actually executed at Salamanca, though, as every night groups of Spaniards were taken out of the prison in a van – which became known as the 'Agony Wagon' – and not brought back again, the five condemned British prisoners greeted the arrival of the truck at 5 o'clock each evening with particular foreboding.[26]

Following their show trial, the prisoners were moved to the Model Prison in Salamanca, where they remained until May 1937. They were then informed that Franco had pardoned them, and that they were to be exchanged for a similar number of Italians captured by Republican forces. Twenty-three British prisoners were exchanged[27] and marched across the frontier at Irun, through a crowd with their arms raised in the fascist salute.[28] The volunteers reached England at the end of May 1937. Of the 23 released prisoners, five were back in Spain fighting with the British Battalion within six weeks, including Harold Fry, Basil Minsk (a Jewish volunteer from London fighting under the name of Basil Abrahams, who later served with the 15th International Brigade staff), Tom Bloomfield, a Scot from Kirkcaldy in Fife, and Jimmy Rutherford, the Edinburgh delegate to the YCL annual conference in 1934.[29]

A small number of prisoners were not released but kept back, including George Leeson, Maurice Goldberg and Robert Silcock, a volunteer from Liverpool, and were moved in with Spanish prisoners. Leeson was released in September after a solidarity campaign in the UK, and Goldberg and Silcock were finally released in November 1937.[30] The reasons for holding back the volunteers are unclear; Bill Alexander suggests it was anti-Semitism,[31] Carl Geiser that it was to ensure that the released prisoners would not say anything unfavourable when they returned home.[32]

The second large group of British volunteers was taken prisoner at Calaceite, during the retreat through Aragon on 31 March 1938, by an Italian column from the crack Italian (Blackshirt) Division, and a number of stragglers were picked up over the following days. The capture of over 100 British volunteers was a disaster for the British Battalion, which, like most of the Spanish Republican Army, was already reeling from the dramatic advances made by the rebel forces. Several prisoners were shot outright, just as some had been at Jarama in February 1937, even though Nationalist aeroplanes had dropped leaflets on the retreating Republicans, encouraging them to desert and guaranteeing their safety.[33] The group of British prisoners were marched to the main square in Calaceite by Civil Guards, where they were lined up against a wall in front of machine-guns. To the prisoners it seemed clear that they were all to be shot; as one said, 'We thought, "this is it."'[34] However, they were spotted by an American journalist who was in the company of several Italian Army officers. The officers, aware of the Internationals' value in an exchange

*Plate 6.1* Members of British Machine-Gun Company captured at Jarama on 13 February 1937, filmed by Movie Tone News: third from right as you look (partly obscured) is Jimmy Rutherford, who later returned to Spain and was shot after being recaptured; Harold Fry, the company commander, is the fourth to Rutherford's right.

*Plate 6.2* Released British and French International Brigade prisoners cross the border at Irun (in May 1937): the Canadian 'Yank' Levy (to the rear in beret) also appears in Plate 6.1 (in front with peaked cap and moustache and his hands behind his back).

for Italian prisoners held by the Republicans, prevented the *Guardia Civil* from shooting them.

The prisoners were gradually all brought to the Italian-controlled prison at Alcañiz.[35] The official battalion report admits that 'Many prisoners were apprehensive and a large number demoralised', and that several blamed the Communist Party and the battalion leadership for their present situation.[36] As the inevitable interrogations began in earnest, it soon became clear that the Nationalist authorities were looking for officers and political commissars. Communist Party and YCL members decided wisely that all should deny party membership or officer rank, and hope that they would not be exposed by 'some of the weaker elements'.[37]

After a number of days at Alcañiz, the prisoners were taken to the military academy at Saragossa, where most British prisoners had arrived by 2 or 3 April. Here the discipline was even harder than at Alcañiz, where prisoners had been beaten and forced to sleep in appalling unsanitary conditions alongside the open lavatory. At Saragossa they were warned that guards had orders to shoot on sight any prisoners showing themselves at the windows. Prisoners were forced to salute in the fascist style, though the Irish Republican leader Frank Ryan, who made no secret of his rank, refused to do this throughout his long period of captivity, and several devout communists, such as Danny Gibbons (later a member of a Soviet spy ring following the invasion of Russia by Germany in June 1941)[38] and Lionel Jacobs, initially spoke out against it.[39] The rebel authorities' rather clumsy and ineffectual attempt to impose the fascist salute on the prisoners at Saragossa is recounted by the American political commissar and prisoner Carl Geiser:

> [The Nationalist Officer] formed us into straight ranks, making certain that each man would have enough room to swing his arm properly. Then he stepped in front of us, drew himself up to his full height, and barked, '*Rompen filas!*'
>
> The number of creative ways nearly two hundred Internationals found to express their opinion of Franco was impressive. After giving the military salute, arms went up in all directions, all out of synchronisation and to all levels. Fingers drooped forward, even formed fists. Some were yelling 'Fran-' while others were yelling '-co.'
>
> The astonished expression on the officer's face told us we had scored. When he made the mistake of again shouting, '*Rompen filas!*' we attained new heights of creativity.
>
> The officer realised it was useless to continue, and with a show of disgust dismissed us. We were jubilant. What had threatened dangerously to divide us had been converted into a morale-boosting victory. We were not asked to salute again.[40]

The prisoners scored a similar success later in their period of captivity. Ordered to chant the Francoist slogan – *¡España Una! ¡España Grande! ¡España Libre!*, they were also to respond to each line with their own cry of '¡Franco!'. Instead many amended the chant to 'Fuck You', or kept quiet for the first two chants then bellowed out

'*¡Libre!*'.[41] When the prisoners were ordered by the prison guards to shout louder, the guards must have been astonished by their willingness to respond.[42]

On the second day in the military prison at Saragossa, the prisoners were interviewed by Merry del Val, who had interviewed the British prisoners captured at Jarama the previous year.[43] One of those at Calaceite was Jimmy Rutherford, who had earlier been taken at Jarama and repatriated, but had returned to fight in Spain. Despite desperate attempts by other British volunteers to shield Rutherford – who had attempted to hide his identity by using the pseudonym Jimmy Smalls – he was recognised by Merry del Val as one of the Jarama prisoners he had interviewed previously.[44] Rutherford was taken away and shot on 24 May 1938 for being in contravention of the agreement, which all the freed British prisoners of war had signed, not to return to Spain following their repatriation to Britain. Following the execution, a letter was sent by the British Foreign Office to Jimmy Rutherford's father confirming that this was the case.

> Your son, Mr. James Rutherford, was taken prisoner on February 13th, 1937 at San Martin de la Vega, but was released on July 5th, having promised to take no further part in future Spanish hostilities. On May 24th last he was captured a second time at Calaceite, tried by court martial and executed.[45]

As the letter went on to explain, Rutherford was in contravention of international law, and the Foreign Office somewhat insensitively enclosed an extract from Oppenheim's *International Law* to demonstrate this. A letter to Willie Gallagher, the communist member of parliament for Fife, on 9 February 1939, explained the government's position in more detail:

> I am very sorry that the enquiries which we have made resulted in this bad news, but I am afraid that a formal protest or a claim for redress would serve no purpose seeing that Mr. James Rutherford was released on a promise that he would not serve again in the Spanish war and broke this promise . . . General Franco's army have as a general practice made this offence a capital one and H. M. G. have no status for demanding special treatment for British subjects serving with the Spanish forces.[46]

Rutherford's execution in April 1938 and Harold Fry's death at Fuentes de Ebro the previous October persuaded the British Communist Party not to allow volunteers who had been prisoners to return to Spain, as George Leeson found when he later attempted to re-enlist with the British Battalion.[47]

Whilst the prisoners were imprisoned at Saragossa they were visited by several international journalists, who had been invited in order to show to the world how the International Brigade had been smashed by the Nationalist Army. Clearly, the rebel authorities recognised that there was far greater propaganda value in keeping the large number of British prisoners alive than in executing them.[48] Amongst the visitors was *The Times* reporter Kim Philby,[49] who gave the impression of 'a rather conservative Englishman with leanings towards fascism',[50] and William Carney of the *New York Times*, who was extremely unsympathetic to the Internationals.[51]

On 6 April the prisoners were marched to Saragossa railway station, where the humming of 'revolutionary marching tunes' by some caused more conflict between the prisoners, as several complained that this would lead to further punishment. Four of the volunteers were particularly unhappy and 'offered to throw in their lot with the Fascists'.[52] The British prisoners were then transferred to Burgos, a two-day train journey, during which they were rarely fed, and allowed even less exercise. Late in the evening of 8 April, the contingent arrived at the prison camp of San Pedro de Cardeña, 8 miles south-east of Burgos, built on the site of the first Benedictine monastery in Spain and the last resting place of El Cid. There they were kept separately from the large numbers of Spanish prisoners of war, who were mainly awaiting transfer to labour battalions.[53]

The prisoners at San Pedro who had been captured at Calaceite in March were later joined by other British prisoners, including Frank West and George Wheeler,[54] who had been apprehended at Sierra de la Val in the Sierra Pandols in Aragon in the autumn of 1938, after the Republican offensive across the Ebro had ground to a halt.[55] At first West, Wheeler and the other prisoners were taken to an overcrowded barn, where they spent the night with no room to lie down. At daybreak the following morning, the prisoners were called up individually in alphabetical order and asked why they had come to Spain and, if they were released, whether they would come back to fight again. The first to be questioned answered, 'Because I am an anti-fascist' to the first question and 'Yes' to the second. Following this brief interrogation he was taken out of the building, and those inside heard a brief burst of machine-gun fire. The process continued with most prisoners giving similar answers. George Wheeler was one of the last to be questioned and led outside. To his astonishment and relief he found that his comrades were alive and well, if extremely shocked. As Wheeler realised, the process was a macabre exercise designed by the rebels to humiliate and terrify the prisoners.[56]

The International prisoners at San Pedro were kept in dormitories approximately 70 metres long by 10 metres wide, with between 300 and 350 prisoners in each dormitory; one group was on the ground floor, and the rest were divided between the first and second floors.[57] On the ground floor, the discomfort caused by insufficient blankets, ventilation and light was exceeded only by the sanitary arrangements, which were, if anything, worse than those experienced at Alcañiz. There was only one tap for 600 men, and 'the lavatories were open, of the crudest style, and were often blocked.'[58] The facilities were outside in the main square and shared with the Spanish prisoners, and the men were required to wait in line, sometimes for hours, to use them. George Wheeler described how the standard of sanitation was so bad that there was 'No water so the faeces were piling up and sometime that was about two feet high . . . It was the most disgusting thing under the sun.'[59]

Joe Norman, one of the British captured at Calaceite, has particular reason to remember the toilets at San Pedro with horror:

> There was no newspaper, no toilet paper. And it was in a sunken room, the toilet. And, of course, they were tearing their clothing and all that sort of thing.

And it got stopped up. So they asked for volunteers to . . . It flooded to a depth of six feet, this place. And they asked for volunteers. The fascists wouldn't clean it out. So the committee asked for volunteers. But we couldn't ask anyone outside the committee because it was such a filthy job. So three of us volunteered. And we'd got to dive in this lot and we cleared it. It took about an hour. One was a Canadian. One was a Scot. Two of them died of typhus.[60]

For those on the first and second floors, the facilities were at least inside the building but, nevertheless, still woefully inadequate. With only three taps divided between the prisoners, it was impossible for them to stay clean, and thus fleas, lice and diseases were endemic. Most prisoners were infested with lice for the entire time they remained at San Pedro:

> People were so ridden with lice, that they got so accustomed to it, that they no longer had to think. If I was talking to anyone and I saw a louse on his shoulder I'd simply put out my hand take off the louse and just squash it straight away.[61]

Many prisoners suffered from sickness whilst they were in the prison camp; a large number of the British prisoners were suffering from a form of dysentery brought on by a poor diet and insufficient and unhygienic food, and were not always able to restrain themselves whilst waiting in the long queues for the toilets, thus adding to their, and other prisoners', misery.[62] Treatment for diarrhoea was rudimentary at best and, as always, there were difficulties caused by language problems, with the few medical workers amongst the prisoners sometimes misunderstanding descriptions of the symptoms.[63] With the medical facilities being somewhat limited – there were five doctors for all the International Brigaders held at San Pedro – those suffering from wounds sustained before their arrival, or diseases contacted during their incarceration, suffered particularly badly, with their condition exacerbated by the general unsanitary conditions.

Several prisoners reported having sores on the lower half of their bodies and brittle teeth, symptomatic of scurvy. Harold Collins, a volunteer from North Kensington, was hospitalised with suspected malaria.[64] Maurice Levitas suffered from swollen knees, which made walking extremely difficult and painful.[65] Joseph Byrne from Liverpool fell ill with enteric fever, for which he was, in the circumstances, lucky enough to be treated with aspirin and the occasional dose of half a cup of goat's milk. Much to his own surprise, he survived. Two other prisoners suffering from similar symptoms did not.[66]

In fact, hospitalisation did not necessarily offer any great improvements on conditions in the camp. Bruce Allender, who, as a first-aider, occasionally helped in the Burgos hospital, described how it was run by priests who 'treated people like pigs', for they believed the Internationals to be 'animals'. Allender was in no doubt that their cruelty was deliberate: 'They were letting people die off. That's what it amounted to.'[67]

Behind many of the illnesses lay the poor diet. The prisoners were fed a thin soup, *ajo*, comprised of warm water flavoured with olive oil, garlic and breadcrumbs, and one small bread roll per day, roughly the size of a man's fist.[68] At lunchtime and in the evening they were also given a spoonful of white beans which, very occasionally, contained a small piece of pork fat.[69] Not surprisingly, food was an issue that stretched the prisoners' self-discipline and was the cause of occasional arguments, particularly on the very rare occasions when the meagre rations were augmented with sardines.[70] These came in large frying pans, which prisoners would crowd around, attempting to scoop up the nutritious oil on their bread. Quarrels over the pans are described by Frank West, one of the British volunteers captured at the Ebro in September 1938, who believed that the strict discipline maintained in the International Brigades temporarily broke down at San Pedro:

> The meals were turned out in big flat frying pans that were put on the floor and the lads just told to come and get it. They fought one another, trod in the food and really messed things up. It was decided two things should happen. One was that all the International Brigaders should be formed into four companies. Each company should have a commander. And second they then organised the food so that it could be served to each company and each company took turns getting what was left over. That stopped the battles.[71]

The arguments could become a real problem on the rare occasions that there was enough food for a few prisoners to have a second portion. Those served first would have enough time to eat their food before rejoining the queue. Thus prisoners competed to be first in the queue, creating crowding around the cauldrons, which led to beatings from the guards. There were also occasional thefts of food, usually bread rolls which prisoners had tucked away to consume later. One prisoner was discovered stealing, tried by a summary court headed by Frank Ryan and punished by the temporary daily confiscation of his own bread ration.[72]

Aware that indiscipline could encourage the authorities to mete out punishment to the prisoners, Communist Party members attempted to group together to form a 'camp committee' to restore discipline and raise the spirits of the demoralised men. The Communist Party members quickly got to know each other, despite the dangers associated with overt political activity. By 4 April 1938, Danny Gibbons had convened a meeting of party cadres, a committee had been organised – known by the other prisoners as 'the secret six'[73] – and Jack Jones (a miner from the Rhondda, not the Labour trade unionist) was designated secretary.[74] The committee was later expanded when it turned out that another group of communists had also formed a committee, and the two groups were first amalgamated and then reorganised following the transfer of the prisoners to San Pedro.[75] The group gradually increased in number, though progress was slow as the party members 'were apprehensive of possible informers and of what measure the Fascist authorities would take if they became aware of the Party Committee and Party members.'[76] By the summer of 1938 the committee at San Pedro comprised eight British party members, plus Bob Dickie, a Canadian. Bob Dickie, together with Jack Jones and Danny Gibbons, were selected to form the secretariat, who would be required to make any decisions too urgent to allow the meeting of the entire committee. This arrangement arose despite the opposition of American communists, who preferred forming members into groups of five who would discuss all matters before decisions were taken. The British committee decided that 'the most effective and safest method was to give the committee full powers, with implicit acceptance of direction by all Party members', and cited the American model as 'false democracy', claiming that it opened them up to the risk of infiltration.[77] The British committee was also critical of the German group, which they claimed was over-cautious, though they did recognise that the Germans had 'special difficulties', for their position was more dangerous than that of any other nationality. The German prisoners were interrogated daily by Gestapo agents and were believed by other prisoners to have been infiltrated by 'unreliable elements' and 'Trotskyists'.[78]

The party committee continued to operate clandestinely throughout their time at San Pedro, with their main objectives being to limit punishment inflicted on the prisoners by the guards and to settle grievances between prisoners without involving the camp authorities. Misdemeanours were assigned punishments – such as extra duties and cleaning lavatories[79] – by the committee, rather than the miscreants being reported to the camp authorities, thus saving everyone a beating. To a certain extent, this necessitated the committee having a realistic attitude towards cooperation with the camp authorities. As Joe Norman, a communist and a member of the camp committee, described:

> The function of the committee, any problems – because we did get problems, surprisingly, you know, people fell out with each other and that sort of thing. You had to pacify them and explain that it's not a thing to do. You don't want to give the fascist guard a chance to come at you.[80]

The negotiation came despite protests from a number of the prisoners that this would only provoke the authorities into further acts of violence. Danny Gibbons was threatened with being thrown out of a window by some of the prisoners who were alarmed by his agitation. Indeed, the party officials were informed categorically by the camp authorities that orders were not to be questioned but to be carried out, or 'serious consequences would result', which the prisoners reasonably concluded meant that those disobeying would be shot.[81]

Maintaining a disciplined military manner when being drilled or paraded could easily be justified, for the prisoners were, after all, members of the International Brigade, but kneeling for Catholic Mass, for example, was not accepted willingly by some prisoners. Two German prisoners who refused to kneel met a swift and brutal response from the authorities: 'They were immediately beaten by an officer, while the other officers "crossed" themselves. The two Germans were further punished by being put in the calabouse [*sic*].'[82]

Another point of contention was the saluting of the Nationalist flag and the shouting of 'Franco', which had to accompany giving the fascist salute.[83] Not surprisingly there was a general unease at this, and many prisoners cooperated half-heartedly at best. This was frequently rewarded with a beating. The committee recognised that here they faced an awkward dilemma, and pragmatically sought a compromise. However, this approach created its own problems, and opened the committee up to criticisms that they were not firm enough in resisting the authorities' demands and succumbed too easily to the latter's threats.[84]

Criticisms of the committee eventually died down when it was realised that they were not making decisions autonomously, but were consulting with committees from other national groups. Certainly the committee's conciliatory approach to the authorities was not an unqualified success; despite their attempts, beatings with sticks, rubber piping and riding crops were a regular occurrence. Occasionally the committee would warn an individual prisoner that his behaviour was 'bringing trouble upon himself' and that, therefore, he alone would have to take responsibility for any punishment meted out. One British prisoner, Robert Beggs from Glasgow, was beaten up on the parade ground and, despite the advice of the committee to the contrary, attempted to complain directly to the commandant. He was intercepted by the sergeants and put into the cells, where he remained until the British prisoners were released from San Pedro.[85] The effectiveness of the committee's approach was demonstrated when they wrote to the commandant about Beggs's treatment, and shortly afterwards the prisoners were informed that if they followed general regulations there would be no more beatings. Eventually, the house committee's policy of negotiation was rewarded by official recognition from the commandant at San Pedro, in part because of their undeniable role in organising various activities, but also because they oversaw the distribution of a fund which was formed by prisoners donating 10 per cent of monies received after the regime was relaxed slightly in August 1938, combined with a large donation of £100 from Clive Branson when he was repatriated in October 1938.[86] The money was used to buy various items, such as tobacco and chocolate for some of the sick prisoners and writing materials for the lectures and classes.[87]

The prisoners soon developed strategies for coping with the harsh nature of the regime, and here the house committee set up by the Communist Party activists played a leading role. In addition to various language classes, there were a number of lectures organised on aspects of political culture, including Marxist philosophy and a history of the International Brigade. A course of lectures on English working-class history was started by one of the members of the committee, Lionel Jacobs, but was forced to be abandoned after pressure was applied by the camp authorities.[88] Various games and tournaments were also organised, and for three months a hand-written newspaper, the *San Pedro Jaily News*, was published, until copies started falling into the hands of the guards, after which it was prudently discontinued.[89] The committee even managed to organise a May Day celebration and a Christmas concert, which consisted of the rendition of a number of old ballads. Whilst the guards applauded the singing enthusiastically, the prisoners' performance of 'The Barber of Seville', a satire of camp life, was less well received.[90] Still, for the prisoners, there was a rather more surreptitious pleasure: 'To the inner amusement of all prisoners, at each performance, some of the fleas in our straw sacks left us and established new residence with our guests.'[91]

However, playing chess, with pieces carved from at first bread and later soap, was, as Walter Gregory explained, 'the most popular way to isolate ourselves from the daily horror of life in the filth of San Pedro.'[92] Towards the end of the British prisoners' stay at San Pedro, reading became an increasingly popular way to pass time, particularly after the delivery of a large shipment of paperback books to the camp, following a request by Jimmy Moon to a friend of his who worked in a library in south-west London.[93] The request did not fall on deaf ears, for one of the directors of the library was Harold Laski, who was also on the editorial panel of the Left Book Club.[94]

The committee also managed to raise issues with the British military attaché in Burgos, Colonel C. C. Martin, on his visits to the camp. The first of these was on 11 June 1938, when the prisoners' refusal to perform the fascist salute in front of Colonel Martin, despite the order being given twice, was met by renewed beatings.[95] Concerned that many prisoners might have their own agendas to raise with Martin, 'the Committee organised responsible comrades to do the talking.'[96] However, some individuals did manage to make contact with Martin. George Wheeler, concerned that his parents believed him to have been killed, was desperate to get news of his whereabouts back to his parents, and brought the matter to the colonel's notice. Martin shook Wheeler's hand and promised he would personally see to it. According to Wheeler, he never did.[97]

The camp committee raised various matters with Colonel Martin, such as the number of prisoners, the beatings, the role of the Gestapo in the camp, and the poor general conditions of the medical facilities, food and quarters. However, there was very little improvement as a result of the visit, and a great deal of bad feeling when Martin stated that the British government would be requesting a levy of £4 per man from the 100 prisoners who had been told they would shortly be transferred in preparation for an exchange with Italian prisoners held by the Republic.[98] The British prisoners were transferred to the Italian-run camp at Palencia on 12 June 1938, the day after the visit from Colonel Martin. On the same day, Frank Ryan, the Irish Republican leader, also left San Pedro, though not to be repatriated. He was led away in handcuffs and sentenced to death at his trial on 15 June, accused by the Nationalists of commanding International Brigaders who had executed Nationalist prisoners captured during the Brunete offensive.[99]

The 100 prisoners being repatriated were held until the Nationalist authorities received notice that the Italians had been released. Finally, on Saturday 22 October 1938, confirmation was received and the British were transferred to Ondarreta prison at San Sebastian in northern Spain, where they were kept for a further two days.[100] Many prisoners considered it to be worse than San Pedro, for the basement of the prison was full of Basques awaiting execution. On the following Monday, 40 of the British International Brigaders were released and allowed to march over the French border to Irun and freedom, led by the London artist Clive Branson.[101] They arrived back in Britain at Victoria Station on the evening of 25 October 1938. The remaining British at Ondarreta were released and returned to Britain over the next few days.

For the prisoners remaining in San Pedro, the most urgent matter was to attempt to limit the use of beatings, which were endemic and used by the rebel authorities to punish and humiliate the prisoners, on top of the hardships caused by deliberate neglect.[102] The sergeants in charge of the British contingent were particularly vicious; one was nicknamed 'Sticky' for his willingness to use a large heavy stick to beat the prisoners at the slightest excuse. The others were little better: 'Tanky', who had been wounded in an Italian tank when fighting against the British Battalion on 31 March 1938,[103] usually referred to the prisoners as *rojos bastardos*;[104] and 'Froggy', named after his 'bulbous blue eyes', appeared to dislike the British in particular.[105] The British prisoners were advised that any unwillingness to obey regulations would result in the offenders being 'shot like dogs';[106] many prisoners believed that the violence of the jailers was a deliberate attempt to provoke them.[107]

Most of the beatings resulted from a belief by the sergeants in control that the prisoners were undisciplined. The beatings increased substantially after the British refusal to salute in front of Lady Austen Chamberlain, a relative of Neville Chamberlain, who visited San Pedro on 8 September 1938. The camp authorities cynically issued clean uniforms and shoes to the prisoners. However, the impression they were attempting to create was somewhat ruined by parading the prisoners in the rain for an hour before the visitors' arrival. Lady Chamberlain was infuriated by the prisoners' refusal to offer her the fascist salute, as was the Spanish sergeant, 'Sticky'.[108] The discipline increased considerably in September 1938, following the arrival of two new sergeants, and the official report describes the regime implemented by the new guards as 'a period of terror'. As the regime increased the level of disciplinary measures, the party committee reacted by recommending that prisoners should be cautious and try to avoid provoking the guards. Before September the prisoners had been left relatively to their own devices, at least within the dormitories, but this ended dramatically. The level of violence was stepped up, with prisoners regularly being taken out at night to receive beatings for alleged infringements of discipline. The use of informants was also extended, and information provided by them led to three prisoners, who had been accused of 'having killed and wounded fascist soldiers and being an officer and having sung revolutionary songs', receiving terrible beatings at precisely the time the British government representative, Colonel Martin, was interviewing the British prisoners for the second time, on 10 September 1938. One man was beaten into signing a confession and kept in solitary confinement for five days without light, food, water or any toilet facilities. He later attempted suicide and was still in isolation when the British contingent left San Pedro.

The daily beatings were usually doled out by 'Sticky'. Every day a handful of men would be arbitrarily selected and given night-time beatings, which often ended in hospitalisation.

> The men would be taken one by one into a small room where there were ten or a dozen Fascists. When the victim entered he immediately received a terrific blow in the face, and he was punched from one man to another right around the room. Then sticks and whips were used. If he fell to the floor he was kicked again to his feet, until finally he could rise no more. After that the hospital.[109]

Prisoners were regularly beaten with rifle butts and riding crops as they reached the foot of the dormitory stairs on their way to parade or meals, so many refused to descend the stairs, preferring to go without food rather than go through the ordeal. Bob Doyle, a veteran of the IRA who was captured at Calaceite, remembered the brutality clearly:

> If you showed discipline they would smash in with rifle butts and with sticks into the rear ranks to throw you into disorder to avoid the beatings. Coming down for your meals and saluting the flag in the morning they would line up at the door so that any attempt to come out in order, to allow one out at a time or two out of the door, they immediately disorganised the ranks. The same way if we made games of chess and sat around with improvised pieces they would raid them and take them away and that would be preceded by a beating of anyone within sight. [110]

Examples of the brutality in the camp abound. Joe Norman, who was a member of the communist committee, was beaten up for mistakenly giving the clenched fist salute to two Gestapo interrogators.[111] In fact many of the prisoners believed, like Bob Doyle, that the beatings were part of a deliberate strategy to break the prisoners' morale and political beliefs.

> I would describe our treatment as brutal, demoralising and of course it was a deliberate strategy in every way to demoralise us and to make out that we were sub-human, that we could not be normal to have come and fought in the International Brigades.[112]

The party committee came under considerable pressure to organise some form of resistance, such as refusing to leave the dormitories, or refusing to take food, but members were convinced that the prison authorities were attempting to provoke the prisoners into some form of reaction. The party committee refused to sanction any form of protest, arguing that there were many other nationals besides the British who would suffer as a result of a unilateral protest. They also argued that amongst the prisoners were volunteers who had attempted to desert from the battalion and others who consistently criticised the party and battalion leaders, who as 'weak elements' could not be relied upon.[113] Instead they decided to include a description of the recent events in a letter home to be given to the British representative, Colonel Martin, on his visit planned for 20 November. The letter stated that, so far, the party committee had acted as a restraining influence on the other prisoners, but could not continue to do so unless the treatment improved. The letter was kept a secret amongst the members of the committee but, in the event, Martin never showed up. Had he done so, the effects could well have been dramatic, for the letter requested that a copy should be sent both to the camp authorities at Burgos and to the commandant. The party committee's assessment of the possible repercussions were that 'We could have taken control of the camp, whatever might have been the result after that, but realised any such action would have had world effect.'[114] Instead a complaint was made to the American consul, which led to a brief and unsatisfactory investigation by the Civil Guard.

Not all the punishments were physical; psychological punishments were also inflicted on prisoners. Morien Morgan describes himself and four others being lined up against the wall as though they were to be executed.

> I remember on one occasion about five or six of us were taken down to the courtyard, made to face the wall; they were going to shoot us. And there we were against the wall and they shoot. Deliberately missing us and having a very good laugh.[115]

Joe Norman was either the victim of this form of psychological torture or very fortunate to survive his time at San Pedro. On two separate occasions he and other comrades were brought out at 3 o'clock in the morning and stood in front of a firing squad for an hour, before being returned to the barracks. Norman believes that the only reason the executions did not go ahead was because Merry del Val intervened, frightened of creating a political furore.[116]

Some guards found other ways to humiliate the prisoners, such as throwing half-smoked cigarettes to them to watch their nicotine-fuelled scrabble or, when the prisoners got wise to the trick and refused to rise to the bait, offering them cigarettes to which cordite had been added.[117] Attempts were also made to indoctrinate the men with Nationalist ideology. Following a visit by a priest, several large shelves were put up in the camp and filled with books of Nationalist propaganda. To many of the prisoners, the handing out and reading of fascist literature by Catholic priests merely provided an object lesson in the Catholic Church's role in Spain's ruling class. When the camp authorities discovered that the books were disappearing off the shelves, yet no prisoners appeared to be reading them, they tried a different tack.[118] Prisoners were forced to listen to speeches and to attend Mass, though, as both were usually conducted in Spanish, their effectiveness was bound to be somewhat limited, even if the prisoners had been susceptible.[119]

Aware that many of the prisoners were by no means proficient in Spanish, the camp authorities attempted to persuade representatives from the various nationalities to read the propaganda aloud in their own languages. This gave the English-speaking contingent an opportunity for a rare victory over the authorities for, when asked, all volunteers at first denied they were English speakers, but maintained instead that they spoke Welsh or 'Scottish', 'Irish' or 'Canadian'.[120] Eventually, of course, the ruse was discovered, and the party committee recommended that all the volunteers should read in turn. This still offered opportunities for prisoners to gain a small measure of revenge. Maurice Levitas, a volunteer from London, was instructed to read Nationalist propaganda to the other English-speaking volunteers. Different prisoners have different recollections of exactly how Levitas managed to make the text sound ridiculous, but there are many references to the puzzled and angry responses by the guards to the ensuing laughter.[121] It is clear that small victories such as these provided important boosts in morale for the prisoners, particularly when after a time the authorities realised the ineffectiveness of the exercise and the readings were discontinued.

At the same time as attempting to imbue the prisoners with Nationalist propaganda, the authorities were also determined to present their version of life in the camp and, particularly, to deny any stories of atrocities. Reports appeared in Britain in newspapers and journals sympathetic to their cause, and this description of the prison camp at San Pedro is typical of the style:

> These prisoners lead an easy life at San Pedro de Cardeña, for, unlike the Spanish prisoners, they are not called upon to work. Reveille sounds at half past seven. After breakfast all form up on the esplanade outside the Monastery, where the red and gold flag is hoisted in the middle of a small garden planted by these Communist prisoners themselves with designs in box of the emblems of Nationalist Spain. Then they are free, for the most part, to stroll about or chat or read. Two hours of drill a day provide the necessary exercise. Food is abundant and consists of vegetables and meat or fish. These two meals a day are probably better than the men ever had in Red Spain. At sundown they form up again to attend the ceremony of lowering the flag, saluting with outstretched arm as they sing the anthems of National Spain. Then, at nine-o-clock the bugle sounds 'Lights out'.[122]

Photographs were carried of healthy prisoners to support denials of ill treatment.[123] William Carney, writing for the *New York Times*, sent back glowing reports of the treatment of prisoners by the Nationalists, which described how 'Foreigners were treated exactly like Spanish prisoners.'[124] His report was bitingly satirised in a cartoon called 'As Mr Carney Saw Us' by James Moon, a laboratory technician from London, which appeared on the masthead of the prisoners' clandestine newspaper, the *San Pedro Jaily News*.[125] The cartoon shows the prisoners relaxing in the comfortable surroundings of San Pedro, spending their time reading, drinking and fishing in the nearby river, with the sick attended by an attractive young nurse. Reports in the Spanish Nationalist media were even more preposterous, describing how the prisoners declared themselves to be, 'most contented . . . this is not a prison, it's a rest home.'[126]

The attempts by the camp authorities to convince the outside world that San Pedro was run under a beneficent and enlightened regime did at least have some advantages for the prisoners. As early as April 1938 the authorities agreed to a visit by the Red Cross and the right of prisoners to send a message home, though the message was restricted to the phrase '*Notificandoles que me encuentro bien.*'[127] To a certain extent the attempts to dupe visitors to the camp were successful, though it could also be that, like the inspectors overlooking the Non-Intervention Agreement, those examining the camps turned a blind eye to any awkward matters. In a letter to Charlotte Haldane, the secretary of the Dependents' Aid Committee, in January 1939, the Foreign Office insisted: 'Mr Jerram [the acting British agent at Burgos] states that he had been informed by Colonel Miracles that the prisoners were well fed.'[128] Similarly, in a letter to the father of Jimmy Moon in early January 1939, the Foreign Office assured Mr Moon that conditions in San Pedro were satisfactory:

> With regards to the question of the conditions in which the British prisoners are being kept, I am to state that when Colonel Martin, a member of the staff of the

British Agency, visited the camp at San Pedro de Cardena [*sic*] in November last he considered that the prisoners appeared to be well cared for. According to earlier reports, Colonel Martin had found the prisoners well nourished and in good health.[129]

Within San Pedro, attempts to demonstrate to the prisoners the error of their ways and the misguided nature of their cause continued. Prisoners were given a pamphlet to read, allegedly written by a former member of the British Battalion, which was critical of the International Brigade.[130] In response, the British leaders claimed that he had been a drunkard and sent back to England. As the American prisoner Carl Geiser remarked sardonically, 'The British thought he had written it for pay. The paper was appreciated.'[131]

Attempts were made by the camp authorities both to assess the success of the Nationalist propaganda on the prisoners and to obtain information from them. A few of the British were questioned by the Gestapo at various times during their incarceration at San Pedro, though the Italian and German prisoners were questioned on a daily basis. Interrogators were keen to determine how the volunteers were recruited, how they arrived in Spain and whether or not they were communists.[132] They also attempted to discover military information about the workings of the brigade: who were the officers, where the volunteers were when captured and whether they were carrying a gun. The response of the party committee to the questioning was to recommend a clear and straightforward response to the interrogations: that 'We had come to Spain to fight for democracy, that we were armed when captured and to refuse any information concerning the battalion and the officers.'[133]

Some volunteers denied they had been carrying a gun; Bernard McKenna from Manchester claimed that he had been in the transmissions department and that he was 'an innocent bystander'.[134] Rather more bizarre were the psychological tests to which the prisoners were subjected during interrogations. In addition to detailed measurements being taken of their physical characteristics, they were required to complete a questionnaire containing 200 bizarre questions dealing with their private lives – intimate personal questions about their families, politics and trade unions. They were also asked rather more philosophical questions regarding their perceptions of the USSR, Francoist Spain and their own countries, what they understood by the meaning of political terminologies such as communism and democracy, and other questions relating to their 'cultural development'. As the prisoners recognised, the aims of these questions were to attempt to provide evidence for three features of rightist ideology and/or propaganda: to justify the Nazi beliefs on race, to show that the International volunteers were the dregs of degenerate Western democracies, and to attempt to discover the identity of the leading elements amongst the prisoners.[135] Or, as one prisoner put it rather succinctly, 'To show to the world what a lot of morons we were. It was a lot of questions related to drink and sex.'[136] The rather formulaic and unsophisticated nature of the questioning meant that the camp authorities were not likely to be successful in their attempts to glean information. In fact, the official report claimed instead that 'Many times the examiners were the ones being tested.'[137] Certainly there was ample opportunity for the prisoners to agree common answers to the questions.

Not surprisingly, a number of prisoners attempted to escape, despite the inherent risks involved. In total there were 16 attempts, of which only two were known by the British committee to have been successful. One of these was particularly audacious:

> One International . . . decided he didn't like the camp, and walked north up a dirt pathway, having picked up a nearby garbage container as if to dump it. The guards allowed him to pass. When he was out of sight, he kept going. The prison authorities had not yet made a list of all the Internationals, so they didn't miss him. Several months later we received a card from him postmarked in France.[138]

The majority of the escape attempts were by the Italian or German brigaders, who were fully aware of the reception waiting for them in their homeland.

> The Gestapo used to go round the camp telling the Spanish fascists that they would shoot the German I.B.ers when they got back to Germany if the Spanish Fascists didn't. There was a German lad who spoke Spanish like the natives, who decided to escape. There was a discussion among the German lads and a bunch of them decided they were going to have a go. But this lad was recaptured. They stood him outside the entrance where we had to come for our meals. He was so battered it was incredible to see. They put him down to a real punishment cell. We had everything arranged so the lads got milk and so on down to him. It took a fortnight to get the pieces of shirt out of his flesh – they'd carved him up with the whip so much.[139]

To discourage escape attempts, the authorities ensured that the escapees were not the only ones to be punished. By the end of the summer of 1938 the authorities had made the prisoners responsible for their own discipline, following the formation of the committees. Each of the two floors in the camp was guarded by three prisoners, so, when there were escapes, the guards would be punished first. Despite this, some escapes were made with the full knowledge of the camp committee: two monitors were supplied with financial assistance as well as information by the party committee, as were the last six German prisoners to escape, on the night of 14–15 November 1938.[140] The six Germans got away by sawing through the iron bars covering the windows and ripping up mattresses to use as ropes. Not surprisingly, the guards concluded other prisoners must have been involved in assisting them to escape, and 'two days of terror' followed at San Pedro. On parade the prisoners were threatened by a captain, in temporary charge of the camp whilst the commandant was on leave, who informed them that his wish was to see all the prisoners shot. During the next few days very few men avoided being beaten, with the six prisoners on watch during the night of the escape receiving particularly vicious treatment. One of the six was David Kennedy from Greenock in Scotland,[141] who was so badly beaten that he was hospitalised for two weeks; if conceivable, the Germans were treated even more harshly. Two German prisoners who had been sleeping near the site of the escape were terribly beaten and thrown into the calaboose, 'the black hole'. Complaints that they were in need of urgent medical attention were ignored by 'Sticky'; they were only released a week later when the major in charge of the camp realised that prisoners dying from beatings would only make his position worse. All six German escapees were recaptured and were thrown back into solitary confinement in San Pedro, following harsh beatings. The Gestapo agents in the camp were brutal in their interrogations of prisoners who had been caught attempting to escape. In many cases they questioned the returning captives on the situation outside the camp, clearly under the belief that prisoners were making contact with Republican supporters on the outside.[142]

The remaining 75 British prisoners stayed at San Pedro until another exchange was arranged. On 23 January 1939 the British, together with around 30 Canadian and a small number of Swiss prisoners, finally left.[143] They were exchanged at the rate of one International Brigader to ten Italian soldiers – a policy which later led to the volunteers' claim that one British volunteer was equal to ten Italian Nationalist soldiers. The prisoners were then transferred to Ondarreta jail in San Sebastian before they finally returned home in early February 1939.[144] On 16 February 1939, the British Consul at Valencia arranged for another 34 British, and 11 Swiss, to be exchanged for 45 Italians.[145] As there were insufficient Italian prisoners, ten British prisoners remained in San Sebastian jail for a further three months, eventually being released in April 1939.

As with the other British volunteers repatriated from Spain, the Foreign Office stated that 'Undertakings to refund the cost of repatriation should be obtained from British prisoners.'[146] Bill Alexander stated that there are no records of any of these requests being honoured,[147] though at least one ex-prisoner later admitted having paid the levy.[148] Many veterans believe that the British government did very little to help the prisoners, and their treatment during the prisoners' repatriation by British Government representatives, such as demands for payment, made many feel extremely bitter. Bruce Allender describes how the released prisoners were met by one solitary British representative in Hendaye, who made it clear how they were viewed by many, if not most, of those working in the Foreign Office:

> They stripped us of our clothing . . . this is the British Embassy, the sods. They were really nasty, you know, the British. Altogether. When I say altogether I only mean one. I only saw one. Who was a toffee nosed little bastard . . . He treated us like dirt.[149]

Likewise, George Wheeler complained that, following their release, all the food and drink on the train through France had been provided by the Canadian government: 'The Canadian Government provided everything. I'm sorry to say that the British Government didn't contribute a thing . . . That was the British Government for you. They didn't care tuppence.'[150]

Two prisoners were still not released even in April 1939: Tom Jones, a Welsh miner from Wrexham, and the Irishman Frank Ryan, who had been sentenced to death. Ryan was connected to the Nationalist movement in Ireland, and it has been suggested that the Nazi regime hoped to make use of him in some manner.[151] The death sentences on both were commuted to 30 years' imprisonment. A powerful campaign to secure their release was launched in Ireland and Britain, which gained support from sympathisers in Canada and America, and huge amounts of mail and food parcels were sent to the two. At one stage appeals were made in parliament for Ryan's release and 'Release Frank Ryan or else' was painted in huge letters alongside the River Thames.[152] A telegram sent from the British representative in Burgos to the Foreign Office in London in February 1939 shows that representatives of the British government were trying get Frank Ryan included in the group to be repatriated – despite his IRA past – but were not meeting with any success.[153] Eventually Jones was released, on 20 March 1940; Ryan, however, was taken to Germany and never returned to Ireland. He eventually died in Dresden in June 1944.[154]

# 7  British volunteers for liberty or Comintern army?

The international movement can and must be regarded as the highest manifestation of progressive humanity's international solidarity with the heroic people of Spain.[1]

The Brigades were, from beginning to end, a Comintern army. The Brigades would never have existed but for the Soviet-Comintern decision to call them into being.[2]

For many years after the end of the civil war, the history of the British volunteers in Spain remained in the safe hands of members of the battalion or their ardent supporters. Thus, Frank Ryan, Bill Rust and Bill Alexander, the authors respectively of *The Book of the XVth Brigade* (1938), *Britons in Spain* (1939) and *British Volunteers for Liberty* (1982), were described accurately by one later observer as 'keepers of the story by which they wanted the battalion to be remembered'.[3] In these works, the legend of the International Brigades was a heroic tale of international working-class solidarity, a lesson in 'strength and unity', to use Bill Alexander's phrase. Over the years, as the full horror gradually dawned as to what the 'new civilisation' of Soviet Russia actually meant, the heroic struggle of the Spanish Republic against the barbarous invasion by Italy and Germany, and the help from democratic supporters around the world for the International Brigades, became, for many, the one thing to be looked back on with pride: 'the last great cause'.

However, many have felt that this view is simplistic in the extreme. As early as 1937, George Orwell had been arguing that the notion of 'good versus evil', or 'democracy versus fascism' was extremely problematic. Orwell's criticisms of the Communist Party's role in Spain – especially the brutal suppression of the POUM – have made their mark, and the argument over 'war or revolution' is still repeated endlessly in classrooms, seminars and, more recently, internet discussion lists.[4] And despite the efforts of Bill Alexander and his cohorts to hold the line established in 1936, the image of the International Brigades has come under a prolonged and sustained attack from both left and right. Alexander's attempt to face down these attacks with the publication of *British Volunteers for Liberty* was both a success and a failure. It was successful in that the book benefited greatly from the intimate personal knowledge of Alexander and other volunteers, which enabled him to rectify many of the weaknesses and omissions in the earlier works to make his book the standard work on the British Battalion. But it was also a failure, for the work was too heavily steeped in the world of the 1930s and either skirted around, or played down, issues – such as the executions of deserters – that challenged the heroic legend of the International Brigades in the Spanish Civil War.

The first major study to begin the attempt to revise attitudes towards the brigades was R. Dan Richardson's *Comintern Army*, also published in 1982. The book, in Richardson's words, challenged 'the appealing idea that the men of those first international contingents, and the thousands who were to follow them into the whirlwind of the civil war in Spain, represented the response of world democracy to the threat of fascism.'[5] Richardson argued that the significance of the brigades went beyond the military, that 'they were a significant political, ideological and propaganda instrument which could be – and was – used by the Comintern for its own purposes, not only inside Spain but on the larger world stage.'[6] For Richardson,

> The origins of the International Brigades are to be found in the working out of a Soviet-Comintern policy of worldwide scope and not, as some would have it, the spontaneous response of world democracy to the threat of fascism in Spain. To put it differently, without the Soviet-Comintern decision to intervene directly in the Spanish war and, as part of that intervention, create a volunteer force for use in Spain, the International Brigades would never have come into existence.[7]

However, the international response to the Spanish war began *before* the Comintern started to organise recruitment and was first and foremost a *reaction* to German and Italian participation, rather than a Soviet creation to further their strategic and political interests. By the time Comintern involvement was making itself felt, many foreigners, such as the English artist Felicia Browne, had already died fighting the rebels. The sophisticated level of organisation of the Communist Party enabled the International Brigades to become a disciplined fighting force, but the will to fight against the uprising was not something the Comintern created, though they could, and did, put the willingness to effective use.

Richardson draws a distinction between the early volunteers who fought with the militia units affiliated to particular political groups such as the anarchists or POUM, and the large number of – overwhelmingly communist – volunteers who fought in the communist-run International Brigades themselves. 'The fact that some of the foreign militiamen were ultimately incorporated into the Brigades demonstrates rather that the Brigades were a new, different, and essentially unconnected development.'[8]

As I have shown, there was a higher proportion of middle-class individuals amongst the early volunteers (that is, those arriving before December 1936), but there is little evidence to suggest that there were substantial *political* differences between the first few and the later recruits, only that the organisational structure provided by the Communist Party allowed those who might not otherwise have been able to travel to Spain easily with the means to do so. As Chapter 3 demonstrated, whilst the John Cornfords and Ralph Foxes had passports and the wherewithal, they were not typical; working-class non-party members and members alike were already leaving for Spain. As Helen Graham argues,

> The way the Comintern stepped in to coordinate the mobilisation of volunteer fighters for the Republic provides a perfect example of Soviet caution . . . the International Brigades were far from being a 'Comintern Army' (i.e. an instrument for the political domination of the Republic). They were shock troops, part of Stalin's emergency planning. The Comintern provided the vital organisational mechanism that made it possible systematically to channel to Spain the military expertise of the international left in order to stave off imminent Republican defeat in the Autumn of 1936. But the political and social motives that took the Brigaders to Spain were as complex as those of the first volunteers who had gone to Spain without organisational back-up. Seen in their full historical context, the International Brigades were no more Stalin's 'invention' than was the dynamic of European Popular Front itself.[9]

Since the opening of the Comintern archive in Moscow, the process of revision has accelerated. Works emanating from the United States, such as Herbert Romerstein's *Heroic Victims* (1994), *The Secret World of American Communism* (1995) by Harvey Klehr, J. E. Haynes and F. I. Firsov, and, more recently, *Spain Betrayed* (2001), edited by Ronald Radosh, Mary M. Habeck and Grigory Sevostianov, make extensive use of the Moscow material to demonstrate communist domination and, more significantly, Comintern control of the brigades.

Clearly communists did dominate the British Battalion for, as Chapter 1 has stressed, the British volunteers were overwhelmingly communist. However, this description, though factually accurate, is too simplistic, for it suggests that the members of the Communist Party were a homogeneous block, a 'phalanx of disciplined Comintern warriors'. In fact, the reasons for joining the party were as diverse as the reasons that led to volunteering for Spain, though most of the volunteers shared a belief that mainstream conventional politics was not serving the interests of working-class people. The high levels of unemployment of the Great Depression – with over 2,000,000 still unemployed in Britain in 1935[10] – means testing, and the rise of Mosley's British Union of Fascists, provided ample evidence for those looking for it. At the same time, the hostile response of the official labour movement to both the National Unemployed Workers' Movement and the hunger marches – not forgetting Ramsay MacDonald's willingness, following the great split of 1931, to sit with the Conservatives in a National Government – led many to look for alternative political cultures.[11] Some joined the Independent Labour Party (ILP), though the ILP was, by 1936, a party in decline, 'a regional (primarily Scottish) political force'.[12] Others turned to the Communist Party, and, though the party never made any real inroads into parliamentary politics, it became a noisier and rather more serious force of resistance once the disastrous policy of 'class against class' had been replaced by 'popular frontism'.[13] For those in Britain who believed that direct action was needed to fight injustice, inequality and the spread of fascism, it is not hard to see why, in the 1930s, the Communist Party would have been a great attraction. As George Leeson, an Irish-born Londoner, explained, his reasons for joining the party and volunteering for Spain were inseparable:

> The reason why I joined the Communist Party is partly the reason why I went to Spain . . . My basic feelings and beliefs made me an anti-fascist, opposed to Hitler and were my reasons for joining the Communist Party and going to Spain . . . I looked around and thought the Labour Party doesn't seem to be doing very much, they are pretty tame anyway and I thought the only people who seem to be doing anything that leads to what I believe in – Socialism – were the Communists, even if they were a small group.[14]

The accusation of Comintern control of the brigades is based upon the indisputable fact that the senior military commanders were Comintern appointments, even though the shortage of middle-ranking officers in the Republican Army is well established, as is the lack of military experience amongst many of the international volunteers.[15] Furthermore, there was no real means of knowing if the loyalty of those Spanish officers who did stay with the Republic could be guaranteed.[16]

Likewise, it is argued that the system of political commissars was instigated by the Comintern to maintain political discipline or, in fact, to suppress heterodoxy. This criticism of the role of the Comintern in the International Brigades – that it fostered a lack of toleration for any form of political nonconformity – is the major theme of James Hopkins's study of the British volunteers, which, whilst considerably more measured than the works of Richardson and Radosh, Habeck and Sevostianov, nevertheless maintains that there was a clear schism between the leadership and the rank and file. Hopkins appears to agree with Romerstein that many of the volunteers were 'heroic victims', facing totalitarianism not just from the rebels, but also from the Comintern, who held the brigades in an iron grip. The communist leadership, at battalion level and higher, comes in for particular criticism, though Hopkins is less critical of the lower echelons of the British Battalion, believing that they had little access to impartial information on which to base their thoughts, as all reading matter was controlled by the party: the *Daily Worker*, 'the newspaper of working-class militants consistently misled or lied to them.'[17] Hopkins argues that the leadership of the Communist Party, at both national and international level, cynically used the International Brigades to further the aims of the party, which, he argues, were inextricably intertwined with the foreign policy of the USSR. Thus the accusation that appeared in the contemporary press that the volunteers were 'dupes' returns. Hopkins's summary is explicit in its criticism: 'If the men on the battlefield sought to live their political ideals on the battlefields of Spain, they were betrayed by the party that made it possible for them to be there.'[18]

However, it seems likely that the level of Comintern control over the British volunteers in the International Brigades has been exaggerated, just as the extent of its control of the British Communist Party has been shown to be overstated.[19] Just as the CPGB was given a certain amount of 'slack in the line', so the British Battalion was allowed a certain degree of autonomy. And just as, 'by the later 1930s, Pollitt was becoming increasingly irked by the Comintern',[20] so many senior members of the British Battalion were feeling irritated by the members of 15th International Brigade staff.[21] Furthermore, as I will show, the British Battalion maintained a much more compassionate attitude towards deserters than some of the other battalions, despite pressure from above.

Likewise, though most volunteers accepted the 'Moscow line' during their time in Spain, this does not mean that they were all blind adherents or 'true believers', but rather fellow travellers who used the Communist Party's resources to get them to Spain.[22] Not all the commanders of the battalion were communists or, at least, not when they volunteered.[23] Sam Wild only joined the party in Spain, as, so he claims, did Fred Copeman, despite his history as a political activist. They were hardly unrepresentative; of the 500-odd members of the Communist Party who list a date of enrolment, over 40 per cent joined in 1936 or later.[24]

The volunteers were not 'dupes'; they went to Spain to fight fascism, and most survivors still believe, with some justification, that they did just that. In this sense the relationship between the Communist Party and the volunteers is more symbiotic than parasitic, for the party greatly facilitated the process of volunteering for, and travelling to, the war in Spain. And whilst they were in Spain the volunteers acknowledged what many commentators seem to ignore: that the Republic was involved in a life or death struggle and that, as George Orwell himself recognised, 'war is bloody'. The myth of the 'last great cause' has prevented many supporters of the Republic from accepting that the censorship, the imprisonment of insubordinates, and the occasionally callous treatment of deserters that occurred within the Republican zone are not necessarily symptoms of the 'Stalinisation' of Republican Spain, but could also be seen as the desperate reaction of the Republican Army in a bitter struggle for its very survival.

But for critics of Soviet intervention in Spain, the suppression in the Republican zone is seen not as a reaction to the war, but as an extension of Stalin's purges in the Soviet Union. As R. Dan Richardson argues, 'The mentality of political suspicion, hatred, terror and murder that was then running its grotesque and bloody course in the Soviet Union and that cast its spell throughout the Comintern spilled over into Spain and the International Brigades.'[25] Likewise, James Hopkins claims that 'Stalin had every intention of achieving effective dictatorship in Spain but behind an anti-fascist façade.'[26] This belief is particularly explicit in the works by Romerstein and Radosh and his colleagues, who have a mutual distrust of the roles of the Communist Party, the Comintern and Stalin, which they seem to consider one and the same. These commentators argue that Stalin supported the Republic, not so much because he wished to prevent Spain becoming another fascist state, but in order to establish a 'people's democracy', along the line of the later Eastern European states.

Despite ample evidence of the extent of Soviet influence in Spain, this seems unlikely; not out of any altruistic motives of 'solidarity' by Stalin, but because the USSR's security lay in the hope of fostering détente with the Western democracies, which Stalin was fully aware would be dashed by any sign of sponsorship of a social revolution by the USSR or the Comintern. Indeed, on this point, there is a rare consensus that the Communist Party in Spain acted as a counter-revolutionary force. Like Chamberlain, Stalin viewed the Spanish war from the context of increasing

German strength and how he might use Spain to limit Hitler's expansionism: first, by keeping Germany involved in the war as long as possible and, later, when it became clear that the Republic would lose, by looking for alternative solutions. Ironically, as Alan Bullock has argued, there are parallels in the attitudes of Stalin and Hitler towards the Spanish war:

> Both Hitler and Stalin valued the diversionary effect of the war, Hitler in allowing Germany to continue rearmament, and Stalin in keeping the other European powers divided and so allowing him to carry out the purges [within the USSR] without anxiety about external threats.[27]

There is also a parallel between Stalin's aims within Spain and his ambitions in the rest of Europe: whilst fostering 'social revolution' might be considered a long-term (almost theoretical) aspiration, for Stalin, the threat of a resurgent Germany was a much more immediate concern. Thus the revolution in Spain was a lower priority than the survival of the Republic, just as a revolution in Europe was a lower priority than the survival of the USSR.

Much of the evidence for the Communist Party's political intolerance in the brigades comes from the large number of files in Moscow containing appraisals of the volunteers, drawn up by their military and political leaders. However, as Cary Nelson has pointed out, the – often highly derogatory – comments were written for party officials back home, and remarks such as 'lumpen element' should be seen in context.[28] The British volunteers had, at best, limited military experience, and were thrown into a brutal war where the likelihood of death or serious injury was undeniable. Viewed in this light, it is perhaps not surprising that a number of individuals failed to measure up to the party's strict criteria, and reacted to the stresses of war by drinking excessively or deserting. The list of terrifying battles in which the volunteers were involved, from the defence of Madrid in 1936–1937 to the Ebro offensive in the summer of 1938, should provide some understanding of the incredible strain they were put under. In many of these battles the battalion fought against the elite of the Nationalist forces; that many volunteers were disgruntled and demoralised, and that a number deserted, should thus hardly be taken as a fundamental disenchantment with their cause and their leaders. As one of the British volunteers, John Longstaff, later observed:

> They'd gone through some very traumatic and severe experiences in the front line. They'd gone without sleep. They had seen their pals being killed or badly wounded. There's a limit to any man's endurance. And it wasn't surprising to me, [that] by the end of some of the campaigns some people needed medical treatment. I suppose one would call them shell-shocked.[29]

As another volunteer admitted, 'I should think that if they were honest, almost every member of the British Battalion wanted to go home at some time or other, because it was a war of unusual hardships, of unusually high casualties.'[30]

The strain was often compounded by contact with relatives at home, for though the post office in Albacete frequently censored letters containing requests to return home, it is clear that some volunteers were fully aware of the worries of their families in Britain. John Tunnah, who fought with the battalion during the first half of 1937, recounts how 'My sisters just wanted to come to bring me back. And I had to tell them in a letter that while you could volunteer in you couldn't volunteer out.'[31]

The volunteers fought in the extremely harsh climates of Brunete and of Teruel on a diet that plainly disagreed with many,[32] frequently against overwhelming military odds. That they actually managed to operate at all, let alone as 'Republican shock-troops', is more a testament to their individual bravery and their collective discipline. As Cary Nelson observes of the reports, 'Often enough these were hasty comments written in battlefield conditions. The language is often hyperbolic, the judgements frequently unsound.'[33] The remarks were often more on their political *potential* than on their actual performance in Spain. Thus even some of the negative statements were tempered, such as the report on Jack Waring-Reid, who was described as 'Weak. Came under the influence of bad elements and deserted'; yet the report concludes: 'may well possibly still do some good work.'[34] As a covering letter to the Central Committee of the Communist Party, dated 20 December 1938, explains:

> The standard set has been a high one. One must bear in mind the fact that the comrades have been tested here in exceptionally severe circumstances during many months of fighting, and this has made a very big demand on their political, moral, and physical resources.[35]

And as Vincent Brome acknowledged:

> There are individual accounts of different sections of the International Brigade which represent them as overrun by criminals and drunkards, but these were in a minority. A high proportion were ordinary working men who might or might not have personal problems which they solved by joining the Brigades, but many of the early recruits fiercely believed in the ideal of fighting Fascism, and were ready, in the long run, to obey orders.[36]

However, it is certainly true that several volunteers have confirmed that, as James Hopkins suggested, the subject of drunkenness was an issue within the battalion:[37]

> During the training period of the battalion at Madrigueras we had some problems arising from drink. A strict order had been issued that during training no drink would be served to any of the internationals. Notwithstanding this there were lads turning up very, very much under the influence. We discovered by pure accident that the way round the problem of getting drink even when there was a complete prohibition was to order what they called *cafe frío*, cold coffee, a mixture of rum and coffee.[38]

In a letter written in August 1937 to Will Paynter, Walter Tapsell referred to his satisfaction that during a recent period of rest there had been no desertions and 'Only one case of drunkenness. (Compare this with the previous position when we were at Mondejar!)'[39] But though the Moscow characterisation list mentions several 'drunkards', it also states that some of them were otherwise good soldiers, suggesting that to some extent heavy drinking was tolerated, or at least understood.[40] After all Sam Wild, probably the best of the British commanders, was known to be a very heavy drinker. As Jan Kurzke, a German volunteer who fought alongside the British in Madrid in 1936, recognised:

> Sometimes comrades became the worse for drink. To deny that would be denying human nature . . . Somehow or other one could not be too hard on the few comrades who drank a glass too much at times. One never knew what the next day would bring.[41]

For a number of the volunteers, of course, the pressures of the war could not be relieved by the occasional drinking spree. Thus the issue of desertions is another major facet of the perceived disaffection with the leadership and the conditions in Spain. As R. Dan Richardson noted, 'From at least as early in the war as March 1937, men were deserting or attempting to desert in large enough numbers to make it a major issue in the brigades.'[42] According to the list of undesirables held in Moscow, there were over 250 deserters from the British Battalion,[43] a lower estimate than Bill Alexander's of 298.[44] It has always been acknowledged that it was a problem for the British Battalion: as Walter Greenhalgh, who served from December 1936 right through to October 1938, admitted, 'There were lots of desertions.'[45] This point is clearly made in a report from the International Brigade base at Albacete, which stated that 'the English battalion has fallen victim to a wave of collective desertions, which has begun to effect [sic] the American battalions. The officers are not excluded from this process of demoralization.'[46]

Fred Copeman, one of the battalion commanders, admitted threatening with grenades a number of deserters who were hiding out in wine vats at Jarama in order to encourage them to return to the line.[47] There were also a number of desertions after Brunete when, as George Aitken, the battalion commissar, described, morale was very low: 'They were lying almost dead to the world with fatigue, with the heat, the thirst and the lack of food . . . they were half dead with exhaustion.'[48] John Angus, later commissar at Camp Lucas, the re-education camp for deserters, agrees:

> After the terrible battering the battalion received at Brunete a number of the survivors, perhaps as many as 60 or 70, though my memory is now hazy, expressed shall we say, a reluctance to return to the front. Many of them claimed, I think honestly, that they had been told when they joined up in England that they were signing-on for only a limited period of some months and would then be able to return home. This would probably have been the most happy solution but it was prevented, at least it was alleged by the new Minister of War, Prieto, issuing a decree which made it impossible.[49]

R. Dan Richardson asserted – repeating accusations printed in newspapers such as the *Daily Mail* and *Morning Post* – that

> Numerous men also claimed that they had been lured to Spain with the promise of high-paying jobs. Once in Spanish territory the brigade authorities took their passports and informed them that they were in the army. When the men complained, the answer given was that since they had no passports they were strictly subject to the Spanish authorities and that if they attempted to 'desert' they would be shot.[50]

However, as I have shown, there is scant evidence for Richardson's accusation. Nor is it likely that the Communist Party refused to allow the British volunteers to return home because they were impossible to replace and that it was feared some would 'make public some of the unsavoury aspects of Communist operations in Spain'.[51]

The reality is that, in the main, the desertions from the British Battalion did not so much represent a dissatisfaction with the political organisation of the battalion, but were a reaction simply to the high casualties sustained in the first half of 1937 and the lack of leave and repatriation. In a sense, the repatriation problem was irreconcilable, for there was a clear contradiction between the volunteers as 'volunteers' and as members of the Republican Army. The problem was undoubtedly exacerbated by some British party figures offering guarantees of limited periods of service in Spain, though it seems unlikely that this was a deliberate attempt to trick potential recruits; what seems more likely is that Robson, and others, simply made promises that they were not in a position to keep.[52]

It is widely recognised that most of the men deserted because of the battalion's refusal to allow leave in England.[53] With many believing that they were volunteering for a limited period of time[54] and that at the end of this period they would be allowed to return home, this was a predictable source of conflict once the International Brigades had been incorporated into the Republican Army and the volunteers were told they must stay in Spain until the end of the war.[55]

> The question of returning comes up ever more frequently and more insistently. The question is raised not only by some bad or demoralized elements, whom consulates sent home; the question comes up in general and is raised by a broad contingent of the volunteers, and in almost every brigade.[56]

The leaders of the battalion were well aware of the importance of the issue. For example, in the period after Brunete there was a move to repatriate a number of volunteers who had been in Spain for some time. Unfortunately, the repatriations were badly organised, and Will Paynter, the commissar at Albacete, complained that:

> The whole policy which I suggested on repatriation has been distorted . . . A list of those for repatriation was read and the comrades were sent down to me whether they wanted to come or not. In short about one half of the effective fighting strength of the battalion was sent down to me for repatriation and at a

time when it was held up!! However, the thing is done now and we will have to make the best of it. On the whole I think it will be best that these men return.[57]

As George Aitken makes clear:

A decision had been reached with the agreement of the Party that all of the men of the original No 1 Company, who had been in Spain from 8 to 9 months, should be given the opportunity of going home. Similarly, the original battalion people had also to be allowed to return home gradually after 8 months service and according to length of service.[58]

According to John Angus, the problem was exacerbated by the belief that the higher ranks were treated differently from the lower:

However, what made the situation infinitely worse, and added to the general atmosphere of cynicism and demoralisation, was that the entire British leadership from the battalion right down to company or even lower level, had, in fact, been allowed to go home either on leave or permanently.[59]

While this may have been the perception of some of the volunteers, it is not an accurate observation. Between July and September 1937 there were six battalion political commissars[60] and five battalion commanders,[61] and, although rapid turn-over must have been extremely disconcerting for the volunteers, the impression that the senior figures of the battalion were being allowed to return home whilst the lower ranks remained in the line is not an accurate one. Walter Tapsell and Fred Copeman did return home briefly in September 1937 (with Bert Williams, George Aitken and Jock Cunningham, who remained in the UK), but this was hardly for rest and recuperation; on the contrary, they were all hauled over the coals by Harry Pollitt for the internal divisions which had been causing great unrest at both battalion and brigade level since Brunete. And Angus clearly did not think that the battalion was full of men who resented the party's influence in the brigades and who deserted in response; as the political commissar at Camp Lucas, the 're-education' camp for deserters, Angus was in a good position to understand their gripes, but, as he states, their complaints didn't prevent them agreeing to return with him to the battalion during the Aragon retreats of spring 1938.[62]

They were not the only deserters to return to the battalion, even though, as Joe Norman explained, 'it was like any other army, if you deserted and got caught you were punished.'[63] George Coyle deserted after Jarama and was sentenced to serve in a labour battalion, but returned to the battalion and later became a political commissar.[64] As Peter Carroll explains:

Brigade policy, with a few exceptions, permitted the return of deserters. Typical punishment was assignment to a labour battalion, which required work on fortifications and trenches. Then, after interviews, men who had completed their sentences were attached to appropriate units.[65]

Some volunteers just slipped off for a weekend, particularly during the long period in the line at Jarama during the spring of 1937, and in these circumstances the usual punishment would be to dig latrines.[66] As an official report stated, 'During the month of March, discipline amongst the Battalion was weak. Many comrades went to the nearby towns (Chinchón, Aranjuez, Morata). Many also left the lines without permission and went on foot to Madrid.'[67] Three volunteers were disciplined for overstaying leave during the end of 1937, for which the punishment was loss of pay for those days. This was hardly a harsh penalty, for there was little to spend the money on anyway.[68]

Some men even returned to the battalion after deserting to Britain.[69] For example, the record of Pat Murphy, a volunteer from south-east London, states: 'Deserted to England March. Returned to Spain 2.6.37. Was with battalion at Brunete and Aragon. Fair soldier in line. Recently deserted to Valencia, but caught and brought back. Now at Intendencia as bricklayer.'[70] According to another file held in London, Murphy absconded once again, on 4 September 1938.[71] Despite his frequent desertions, he appears to have been punished by nothing worse than imprisonment. He is not unique. Albert Rabone from Gosport in Hampshire also returned to Spain after deserting in May 1937.[72] Charles Jefford from Dagenham was sent home on 4 September 1937 with a reputation as 'A bad grumbler and agitator',[73] but returned to Spain on 15 November 1937. He again got himself into trouble and was 'Arrested for organising desertion. Now in jail Albacete.'[74] He too survived his run-in with the authorities. Albert Charlesworth left of his own accord via Barcelona, but returned to Spain six weeks later over the Pyrenees in time to join the fighting at Teruel.[75]

This apparently liberal attitude to deserters flies in the face of the claims that British volunteers were shot for desertion. Several volunteers, such as Hugh Sloan (known in Spain as Hugh Smith), a member of the British Anti-Tank Battery, have denied that any British volunteers were executed for desertion,[76] and Fred Copeman has stated that Harry Pollitt was firmly opposed to the shooting of deserters.[77] Copeman strongly resisted communist demands for the use of the death penalty and deliberately put discipline in the hands of Bill Alexander and Sam Wild, who he believed didn't support it either.[78]

However, despite this opposition, at least two British volunteers were certainly executed and another two were put in positions that virtually guaranteed their deaths. Yet it was not the deserting alone that led to their deaths; in all of the cases it was because the desertions were exacerbated by actions which caused, or had the potential to cause, extensive casualties amongst their comrades. The clearest example of this occurred in January 1938, when two British volunteers were captured attempting to desert to the rebel lines and were found to be carrying plans of the layout of the British positions at Teruel, including the machine-gun positions.[79] There is no doubt that this information would have enabled the rebel forces to inflict a heavy defeat on the British Battalion. After their arrest and the report to brigade headquarters of the attempted desertion and betrayal, General Walter, the 15th International Brigade commander, came to the battalion to say that they had been found guilty of desertion to the enemy. In a battalion meeting that followed, the verdict was unanimous that they should be executed,[80] and, according to John Dunlop, several members of the battalion were selected for the execution party.[81] The outcome of this act of treachery was probably inevitable, though Bill Alexander is somewhat circumspect about what actually happened. Alexander remarks on the bitterness felt by the volunteers and states that:

> They were taken to the rear, court-martialled and sentenced to death. It has been said that the sentence was commuted to service in a labour battalion and they were killed later in an artillery barrage while digging fortifications. It has also been said that the sentence was carried out.[82]

Despite his equivocation, the implication is pretty clear, and, as Alexander was battalion commander at this time, it seems rather unlikely that he would not know whether (or not) the sentence had been carried out. Bob Cooney, who was then working in the brigade commissariat, states that one of the deserters, Allan Kemp, a baker from Glasgow, was executed,[83] though according to a file held in the IBA he was killed by shellfire 'on the Ebro front'.[84] His file in Moscow states simply that he was 'killed Jan 20'.[85] Cooney states very clearly why the offence was taken so seriously:

> Kemp was shot by firing squad, but not for desertion. He was shot because in order to carry out his desertion he was prepared to betray the lives of his comrades by giving information to the fascists. It was the one single incident of its kind.[86]

It was believed that Kemp, the elder of the two, was the real instigator of the plan and the other deserter, Patrick Glacken, also from Scotland, was not shot and was probably, as Bob Cooney and John Dunlop claim, killed by shellfire.[87]

> One was an older man who was what we described as a bad type and apparently he'd influenced this younger fellow and he persuaded him to go along with him. And they deserted towards the enemy. Fortunately they were caught by a republican patrol and they were brought back . . . In fact only one of the deserters was executed. That was the older man, because the younger chap was really quite young and we thought it was unfair that he should be punished because he had been so strongly influenced by the other man. He was sent to a labour battalion and I heard he was killed later on.[88]

Though sending a volunteer into a situation in which he was virtually certain to be killed now seems akin to murder, it is unlikely that the volunteers would have seen it that way. After all, as the casualty rates show, they regularly faced odds that were not much better.

The other member of the battalion definitely executed in Spain was Maurice Ryan,[89] an Irishman who had volunteered claiming that he wanted to kill his brother who was serving with the Nationalists under General O'Duffy.[90] Ryan had served with the Irish Free State Army, was believed to have at one time had fascist leanings, and whilst in Spain had been jailed for disruption.[91] There were various accusations of sabotage levelled at Ryan,[92] who appears to have opened fire on his comrades with a machine-gun, but, according to John Dunlop, it seems that his activities may have owed as much to drink as to espionage. Dunlop describes how during an attack on Hill 481 near Gandesa in the Ebro offensive of 1938, he:

> was just at the edge of a small hill. Right above my head, just inches above my head, there was a long burst of machine-gun fire but it was coming in the wrong direction. It wasn't coming from in front of me, it was coming from behind me and it was just hitting the top of this ridge, just above my head. I looked back and I could see this gun, one of our own machine-guns, actually firing. It appeared to be firing on us, so that more or less ended our attack.[93]

Dunlop reported this to Sam Wild, who discovered that Dunlop had been fired upon by Ryan: 'He was flaying drunk. I don't know how many of our blokes had been hit and wounded by this gun, but he was overpowered and arrested.' Divisional headquarters gave orders for him to be executed by members of the British Battalion:

> I was told later that Sam Wild, the commander of the battalion and George Fletcher the second in command took Ryan for a walk and told him to go ahead of them and then they shot him in the back of the head. I also heard that George Fletcher was in tears over that.[94]

Tom Murray, the political commissar of the Machine-Gun Company, refused to identify who carried out the execution, but admitted that 'There was a decision taken to get rid of him . . . At any rate he was got rid of, just shot in the back of the head.'[95]

One allegation that needs to be addressed is the case of Bert Overton, commander of No. 3 Company at Jarama, who deserted his post on the second day of the battle. Fred Copeman claims that 'Towards the end of the war Sam Wild agreed to shoot two British. Of all the people one of them was Overton.'[96] However, despite this claim by Copeman, there is no real evidence to suggest that he was executed. More likely is that, following his court martial, Overton, like Glacken, was placed deliberately in an extremely hazardous situation where he was killed carrying ammunition 'to a forward position'.

There are a number of other uncorroborated rumours of executions. James Hopkins cites the case of William Meeke, a labourer from County Antrim, as a deserter who was 'shot whilst attempting to escape'.[97] Meeke was certainly imprisoned in Spain, as his Moscow file states: 'Served in the British Battalion. Was imprisoned 2 May 1938 near Figueras with an American. Escaped the following day but was recaptured.'[98] However, information that he was shot, drawn from the Moscow files, is contradicted by a file in the PRO, which states that, in fact, Meeke was repatriated around the end of 1938 or the beginning of 1939.[99]

Likewise, one anonymous volunteer claimed that one of the English contingent was executed in January 1937 for possession of fascist literature.[100] There is no other evidence to support this, and, coming from a disaffected ex-member of the International Brigade who, by his own admission, spent a portion of his time in Spain imprisoned for drunkenness, it can probably be seen as anti-communist propaganda. However, the case of one Scottish volunteer, James Donald, is slightly more mysterious. Donald appears in the official roll of honour as having died at Belchite in March 1938 during the retreats. Donald had deserted in March 1937 from Jarama, and was captured before deserting again. He was put in jail in Valencia, along with Bob Smillie, the ILP volunteer who died in prison.[101] At the alleged time of his death at Belchite, Donald was in Valencia jail, and what actually happened to him remains unclear; there is no listing of his return to Britain, so it is not impossible that he was shot after deserting again. Likewise, Michael Browne, a volunteer with two years' experience in the colonial police, and known in Spain as 'Poona' Browne, is alleged to have been executed by his company commander, 'Taffy' Evans, after deserting.[102] Again, there is no other evidence for this, though there is no record of his returning to Britain. The last rumour concerns a volunteer from Devon, J. A. C. Browning, of whom virtually no information still exists.[103] Yet, according to documents held in the PRO, his father travelled to Spain to try to discover his whereabouts, having received a photograph of him in Republican Army uniform before he disappeared without trace.[104]

Despite the rumours, there is no doubt that the belief that the battalion was ruled with rigid and merciless discipline, including the execution of deserters, is an exaggeration. As Peter Carroll argues of the American volunteers:

> Even if *all* the other charges of assassination proved true, the number of Americans killed outside combat would total less than ten. The rarity of these killings undermines the notion, made popular by George Orwell's *Homage to Catalonia*, that the International Brigades enforced discipline by terror.[105]

Despite the numbers of 'unreliables', the real level of disaffection in the battalion was probably not as high as Hopkins and others suggest.[106] In a letter written to Harry Pollitt and R. W. Robson on 21 December 1936, the battalion commissar, Walter Tapsell, names a number of 'bad eggs' in the battalion before stating categorically that, 'of course, [the] great majority are magnificent.'[107] Likewise, General Walter, commander of the 35th Division, in a report to Marshal Voroshilov (therefore for internal rather than external viewing), stated that:

> One can and must confirm that with the exception of a small group of rogues, adventurers, and scoundrels, a hugely overwhelming majority of the inter-nationalists in Spain were fulfilling their duty as revolutionaries and were conscious of the need for an armed defence of freedom and of their national and class interests.[108]

Cary Nelson's remarks on the importance of putting the complaints in context should be borne in mind, as should the traditional culture of 'grumbling' associated with the British Army.[109] There is no doubt that some volunteers clearly resented the hierarchical structure of the brigades, and that a small number, such as the Glasgow tailor Alec Marcovitch,[110] were singled out for their dissenting political views.[111] However, the complaints and the critical reports should be viewed alongside the use of the familiar form of 'tú' by British volunteers to their commanders (to which General Walter referred in exasperation),[112] the employment of the term 'comic stars' for political commissars,[113] and the shouts of 'no bloody pan' instead of *No pasarán*,[114] which are all symptomatic of the British volunteers' reluctance to swallow what many wrote off simply as 'party bullshit'.[115] As John Peet, who served with the British Machine-Gun Company in Spain (and later defected from his post as Reuters correspondent to East Germany in 1950), explains: 'this was just the curious British habit of taking the piss, in a friendly way, out of hallowed symbols and slogans, patriotic or political.'[116] No doubt some inexperienced or excessively officious political commissars over-reacted to the grumbling, perhaps by including a criticism in the volunteer's file, but those who did not and turned a blind eye, like Bob Cooney or Walter Tapsell, were generally popular with their men.[117]

However, there is no doubt that the retreats of the spring of 1938 and the subsequent failure of the Ebro offensive in the summer did have a very detrimental effect on the morale of the battalion.[118] By this time it was readily apparent that the Republic was heading for defeat, and many volunteers clearly wished to return home; some were prepared to go to great lengths to ensure that this happened. One Scottish recruit at Tarazona was alleged to have 'deliberately contracted venereal disease in order to escape front service',[119] and some volunteers were repatriated with what were clearly self-inflicted injuries,[120] despite the seriousness with which these offences were viewed.[121]

Ironically, suggestions have been made that the target of much of the unhappiness in the battalion (and in other International units in Spain) was not the Communist Party, but their Spanish comrades in the Republican Army. General Walter, the commander of the 35th Division of which the British Battalion was part, saw this as one of the International Brigades' greatest failings:

> All of our difficulties, weaknesses, and failures were excused by the fact that there were Spanish present in our brigades. 'The Spanish are cowards', 'they always flee', 'they never want to fight' and so on and so forth, became the Internationalists' favourite and most frequent leitmotiv.[122]

A number of the British volunteers, such as David Hooper, expressed the feeling that the regular Spanish forces were not as committed as the International and communist brigades: 'It was only the International Brigade soldiers who did the fighting. We could never see a Spanish unit anywhere, at any rate where the big action took place.'[123] One Scottish volunteer, Hugh Sloan, refers to resorting to strong-arm tactics to keep some young Spanish soldiers from running:

> Some of the younger boys in Spanish units had broken and an emergency arose. They had just been drafted in and had no experience of any battles before.

Obviously their inexperience caused some concern. Anyway, we had to shoo them back into position. I don't think I should say very much about that . . . In shooing the Spanish boys back Bill [Cranston] and the American [volunteer] had lifted hand-grenades to try and encourage the youngsters to go back. And when they went back the American comrade discovered that he had pulled the pin on his hand-grenade.[124]

According to John Angus, disillusion with their Spanish comrades extended even to Bob Merriman, the commander of the Lincolns, who remarked bitterly to him that 'the only people who do not run away are the English and the Germans.'[125] Hamish Fraser, who served as a commissar and brigade staff officer, went further still and claimed that 'the Achilles heel of the Republic was the indifference of the ordinary Spaniard.'[126] As a later convert to Catholicism, Fraser might be expected to argue that the Republic lacked support from the majority of the Spanish people; nevertheless, the belief that the International Brigades were used as shock-troops and were more dedicated than some of the Spanish forces seems to have been widely held.[127] Indeed, as documents cited by Radosh and his colleagues show, the belief had some foundation, for, at least until after the battle of Brunete, the International Brigades were some of the best Republican units.[128] Walter Tapsell, in a letter defending himself against accusations by George Aitken that he was 'whipping up discontent against the Spanish troops', argued that:

> In plain fact, and it is hard to state this, on every occasion we were with Spanish troops in this engagement they let us down. Their behaviour on every occasion either resulted in serious casualties, or the immediate loss of positions won by us at heavy cost. This is a fact.[129]

Tapsell raged against 'pious prattle' that, he believed, was not facing up to this fundamentally important issue and was avoiding any criticism of the Spanish forces.[130] However, Peter Kerrigan, in a report to Harry Pollitt after the horrendous level of casualties inflicted on the British volunteers on the last two days of active service, between 22 and 24 September 1938, admitted that 'many of the Spanish reinforcements we had received deserted over to the enemy or ran away, and this applied to the new Spaniards with the Mac–Paps and other battalions.'[131] However, he went on to state categorically that 'our own Spanish comrades fought like lions without exception.' There is, of course, a distinction to be made between the battle-hardened and highly politicised Spanish volunteers in the International Brigades and the conscripted Spaniards, who, towards the end of the civil war, were necessarily becoming younger and younger.[132] In general, there seems to have been a healthy respect for the Spanish communist regiments of Lister, El Campesino and Modesto.[133] On first sight it might appear strange that the Internationals were critical of the very people they had come to help. However, to the Internationals, the war was not a civil war between Spaniards, it was an anti-fascist war. Thus, to the Internationals, this was just as much their fight, and the fact that it was being fought in Spain was almost immaterial. Spain was just the latest front on the European battlefield.[134]

The difficulties were probably aggravated by the infamous problem of language; not without good reason was one study of the International Brigades entitled *Legions of Babel*.[135] However, like the other nationalities, the British volunteers did include a small number who were fluent in other European languages.[136] Several senior figures, such as Paddy O'Daire, the battalion commander at Quinto in 1937, and Tony McLean, who worked as a research clerk and military censor at Tarazona, either already spoke Spanish or learnt it in Spain. Bill Alexander spoke French, as did a number of others, including Alex Cummings, the battalion adjutant at Brunete, who was killed on the Ebro in September 1938, and Alan Gilchrist, the political commissar in the Anti-Tank Battery. There was also a number who were familiar with several languages: Hercules Avgherinos, a Cypriot, spoke English, French, Spanish, German and Greek and served as battalion interpreter.[137] Peter Harrison, who worked as an administrator at the hospital at Huete under Dr Alex Tudor-Hart, knew French, German, Spanish and Siamese. However, the outstanding linguist amongst the British volunteers was Jim Ruskin; his file in Moscow lists his languages as English, French, Spanish, German and Russian, all of which were 'excellent'.[138] Though one commentator remarked that the International Brigades showed that a multi-national force could be effective, as 'one man in each company had a rudimentary knowledge of several languages',[139] a large number of those in the British Battalion understood little, if any, Spanish. The Irish volunteer Joe Monks claimed that this was because there was 'a superstition that anybody that started to study Spanish grammar got killed', but he went on to admit that this was, in fact, 'just an excuse for not doing it'.[140]

And it seems the antipathy between the Spaniards and Internationals could go both ways.[141] A confidential report drawn up at the end of July 1937 (probably by Vital Gayman, the base commander at Albacete) testified how

> The International Brigades are considered to be a foreign body, a band of intruders – I will not say by the Spanish people as a whole, but by the vast majority of political leaders, soldiers, civil servants and political parties in Republican Spain . . . It is the prevailing opinion among high officers in the Spanish army, more or less irrespective of political affiliation, that the International Brigades are nothing but a foreign legion, an army of mercenaries fighting for money.[142]

Gayman's feelings are not unique; this was clearly an important issue for the Republican Army.[143] One British volunteer, James Jump, recounts how an officer in a Spanish brigade had rather different ideas of rank and discipline from the British used to serving in the rather less rigid International Brigades:

> [The Spanish Republican Army officer] was immaculately dressed in a spick and span uniform. He wore white gloves all the time. He carried a swagger stick and the Spaniards in the army were standing to attention and saluting him and saying, '*Sí, sí mi capitán*' and things like that and when he saw us . . . We must have given him as big a shock as he gave us, because we used the familiar *tu*

form of address to him which made him wince. We called him comrade, which nearly gave him an apoplectic fit. He remonstrated with us for not calling him sir and saluting him and we said in the International Brigades we never saluted our officers and they were our comrades and we called them by their names or we called them comrade and if he didn't like it, well, you know, too bad on him.[144]

The Comintern advisor, General Stern, believed that this antipathy between national groups was caused mainly by the high casualty rate in the International Brigades, which had dramatically reduced the proportion of foreigners. Most British volunteers in Spain were wounded at least once, and the mortality rate exceeded 20 per cent.

> It is not conceivable that a brigade that consists of no less than 80 per cent Spaniards should be led only by international officers, who as a rule do not command the Spanish language and consequently cannot bring about the proper contact with the soldiers. Imagine yourself in the position of the Spanish soldiers, and you will easily understand that the Spanish soldiers must have the impression that their national pride has been hurt.[145]

However, it is important to put these complaints into perspective. In general, as Bill Alexander testifies, large numbers of Spaniards volunteered to fight in the International Brigades, despite the high casualty rate. And in any case, as the report by General Walter points out, complaints were not directed only at Spanish comrades; there was also a level of intolerance between the national groups within the International Brigades:

> The nationality question is the weakest spot in the international units and is the main hindrance impeding the growth of our potential. Very little is said about relations between the nationalities within the international units, or more truthfully, it is completely hushed up, but it is just this which gives rise to almost all our weaknesses . . . the francophobia was most transparently obvious . . . anti-Semitism flourished . . . At the very same time as the volunteers were unifying, this petty, disgusting, foul squabble about the superiority of one nationality over another was going on. Everyone was superior to the French, but even they were superior to the Spanish.[146]

These criticisms of other nationalities within the 15th International Brigade do appear to have been relatively widespread. The arguments between the Irish volunteers and the British that preceded the split in January 1937 have already been commented upon;[147] likewise the rivalry between the American and British volunteers is well documented. The British felt the American influence in the 15th Brigade was too powerful, and the Americans harboured resentments against particular British individuals.[148] Although the claim by an anonymous volunteer – 'I found that national pride was one of the chief features in the life of the International

Brigade' – was probably an exaggeration, clearly it did play a role.[149] Walter Gregory, whilst admitting that it might have been his 'personal bias', nevertheless believed that, during the retreats through Aragon in the spring of 1938, the British Battalion 'managed to retain a greater sense of purpose and exhibited more resilience than was evidenced by other battalions in the 15th International Brigade.'[150] Likewise, Fred Copeman claimed that the Thaelmann and Dimitrov Battalions ran

"THEY WENT BECAUSE THEIR
OPEN EYES
COULD SEE NO OTHER WAY"

*Plate 7.1* The memorial to the British volunteers killed in Spain, in Jubilee Gardens on London's south bank.

and 'left them in the lurch', that 'it never ended in the war, we always found ourselves stuck up in front of everybody else.'[151]

Clearly, then, it is true that the 'official' histories of the British Battalion have been guilty of either avoiding or at least playing down some of the more awkward issues surrounding the role of the International Brigades in Spain, such as the rivalries between national groups and the desertions. But the disaffection, the desertions and other issues that official histories of the International Brigades skirted around always need to be placed in the context of a war in which the Republic was fighting desperately for its very survival.

It is also true that many of the surviving British volunteers do not feel that the picture of the conflict presented in recent works bears much resemblance to their experiences of the Spanish war. They argue strongly that the volunteers were not Moscow's dupes; they went to Spain to fight fascism, and by their definition of fascism they did just that. Most volunteers (including those who have left the Communist Party) still look back with pride both on their own involvement in particular, and the involvement of international support in general, for the Republicans in the war, despite trenchant criticisms of the Communist Party's role in Spain. Like the Spanish Republic itself, the volunteers who fought in Spain had little official support, and thus were eternally grateful for what help they did receive from the Communist Party and the Soviet Union. And the volunteers' analysis was, after all, proved correct. These 'premature anti-fascists' *were* fighting an illegal military rising launched against a legally elected government, the rising *was* supported by the might of the European fascist powers of Italy and Germany and the war *was* the precursor for the wider European conflict that the Western democracies had sacrificed the Spanish Republic to avoid. In September 1939 the governments of Europe could hardly say they had not been warned.

# Appendix 1: Commanders of the British Battalion

| Surname | Forename | Date | Comments |
|---|---|---|---|
| McCartney | Wilfred | December 1936 to 6 February 1937 | Perhaps not at home with the militant volunteers – apparently referred to them as 'Harry's Bolshies' |
| Wintringham | Tom | 6 February 1937 to 13 February 1937 | Replaced Wilf McCartney after the pistol incident |
| Aitken | George | 13 February 1937 | Stepped in temporarily after Wintringham was wounded until Cunningham returned from hospital shortly after |
| Cunningham | Jack | 13 February 1937 to 17 March 1937 | Promoted after Tom Wintringham was wounded at Jarama |
| Copeman | Fred | 17 March 1937 to 19 July 1937 | Commander after Jock Cunningham's injury |
| Hinks | Joseph | 19 July 1937 to 12 August 1937 | Temporary field promotion at Brunete after Fred Copeman was taken sick |
| Daly | Peter | 12 August 1937 to 24 August 1937 | Promoted Battalion Commander on the eve of the Aragon offensive; Battalion Commander at Quinto |
| O'Daire | Patrick | 24 August 1937 to 29 September 1937 | Commander of battalion and 'Director of Operations' at Quinto after death of Peter Daly on 25 August 1937 |
| Fry | Harold | 29 September 1937 to 16 October 1937 | Replaced Paddy O'Daire as Battalion Commander when O'Daire was sent for training for higher command |
| Fletcher | George | 16 October 1937 to 6 November 1937 | Temporarily replaced Sam Wild (who was on a few days sick leave) at Gandesa/Calaciete until he was himself injured, and again deputised at Fuentes de Ebro in October 1938 |
| O'Daire | Patrick | 6 November to 9 November 1937 | |
| Copeman | Fred | 9 November 1937 to 26 December 1937 | |
| Alexander | Bill | 27 December 1937 to 17 February 1938 | Commander of British Battalion at Teruel after George Fletcher's injury or, according to Bill Rust, Copeman's appendicitis |
| Wild | Sam | 17 February 1938 to 1 September 1938 | Battalion Commander after Bill Alexander's injury; George Fletcher took over when he was hospitalised for a few days in August 1938 |
| Fletcher | George | 1 September 1938 onwards | |

# Appendix 2: Political commissars of the British Battalion

| Surname | Forename | Date | Comments |
|---|---|---|---|
| Springhall | Dave | December 1936 to February 1937 | |
| Aitken | George | February 1937 to 23 March 1937 | Usually referred to as the first political commissar with the British Battalion, though he replaced Dave Springhall |
| Williams | Bert | 23 March 1937 to 31 July 1937 | Replaced George Aitken when Aitken was promoted brigade commissar |
| Coyle | George | 31 July 1937 to 23 August 1937 | |
| Roberts | Jack | 23 August 1937 to 25 August 1937 | |
| Torrance | Alec | 25 August 1937 | Replaced Jack Roberts at Pulburell Hill, Quinto |
| Bourne | Jim | 25 August 1937 to 22 September 1937 | American brigade commissar; took over following death of Torrance until appointment of Whalley |
| Whalley | Eric | 22 September 1937 to 13 October 1937 | At Fuentes de Ebro; selected for job as commissar in England; replaced the American Jim Bourne; killed in action on 13 October 1937 |
| Dobson | Harry | 13 October 1937 to 6 November 1937 | Later killed at Gandesa in the Ebro offensive |
| Tapsell | Walter | 6 November 1937 to 31 March 1938 | Killed at Calaceite |
| Oldershaw | Thomas | March 1938 | Temporary battalion commissar when Walter Tapsell was taken to hospital sick; missing in action at Caspe on 16 March 1937 |
| Cooney | Bob | 1 April 1938 onwards | Promoted at Gandesa after death of Walter Tapsell; position confirmed in the summer |

# Notes

## Introduction

1  As Paul Preston points out: 'Ultimately, the new regime was to fail because it neither carried through its threatened reforms nor fulfilled the utopian expectations of its most fervent supporters.' Preston, *A Concise History of the Spanish Civil War*, p. 24.

2  Gabriel Jackson, *The Spanish Republic and the Civil War, 1931–1939*, p. 157.

3  Raymond Carr, *The Spanish Tragedy. The Civil War in Perspective*, pp. 87–89.

4  Piers Brendon, *The Dark Valley: A Panorama of the 1930s*, p. 307.

5  Robert Whealey, for example, points out that had the airlift not taken place, 'the military Rebellion might have been overcome in a few weeks.' Whealey, 'Foreign Intervention in the Spanish Civil War', p. 218.

6  The boost in morale of the population of Madrid caused by the arrival of a disciplined group of soldiers marching with precision must have been dramatic. Geoffrey Cox, a reporter of the battle for Madrid for the *Daily Express*, claimed that there were over 3,000 International Brigaders in Spain by November 1936, of whom about 60 were British, and that 'trained men were fighting trained men at last.' Cox, *Defence of Madrid*, pp. 69–76. However, Hugh Thomas argues that their influence was, at first, more psychological than military. Hugh Thomas, *The Spanish Civil War*, 3rd edn, pp. 479–481.

7  Though Franco's political rather than military decision to divert to Toledo to relieve the besieged garrison played an important role in allowing time to prepare Madrid's defences.

8  Stalin was at first tempted to leave it to France to support the Republic. Alan Bullock, *Hitler and Stalin*, p. 578. There were two factions within the Comintern. The moderates, of whom Stalin was originally a member, opposed intervention in the war. See E. H. Carr, *The Comintern and the Spanish Civil War*, p. 15, and Denis Smyth, 'Soviet Policy Towards Republican Spain: 1936–1939', in P. Preston and A. Mackenzie, eds, *The Republic Besieged: Civil War in Spain 1936–1939*, pp. 91–92. According to Walter Krivitsky, the Russian intelligence officer, Stalin decided to help the Republic militarily on 31 August at a Politburo meeting in Moscow. Thomas, *Spanish Civil War*, p. 441. However, Alexander Orlov, the senior NKVD representative in Spain, claimed in an interview with Stanley Payne that it was a few days earlier, on 26 August 1936. Text of interview cited in Frank Schauff, 'The NKVD in Spain. Questions by Stanley Payne, Answers by Alexander Orlov'.

9  Vincent Brome, *The International Brigades: Spain, 1936–1939*, p. 15.

10  It was widely believed by supporters of the Republic that pressure had been put on the French government. See 'Spanish War Brings Powers into Conflict', *News Chronicle*, 27 July 1936, p. 1, which claimed that 'there is reason to believe that during M. Blum's visit to London it was hinted to him that the British Government would consider it a friendly gesture if France declined materially to assist the Spanish loyalists.'

11  Hugh Thomas, 'The Spanish Civil War', in A. J. P. Taylor ed., *History of the Twentieth Century*, p. 1601.

12  Sir Robert Gilmour Vansittart, permanent under-secretary at the Foreign Office, pointed out in 1939 that 'the whole course of our policy on non-intervention has in reality as we all know worked in an extremely one sided manner.' FO 371/2415-W973/5/41, Vansittart to Halifax, 16 January 1939, cited in Jill Edwards, *The British Government and the Spanish Civil War*, p. 212. This was also acknowledged in Nationalist Spain: Pedro Sainz Rodríguez, a monarchist conspirator, declared that 'The fundamental reason for us winning the war was the English diplomatic position opposing intervention in Spain.' Enrique Moradiellos, 'The Origins of British Non-Intervention in the Spanish Civil War: Anglo-Spanish Relations in early 1936', p. 340.

13  Douglas Little, 'Red Scare, 1936: Anti-Bolshevism and the Origins of British Non-Intervention in the Spanish Civil War', p. 292. Little explains that 'What one critic has labelled Britain's "malevolent neutrality" in the Spanish Civil War, then, stemmed more from ideological than from strategic considerations. Despite considerable evidence that Germany and Italy were much more deeply involved than Russia during the early days of the Spanish strife, Britain quickly adopted a "better Franco than Stalin" approach, which probably helped shape the strategy of appeasement over the following two years. Given disturbing signs from Madrid to Athens of a new wave of Soviet subversion in early 1936, by August, Whitehall clearly believed that republican Spain was better dead than red.' Little, 'Red Scare', pp. 306–307.

14  IBA Box C, File 1/1. See also Bill Alexander, *British Volunteers for Liberty*, pp. 29–30.

15  See Chapter 5.

16  Bill Alexander recounts that 'a passport, the fare of £5–8–0, and a determination to fight were enough for the first few.' Alexander, *British Volunteers*, p. 43.

17  See S. P. Mackenzie, 'The Foreign Enlistment Act and the Spanish Civil War, 1936–1939'.

18  William Rust, *Britons in Spain*, p. 9.

19  Alexander, *British Volunteers*, p. 45.

20  Robson was moved from the Communist Party's office in King Street to Litchfield Street in February 1937 following the British government's implementation of the Foreign Enlistment Act, which made it a criminal offence to volunteer for Spain. The office was, from June 1937, the headquarters of the International Brigades Dependents' Aid Fund. Hywell Francis, *Miners Against Fascism: Wales and the Spanish Civil War*, p. 157.

21  Alexander, *British Volunteers*, p. 44.

22  Interview with Charles Morgan, Imperial War Museum Sound Archive (IWMSA) 10362/2/1.

23  Walter Gregory was followed from his home town, Nottingham, to London and on to Dover. He also believed himself to be being watched whilst he was in Paris but, again, nothing was done to stop him travelling to Spain. Walter Gregory, *The Shallow Grave: A Memoir of the Spanish Civil War*, p. 24.

24  Brian Lewis and Bill Gledhill, *A Lion of a Man*, p. 36.

25  Interview with John Longstaff, IWMSA 9299/13/3–4.

26  Interview with Edwin Greening, IWMSA 9855/7/2.

27  The act required that both sides, first, were at peace with Britain and, second, were recognised by Britain as *de facto* foreign states. As rebel Spain was not recognised, this made the application of the act legally questionable. As S. P. Mackenzie states: 'While the volunteers could be questioned and some turned back, and confrontations might be heated, nobody was ever arrested.' Mackenzie, 'Foreign Enlistment Act', p. 63.

28  See 'Diary of Sid Hamm', in Frank Thomas, *Brother Against Brother*, p. 155.

29  Charlotte Haldane, *Truth Will Out*, p. 113. Her son fought under the name of his father, Burgess, who had been Charlotte Haldane's previous husband.

30  Alexander, *British Volunteers*, p. 46 and Rust, *Britons in Spain*, p. 10.

31  For this reason, in December 1936, Walter Tapsell, later a British Battalion commissar, wrote back to Robson, responsible for recruitment in London, recommending that the sum of money given to volunteers be reduced. He also complained that a number of volunteers were arriving in Spain suffering from venereal diseases. IBA Box C, File 8/2.

32   See, for example, the interview with Frank McCusker in Ian MacDougall, ed., *Voices from the Spanish Civil War: Personal Recollections of Scottish Volunteers in Republican Spain, 1936–1939*, p. 42. McCusker was arrested in Perpignan on the Franco-Spanish border, charged with vagrancy, and repatriated to Britain. 'They put me on the train, then they put me on the boat and put me back into London again. That was on the Wednesday. On the Friday I was back on the boat tae France again and I got right through then.' Alun Williams, a Welsh nurse, was arrested in the Pyrenees with another Welshman, Jack Roberts, for vagrancy. However, as both Williams and Roberts had money, the authorities were forced to let them go. They continued on their way. Both served in Spain and survived the war. Interview with Huw Alun Menai Williams, IWMSA 10181/5/2 and IBA Box D-7, File A/1.

33   See, for example, interview with George Murray in MacDougall, *Voices*, p. 101, and Alexander, *British Volunteers*, pp. 46–47.

34   Interview with William Feeley, IWMSA 848/4/1.

35   Mackenzie, 'Foreign Enlistment Act', p. 63.

36   Interview with Harold Fraser, IWMSA 795/5/2. See also, for example, interview with John Dunlop, IWMSA 11355/13/3.

37   See, for example, the description of a volunteer who collapses from the strain of the climb, Rust, *Britons in Spain*, p. 11; and Steve Fullarton's remark, 'I can't remember an awful lot about climbing the mountains, except that it was very tiring.' Interview with Steve Fullarton, in MacDougall, *Voices*, p. 291.

38   Conversation with Richard Baxell, 26 February 2001.

39   Interviews with Steve Fullarton and Tom Murray, in MacDougall, *Voices*, pp. 291 and 309.

40   For example, see interview with James Jump, IWMSA 9524/6/2.

41   James K. Hopkins, *Into the Heart of the Fire: The British in the Spanish Civil War*.

# 1   Who were the British volunteers?

1   Judith Cook, *Apprentices of Freedom*, p. 23.

2   Typical is the claim by Harold Cardozo that 'at least 10,000 volunteers' had passed through Perpignan alone by the end of November 1936. Cardozo, *The March of a Nation*, p. 184. Estimates of the level of *matériel* supplied to the Republic have also been shown to be gross exaggerations. As Gerald Howson's meticulous study demonstrates, 'The material strengths of the two sides were balanced so unequally against the Republicans that a great deal of what has been published about the Spanish Civil War in general and of the various battles in particular will have to be rewritten.' Howson, *Arms for Spain: The Untold Story of the Spanish Civil War*, p. 250.

3   Arthur F. Loveday, *World War in Spain*, p. 134. Loveday was a Conservative MP and a devoted follower of Franco and dedicated his book to: 'Spain the saviour of Western Europe from the Crescent, Lepanto, 1571 and from the Sickle and Hammer, 1936–1939'. Loveday was a regular contributor to the pro-Franco newspaper the *Morning Post*, whose views were probably a fairly accurate representation of his own. The first of many letters from him appeared on 29 July 1936, p. 9, complaining of the use of the term 'loyalists to describe Republicans who have discarded God and their King, destroyed Churches, persecuted priests, are supported by irregulars wearing the red shirt of communism and professing its doctrines, and do, in theory and in fact, represent anarchy. The side described as "rebels" represent the maintenance of law and order, the bulk of the regular army, and those people who are loyal to God and the Christian Church.'

4   Figures from Spanish Foreign Ministry and Andreu Castells, *Las brigadas internacionales de la guerra de España*, 1974, cited in Thomas, *Spanish Civil War*, 3rd edn, p. 982, n.2.

5   Interview with John Peet, in D. Corkhill and S. Rawnsley, eds, *The Road to Spain: Anti Fascists at War 1936–1939*, p. 104.

6   For example, after Brunete, in July 1937, estimates suggest that between 60 and 70 per

cent of the 12th International Brigade were Spanish. R. Dan Richardson, *Comintern Army*, p. 89.

7  A copy of this decree, in English translation, appears in Arthur Landis, *History of the Abraham Lincoln Brigade*, pp. 331–335.

8  Numbers of British in the battalion fell after costly battles such as Jarama, then gradually rose again as new recruits arrived to replace them. As Tom Wintringham, one of the commanders of the British Battalion, explained, 'The number of "English" in our battalion in this period [February to May 1937] varied from three-hundred to thirty-five.' Tom Wintringham, *English Captain*, p. 141.

9  John Peet's estimate, drawn from the index cards at the post office in the International Brigade base at Albacete, was just over 40,000. Interview with John Peet, in Corkhill and Rawnsley, *Road to Spain*, p. 105. Bill Alexander, who served as a political commissar and later commander of the British Battalion, originally claimed that the figure was around 42,000, though his most recent estimate of 35,000 was very near the contemporary estimate by the League of Nations, which put the number near 32,000. For the original estimate, see Alexander, *British Volunteers for Liberty*, p. 29. His revised estimate was mentioned in an interview with the author on 5 November 1997.

10  A huge number of foreigners arrived in Spain to fight for the Nationalists, of which a few were volunteers, though by far the majority were not. Hugh Thomas estimates that roughly 17,000 Germans, 75,000 Italians and 75,000 troops from Spanish Morocco fought in Spain with the Nationalist armies. Thomas, *Spanish Civil War*, p. 985.

11  Haldane, *Truth Will Out*, pp. 87–93.

12  Thomas, *Spanish Civil War*, p. 454; K. W. Watkins, *Britain Divided: The Effect of the Spanish Civil War on British Political Opinion*, p. 175; Richardson, *Comintern Army*, p. 32; Hopkins, *Into the Heart of the Fire*, p. 157; and César Vidal, *Las Brigadas Internacionales*, p. 63, n.19.

13  Francis, *Miners Against Fascism*, p. 159.

14  R. Dan Richardson quotes Harry Pollitt, promising that 'the seven hundred and fifty men in the British men in the Brigades will soon become a thousand'; Richardson, *Comintern Army*, p. 32. There is also a reference to a numerical target in a letter from Ralph Bates to Harry Pollitt, probably written in December 1936, in which Bates remarks, 'Remember that even if you give us two battalions we shall need drafts to replace casualties.' However, neither statement really qualifies as firm evidence for a numerical quota. See IBA Box C File 8/2.

15  Based upon records kept in the International Brigade Collection in Moscow, the International Brigade Archive in London and the Public Record Office in Kew, a computerised database of British volunteers for the Republic has been compiled by the author, which includes those that fought with the militias, members of the various medical units, and volunteers from the myriad outposts of the British Empire. The database suggests that just over 2,300 arrived in Spain, which tallies very closely with the estimate by Bill Alexander of 2,340. The main files used to comprise the database were: Moscow 545/6/89-99; IBA Box 21, File A, Box C, File 1/2a, Box D-7, Files A/1 and A/2; PRO FO369/2514-K14742/12563/241 and FO371/22654-W13505. A copy of the database is held in the Marx Memorial Library in London.

16  Some volunteers believed that they were signing up only for a limited period of time and would be able to return home in a few months. See John Angus, *With the International Brigade in Spain*, p. 7. Many volunteers travelled without passports, or surrendered them on their arrival in Spain, though some, such as Jason Gurney, decided prudently to hold on to their passports. See Gurney, *Crusade in Spain*, pp. 55–56.

17  As Tom Murray, one of the political commissars in the British Battalion, later stated, 'Casualty rates in the Spanish war were terrible.' Interview with Tom Murray, in MacDougall, *Voices from the Spanish Civil War*, p. 327. Several senior figures, including Fred Copeman, one of the Battalion commanders, and Billy Griffiths, the Communist Party representative within the battalion in Spain, have remarked upon the high casualty rates and their slowing down of recruitment.

18  Francis, *Miners Against Fascism*, p. 158.
19  Richardson, *Comintern Army*, p. 88. See also Vincent Brome, who argues that by the end of 1937 recruitment was becoming a problem, for returning brigaders did not always present a pretty picture and the chance of death was clearly high. Brome, *The International Brigades*, p. 228.
20  Francis, *Miners Against Fascism*, p. 172. Between April and September 1937, 6,464 volunteers arrived at Albacete, compared to 18,000 between October 1936 and March 1937. P Pagès, 'Marty, Vidal, Kleber at le Komintern. Ce que nous apprennent les Archives de Moscow', *Colloque International sur les Brigades Internationales* (Lausanne, 18–20 December, 1997), pp. 14–15, cited in Andy Durgan, 'Freedom Fighters or Comintern Army?', p. 6.
21  Source for arrival data: Moscow 545/6/89–91 and IBA Box D-7, File A/1.
22  Walter Gregory, for example, a party member and organiser from Nottingham, was asked by Clarence Mason, the paid CP organiser for the Nottingham area, 'Would you like to go to Spain?' Interview with Thomas Walter Gregory, IWMSA 8851/9/1, and Gregory, *The Shallow Grave*, p. 19.
23  Interview with Bob Cooney, in Corkhill and Rawnsley, *The Road to Spain*, p. 118.
24  Billy Griffiths, MS, p. 1.
25  Interview with Tom Murray, in MacDougall, *Voices*, p. 308.
26  Ibid., p. 310–311.
27  Francis, *Miners Against Fascism*, p. 164.
28  Letter from George Aitken to the party bureau, undated, but probably September 1937, IBA Box C, File 17/7. It is also true that the creation of the commissariat at Albacete was partly an attempt by André Marty to preserve the lives of valuable communist cadres following the deaths of Ralph Fox and Hans Beimler, a communist ex-deputy of the Reichstag, in the battles for Madrid in December 1936. Letter from Peter Kerrigan, the brigade commissar at Albacete, to Harry Pollitt, 4 January 1937, CP/IND/POLL/2/5–6, NMLH Manchester.
29  Watkins, *Britain Divided*, p. 176.
30  Huw Williams served as a nurse and first-aider in Spain, and remembers that, at Brunete, 'A lot were dying. [There were] no identity tags. Nobody to report [casualties] to.' His belief was that all details of casualties were highly vague and inaccurate. Interview with Huw Alun Menai Williams, IWMSA 10181/5/4.
31  IBA Box 21, File B2/d.
32  IBA Box 21, File B2/i.
33  Ibid.
34  See, for example, Moscow 545/6/89, pp. 80–84.
35  IBA Box 21, File A.
36  PRO FO889/2-76.
37  Alexander, *British Volunteers*, p. 83.
38  As McGarry has shown, tracing the Irish volunteers faces similar problems. Fearghal McGarry, *Irish Politics and the Spanish Civil War*, p. 55.
39  There is also a particular problem differentiating between the large number of Scottish and Welsh volunteers with identical surnames, and sometimes forenames. The large number of Joneses, Evanses, Robertses and Prices also caused confusion at the time. Miles Tomalin's journey to Spain with a group of Welsh – Bill Price, Goff Price, Leo Price, Jack Roberts and Tom Roberts – led him to compose this simple, witty limerick:

> There was a young fellow named Price,
> And another young fellow named Price,
> And a fellow named Roberts,
> And a fellow named Roberts,
> And another young fellow named Price.

Francis, *Miners Against Fascism*, p. 232 and p. 245, n.36. There are also problems differentiating different members of the same family from each other. For example, Bill Alexander states that Danny Gibbons was wounded at Brunete, whereas it was actually his brother Tommy. Alexander, *British Volunteers*, p. 122.

40  IBA Box 21, File A, Box D-7, Files A/1 and A/2; and PRO FO371/22654-W13505.

41  Lesser was ordered to change his name for slightly different reasons. Lesser/Russell served with the International Brigades from October 1936 to January 1937, before being injured on the Córdoba front. After a stint in Britain he returned to Spain to work for Radio Barcelona, where there was another man with the same surname, so the Communist Party suggested he change it ('Russell' is essentially 'Lesser' backwards). Sam Russell was the name he wrote under as *Daily Worker* correspondent in Spain. Interview with Sam Russell, IWMSA 9484/6/1.

42  Judith Cook, *Apprentices of Freedom*, p. 119.

43  IBA Box 21, File A.

44  Moscow offers an extremely rich source of information on the background of the volunteers. In addition to numerous lists of names and details such as occupation, political affiliation, date of entry into Spain and age, there are a number of questionnaires completed by volunteers during 1937 and 1938. Though only a minority of volunteers completed the forms they are, nevertheless, an invaluable source. The first four sections are concerned with the volunteers' background: personal details, occupational background, trade unionism and social, cultural and sporting information. The fifth and final section is itself divided into five sections: affiliation and political activities; political and moral questions, probably to establish any deviationist or Trotskyist tendencies; educational, intellectual and cultural background; military experience; and details of the time in Spain, such as date of entry, campaigns, promotions etc. See Moscow 545/6/100-218 and 454/6/51, pp. 89–218

45  Ralph Fox, the battalion commissar of No. 1 Company, who was killed at Lopera in late December 1936, had argued that military experience was essential and that only a small number of 'good, loyal and tried comrades' should be taken on. He was somewhat scathing in his remarks, stating that there should be no more 'odds and sods from Bloomsbury, of whom we have had a few'. IBA Box C, File 8/2.

46  There is some debate over Bates's role within the Communist Party. Bates always maintained he was not a party member, yet he clearly had considerable influence in Barcelona. Whilst it is conceivable that Bates could have been editor of *Volunteer for Liberty* and have been a confidante of Harry Pollitt without actually being a party member – witness the British Battalion commander Fred Copeman, who claimed he didn't join the CP until 1937– the role and influence of Bates suggests that, if he was not actually a member of the party *de jure*, he was certainly a member *de facto*. For Bates's background, see Hopkins, *Into the Heart*, pp. 66–71.

47  IBA Box C, File 8/2.

48  Russell argued the Leninist line, that 'a working-class which doesn't learn the use of arms deserves to be slaves.' Interview with Sam Russell, IWMSA 9484/6/1.

49  Ibid.

50  Interview with Phil Gillan, MacDougall, *Voices*, p. 13. As Bill Alexander put it, 'those who had previously served in the regular forces had enlisted because the food and pay provided an escape from unemployment and hardship.' Alexander, *British Volunteers*, p. 133.

51  Letter from Will Paynter to Harry Pollitt, IBA Box C, File 17/1.

52  Moscow 565/9/90-91.

53  Drawn from a sample of 582 volunteers who were asked whether or not they had military experience before their time in Spain. Moscow 545/6/91.The American recruiters also aimed to recruit volunteers with military experience. However, the stipulation was soon dropped: 34 per cent of the US volunteers had formal military training, another 23 per cent had fired a gun, and 42 per cent had no military experience. Carroll, *The Odyssey of the Abraham Lincoln Brigade*, p. 65.

54 Hugh Thomas estimates that over 60 per cent of volunteers were members of the Communist Party. Thomas, *Spanish Civil War*, p. 455. A study of a small number of the British volunteers gave a similar proportion. See M. J. Hynes, 'The British Battalion of the XVth International Brigade', p. 35.

55 Interview with John Tunnah, IWMSA 840/9/6.

56 Of the roughly 1,500 of whom there is information on political affiliation, 1,105 were members of the CP or the YCL and 109 were in the Labour Party. It is very difficult to establish a precise figure for the number of CP members. The reasons mentioned above are likely to underestimate the numbers, whereas other sources, as diverse as the *Daily Worker*, the Communist Party newspaper, and the *Daily Mail* (which at one stage carried advertisements for the British Union of Fascists), are likely to have inflated numbers in order to exaggerate the Communist Party's role in the conflict. A recent study of the British Battalion estimated that only half the British volunteers were party members; in fact this is an underestimate of the level of party membership. See Hopkins, *Into the Heart*, p. 54.

57 Alexander states that, 'on 22 December 1936, of the 23,000 International Brigaders in Spain, 60 per cent were Communists.' Whilst the number of volunteers may be an overestimate, the proportion is probably about right. See Alexander, *British Volunteers*, p. 67. It also conforms to an analysis of the American volunteers, of whom between two-thirds and three-quarters belonged to the Communist Party or affiliated organisations. Carroll, *Odyssey*, p. 19.

58 IBA Box 21, Box 21a, Box D-7, File A/2, and Moscow 545/6/89-94.

59 See, for example the passbook of Fred Copeman, held in the Imperial War Museum, or of Sam Wild, a photograph of which appears in *Images of the Spanish Civil War*, p. 93, and the numerous copies held in the personal files in Moscow.

60 Interview with Jack Jones, 25 August 1978, Manchester 11, 17–18, cited in Hopkins, *Into the Heart*, p. 250.

61 See Fred Copeman, *Reason in Revolt*, p. 107, and Angus, *With the International Brigade*, p. 3.

62 Interview with Albert Charlesworth, IWMSA 798/4/1.

63 George Orwell believed that Smillie died in suspicious circumstances. Recent research, however, suggests that, though his medical treatment was unsatisfactory, to put it mildly, Smillie was not actually murdered. See Tom Buchanan, 'The Death of Bob Smillie, the Spanish Civil War, and the Eclipse of the Independent Labour Party'.

64 Interview with Bruce Allender, IWMSA 11300/4/1.

65 Tom Buchanan, *Britain and the Spanish Civil War*, p. 141.

66 Louis Hearst, MS, p. 57.

67 Alexander, *British Volunteers*, p. 33.

68 Source of age data: IBA Box D-7, File A/2, and Moscow 545/6/91.

69 This correlates very closely with the profile of the French volunteers, whose average age on arrival was recently established to be 29 years and 9 months. Rémi Skoutelsky, *L'Espoir guidait leurs pas: les volontaires français dans les Brigades internationales 1936–1939*, p. 141. This data is available in translation in Skoutelsky, 'French Combatants of the International Brigades', p. 10. The Americans were only slightly younger, with an average median age of 27 years. Carroll, *Odyssey*, p. 15. The age profile also mirrors a profile of 60 Welsh volunteers by Hywell Francis, which estimated an average age of 30 years. Hywell Francis, 'Welsh Miners and the Spanish Civil War'.

70 Roughly three-quarters of recruits, 76.5 per cent, were between the ages of 21 and 35, and half, 49.9 per cent, were between 25 and 35.

71 For the French data, see Skoutelsky, *L'Espoir guidait leurs pas*, p. 142. For the American, see Carroll, *Odyssey*, p. 16.

72 However, some under-age volunteers from Britain still got through the net. Thomas Hurley, an 18-year-old miner from Wales, is listed as joining the British Battalion on 10 March 1938, and Charles Matthews, a 19-year-old clerk from London, joined the battalion as late as 24 March 1938. Moscow 545/6/91, p. 164 and p. 166. It seems that the Americans were more rigorous, with the youngest volunteer being 18 years old. Carroll, *Odyssey*, p. 15.

73 Alexander, *British Volunteers*, p. 33. After serving as a member of No. 1 Company, the 14th International Brigade, and with the British Battalion, Hutchinson became a driver in 5 Army Corps.

74 'Some of the older men had lied as cheerfully about their ages as the youngsters. Officially our age limit was forty; there were men of over fifty who did as well as those half their years.' Wintringham, *English Captain*, pp. 114–115.

75 Alexander, *British Volunteers*, p. 33.

76 In a letter enquiring about her son, Michael Patton (real name Weaving), who joined in January 1937, Mrs M. Weaving of Colchester states that his age was 17, though he told recruiters that he was 19. PRO FO889/2-46.

77 Interview with John Longstaff, IWMSA 92219/13/3.

78 Alexander, *British Volunteers*, p. 36.

79 Ibid.

80 Watkins, *Britain Divided*, p. 168. This would estimate the total Jewish volunteers to number between approximately 60 and 80.

81 See Martin Sugarman, 'Against Fascism – Jews who served in the Spanish Civil War', p. 2. Peter Carroll's analysis of the American volunteers suggests an even higher proportion, with over a third being Jewish. Carroll, *Odyssey*, p. 18. Other estimates record similar figures: Edward Lending suggests that somewhere in the region of a quarter of all International Brigaders were of Jewish extraction, with a figure of between 10 and 15 per cent for the British volunteers. Lending, 'Jews Who Fought'.

82 For example, IBA Box D-7, File A/1, lists only an approximate area next to the volunteer's name. In some cases it is as precise as 'Shoreditch' or 'Lambeth', in others merely 'London'. There is no confirmation in this source whether this is the place of birth, home address, or a next of kin's address.

83 For example, Moscow 545/6/91 gives the volunteers' addresses alongside a listing of their precise nature, e.g. Wife's address, Mother's address, etc.

84 Approximately 200 addresses are either missing, or so vague or ambiguous as to be unusable for any meaningful analysis, though as this comprises less than 10 per cent of the total it is unlikely to skew the results significantly.

85 IBA Box D-7, File A/7.

86 IBA Box D-7, File A/2. Fortunately in this case there is a full address listed: Mrs Forbes, 50 Leslie Road, Tholte Heath, St Helens. This must be either a care-of address or a next of kin. As Connaughton was 39 years old in 1937 it seems unlikely that it would have been the address of his mother.

87 For example, Basil Paul Abrahams, who briefly used the name Basil Minsk during his first period in Spain, gives three separate addresses. As all three are within the Hackney area – one in Mare Street, Hackney, one in Cecil Street, Whitechapel, and one in Braydon Road, Stamford Hill – it seems very unlikely that they could refer to different volunteers. The three addresses come from PRO FO371/22654-W13505 and IBA Box D-7, Files A/1 and A/2.

88 This was chosen to be IBA Box D-7, File A/2, as it contains more details, on a larger number of the volunteers, than any other single source. A rather more legible and complete version of this list appears in Moscow 545/6/40.

89 The total estimate of Scottish volunteers taken from the database of volunteers and including those from Glasgow, Edinburgh and Dundee is 549. IBA Box 21, Files A and C/2, Box C, Files 2/1 and 2/2, Box D-7, Files A/1 and A/2, and PRO FO369/2514-K14742/12563/241. This estimate is higher than both Tom Buchanan's figure of 437 and Ian MacDougall's of 476. See Buchanan, *Britain and the Spanish Civil War*, p. 126 and 'In the Valley of Sorrow: Scots Voices from Spain' compiled and presented by Ian MacDougall and first broadcast on BBC Radio 4, 1986, taken from IWMSA 12943/2.

90 There is little doubt that these numbers are not representative. Those volunteers from Manchester, Liverpool and Glasgow were probably higher, and the numbers from London perhaps 25 per cent lower. Over 80 per cent of the American volunteers came

from the USA's eleven largest cities, with nearly 20 per cent from New York alone. Carroll, *Odyssey*, p. 15.

91   Probably no more than 350 volunteers were actually Londoners.

92   See Don Watson and John Corcoran, *An Inspiring Example: The North East of England and the Spanish Civil War 1936–1939.*

93   Stevenson and Cook, *Britain in the Depression*, p. 51.

94   108 volunteers give addresses in Tyneside.

95   131 volunteers give addresses in Merseyside, and 192 are from Manchester, Lancashire and Cumberland combined.

96   12 volunteers listed their address as Oldham.

97   Francis argues that 'Parts of South Wales in 1935 had more in common with parts of France and Spain than with the rest of Britain . . . The social and political unrest in South Wales can in many ways be seen in a European context, and in particular, as comparable with the Asturian miners' rising in Spain the previous year: both were primarily working-class rebellions against an authoritarian central government, even though the one was a full scale military rising and the other was a largely peaceful "demonstration" of resistance.' Francis, *Miners Against Fascism*, p. 68.

98   Stevenson and Cook, *Britain in the Depression*, p. 161.

99   Stevenson and Cook describe how 'entering "Red" Rhondda meant much the same as marching through the Jewish communities of the East End of London.' Ibid., p. 90.

100  Ibid., pp. 144–152.

101  Estimates gleaned from IBA Box C, File 2/2, Box 21, Files A and C/2, Box D-7/A/2 and Francis, 'Welsh Miners and the Spanish Civil War' suggest that there were approximately 170 volunteers from Wales. However, recent analysis suggests that the number may be nearer 150. (My thanks to Robert Stradling for this revised estimate.)

102  A total of 437 for the number of Scottish volunteers appears in IBA Box C, File 1/1, which Tom Buchanan quotes. Buchanan, *Britain and the Spanish Civil War*, p. 126. However, after an examination of the lists of volunteers in the IBA, PRO and Moscow, this would appear to be an underestimate.

103  Sources, see above, list 60 volunteers from Dundee and 33 from Edinburgh.

104  Stevenson and Cook, *Britain in the Depression*, pp. 151–154.

105  IBA Box C, File 1/1. The actual number was probably nearer 100.

106  Stradling claims that 'The substantial majority – 66 per cent – of the approximately 200 Irishmen who fought for the Spanish Republic were working-class men from the slums of Belfast and Dublin, along with other substantial urban centres like Cork and Waterford . . . About 60 Dubliners, many of them unemployed, along with some 25 Belfast men went to join the International Brigades. In contrast, only about a quarter hailed from rural backgrounds.' Stradling, *The Irish and the Spanish Civil War 1936–1939*, p. 137. Ciaran Crossey's recent estimate of 250 is slightly higher than Stradling's. It includes all volunteers born in Ireland or those with one parent born in the country. For a list of volunteers see http://members.lycos.co.uk/spanishcivilwar/Contents-Rep.htm

107  IBA Box 21, File A, Box D-7, Files A/1 and A/2, Box C, File 2/2, and PRO FO371/22654-W13505.

108  For a good example of a British communist official's interpretation of this dispute, see Alexander, *British Volunteers*, pp. 68–69. Although Robert Stradling refers to this event as a 'crisis and split', Alexander stresses instead the 'powerful arguments' that were put by several of the Irish opposed to leaving the British Battalion. Whilst Alexander accepts that 'there was a short period of tension', he claims that 'these tensions, inevitable against the background of Irish oppression, vanished in action.'

109  The American unit is often referred to as the Abraham Lincoln Brigade, though it was a battalion within the 15th Brigade.

110  See Chapter 3 for an examination of the circumstances surrounding this issue.

111  See McGarry, *Irish Politics*, p. 55.

112  There are several works written by Irish volunteers. For the Republicans, see Michael

O'Riordan's *Connolly Column*, and for the Nationalists, see the memoirs of General Eoin O'Duffy, the leader of the Blueshirts, *Crusade in Spain*. Seamus MacKee, a volunteer for O'Duffy who regretted his experiences, describes his tale in *I Was a Franco Soldier*, which bears the mark of either a rather zealous convert to Marxism or, more likely, a ghost writer. Secondary works on the volunteers from Ireland include Seán Cronin's study of one influential figure amongst the Irish republican volunteers, *Frank Ryan*. On the Nationalist volunteers there are Maurice Manning's *The Blueshirts*, Robert Stradling's, *The Irish and the Spanish Civil War* and McGarry, *Irish Politics*.

113 I am grateful to Michael O'Shaughnessy for information on the volunteers from New Zealand.

114 For the Australian volunteers, see Amirah Inglis, *Australians in the Spanish Civil War*.

115 Information relating to occupations has been gleaned mainly from Moscow 545/6/90–91, from the trade union membership lists held in the IBA in Box C, Files 2/1 and 2/2, and Box 21c, File 2, and from miscellaneous lists such as the record of wounded volunteers from Liverpool in IBA Box D-7, File A/7. The various interviews with volunteers, both published and unpublished, have also been helpful here. Certain occupations, such as labourers and general labourers, miners and coal miners, and writers, novelists and authors have been combined for the sake of clarity.

116 Stevenson and Cook, *Britain in the Depression*, p. 51.

117 Thomas, *Spanish Civil War*, pp. 454–456.

118 Angus, *With the International Brigade*, p. 3.

119 Alexander, *British Volunteers*, p. 32.

120 IBA Box 21c, File 2.

121 Wintringham, *English Captain*, p. 330.

122 Alexander, *British Volunteers*, p. 37.

123 Tom Buchanan, 'Britain's Popular Front? Aid Spain and the British Labour Movement', p. 61.

## 2 Why did they go?

1 Interview with Bill Alexander, December 1997.

2 Interview with Freddie Brandler, May 2000.

3 For the British government's reactions to the war, see Edwards, *The British Government and the Spanish Civil War*; Douglas Little, *Malevolent Neutrality* and 'Red Scare, 1936', and Enrique Moradiellos, *La perfidia de Albión: el gobierno británico y la guerra civil española*.

4 Cited in Edwards, *British Government*, p. 38.

5 Even though the Popular Front government elected in 1936 did not actually include any communists. As Enrique Moradiellos has pointed out, 'The rigid adhesion by Britain to the Non-Intervention Pact signed by the European states in August 1936, with the corresponding imposition of a strict embargo on arms and munitions, produced uneven effects on the two Spanish camps.' Moradiellos, 'The Origins of British Non-Intervention in the Spanish Civil War: Anglo-Spanish Relations in early 1936', p. 339. For an examination of the level of inequality between the *matériel* supplied to the Republic and the rebels, see Howson, *Arms for Spain*.

6 E. H. Carr, *The Comintern and the Spanish Civil War*, p. 17.

7 Hugh Sloan, 'Why I Volunteered', p. 31.

8 In a letter to the general secretary of the British Communist Party, Harry Pollitt, dated 4 January 1937, Peter Kerrigan, the British political commissar at the International Brigade headquarters at Albacete, described how 'the embargo is certainly affecting us here when you know that rifles are not available in sufficient numbers for effective training.' NMLH Manchester, CP/IND/POLL/2/5-6.

9 Corkhill and Rawnsley, *The Road to Spain*, pp. 139–140.

10 Interview with Roderick MacFarquar, in MacDougall, *Voices from the Spanish Civil War*, p. 85.

11  Hearst, MS, pp. 6–7.
12  Rumours of a communist plot to launch a revolution in the summer of 1936 in Spain were widely cited by rightists as a justification for the rising. Arthur F. Loveday produced documents he claimed proved the existence of a communist conspiracy in Spain to launch a Bolshevik revolution that, he believed, Franco pre-empted with his own coup. Loveday included a translation of the documents in an appendix to his book, entitled 'Secret Documents detailing the plan for the establishment of a Soviet in Spain, the discovery of which was one of the immediate causes of the counter-revolution and the civil war'. See Loveday, *World War in Spain*, pp. 176–183. General O'Duffy, the leader of the Irish contingent that fought – briefly – with the rebels, also refers to a Russian 'Manual of Action' for Spain, which he blamed for the spate of church burnings that followed the declaration of the Republic in 1931. Eoin O'Duffy, *Crusade in Spain*, p. 43. This theory has been systematically demolished by Herbert Southworth. See Southworth, *Disinformation and the Spanish Civil War: The Brainwashing of Francisco Franco*.
13  Interview with John Henderon, in Don Watson and John Corcoran, *An Inspiring Example: The North East of England and the Spanish Civil War 1936–1939*, p. 53.
14  Hopkins, *Into the Heart of the Fire*, p. 106, and Buchanan, *Britain and the Spanish Civil War*, p. 121. Byron had himself volunteered to fight for the Nationalist cause in Greece in 1823–1824.
15  Buchanan, *Britain and the Spanish Civil War*, p. 122.
16  Cited in Hopkins, *Into the Heart*, p. 106.
17  Walter Greenhalgh, who was with Cornford when he was killed, remarks on this 'Byronesque image' of Cornford, ironically claiming that it was the 'heroic and romantic' (in the words of another volunteer, Sam Russell) bandage that was responsible for his death. See the following chapter.
18  Buchanan, *Britain and the Spanish Civil War*, p. 127.
19  Rust, *Britons in Spain*, p. 7.
20  Nick Gillain, *Le Mercenaire: carnet de route d'un combattant rouge*, Paris: Arthème Fayard, 1938, quoted in Thomas, *Spanish Civil War*, 3rd edn, pp. 454–455. In the Spanish edition, *El mercenario: diario de un combatiente rojo*, Tanger: Editions Tanger, 1939, p. 3, Gillain refers to his 'boredom', *aburrimiento*. In Thomas's portrayal of motivations in his earlier 1961 edition, p. 299, he referred to volunteers 'purging some private grief or maladjustment'. This was removed from later editions.
21  See, for example, Bob Clark, *No Boots to my Feet*, p. 22.
22  Wintringham, *English Captain*, p. 66.
23  Interview with James Jump, IWMSA 9524/6/2, also cited in Philip Toynbee, ed., *The Distant Drum: Reflections on the Spanish Civil War*, pp. 112–113.
24  All those involved in recruitment for the International Brigades deny this charge and point out that what was wanted was determined and disciplined volunteers, preferably with military training. However, Douglas Hyde, an International Brigader who later converted to Catholicism, claimed that, 'When cannon-fodder was needed, one Party organiser's job was to go around the Thames Embankment in London at night looking for able-bodied down-and-outs. He got them drunk and shipped them over the Channel.' André Marty also referred to the issue: 'There should be a stop to recruiting in hostels and parks, Embankments etc. We want men from the working class movement, class-conscious comrades [not] drunkards, down and outs, criminals.' Whilst Hyde's remark is clear in his accusation, Marty's makes no reference to hoodwinking, only recruiting; thus this point rests on the reliability of Douglas Hyde's testimony, and he was certainly a hostile witness. How the men were shipped across the channel, let alone into Spain, is not clear. See Douglas Hyde, *I Believed*, p. 60, and 'Records in London – Observations', enclosed in Marty to Pollitt, 22/12/37, Moscow 545/6/87/39-40.
25  The *Morning Post* often argued that those leaving Britain were misguided rather than heinous criminals. A satirical poem appeared on 2 March 1937, p. 12, that typifies their portrayal of volunteers as 'dupes':

I grant that you will seek in vain,
Among the volunteers in Spain,
Defying death and wounds and dirt,
One with 'S. Cripps' upon his shirt.
Not Labour's leaders, but its dupes
Are Caballero's British troops
Who volunteered – it sounded fine –
For well paid work behind the line,
But when they reached the actual spot,
Were told to fight or else be shot.

26  See, for example, 'Britons Lured to Red Front', *Daily Mail*, 18 February 1937, p. 13, which claims that a Scottish volunteer, John Bruce, who had been captured by the Nationalists, had been told he would be working in Spanish vineyards for £6 per week and that he had only been informed he would be required to fight once he arrived in Spain. It seems probable that Bruce recounted this story hoping it might save his life. If so, he was to be proved mistaken: he was executed by the rebels in February 1937. The rumour that down-and-outs were picked up on London's Thames Embankment, drugged and smuggled across to Spain was another story that originated in the right-wing press. See also Alexander, *British Volunteers for Liberty*, p. 31.

27  Ibid., p. 32.

28  Hopkins, *Into the Heart*, p. 211.

29  Interview with John Longstaff, IWMSA 92219/13/4. Longstaff's experience was not unique. Baruch Ramelson, a Canadian who served with the Mackenzie–Papineau Battalion but who was recruited through Britain, described how Robson 'Pointed out all the difficulties, all the hardships, "Was I certain I knew what I was letting myself in for?" He wanted to assure himself absolutely that I quite knew what I was doing, that I was aware both politically and physically, that I was not going to Spain for a picnic or just to visit Spain to see what it was like, that my intentions were serious.' Interview with Baruch 'Bert' Ramelson, IWMSA 6657/6/1. See also Gurney, *Crusade in Spain*, pp. 37–38: '[Robson] delivered himself of a short and rather threatening lecture. He was completely fair and frank in what he had to say. It was a bastard of a war, we would be short of food, medical services and even arms and ammunition. If any of us believed that we were going into a fine adventure we might as well pack up and go home right away.'

30  'We had another medical there [Paris], by the way, and we all were given the opportunity, I must state this, we were all given the opportunity, if you wished to return, now is the time. We were told that before we left London, when we got to Paris and when we got to the Spanish frontier. Even when we got to Spain we were told, "If you want to go back, you can go back. There's no shame in going back."' Interview with Hugh MacKay, IWMSA 12025/5/2.

31  Interview with James Jump, IWMSA 9524/6/1.

32  Jan Kurzke, MS, p. 18.

33  This number is an estimate based upon lists of British men repatriated from Spain held in PRO FO369/2514-K14742/12563/241 and FO371/22654-W13505.

34  For example, in a letter to Alec Cummings, on 5 February 1937, Mike (probably Econo-mides) relates that eight British volunteers have been held back at Figueras, for 'they have always been and are a liability . . . They [have] got to be sent back to [*sic*] quickest possible as you will understand they cannot be kept here indefinitely.' Moscow 545/6/89, p. 4.

35  Interview with Chris Smith, IWMSA 12290/9/3.

36  Interview with Fred Copeman, IWMSA 794/13/9.

37  Greening recounts how 'my uncle Gwillam had twelve magnificently illustrated volumes of the First World War, so I knew exactly what war was all about. I had my eyes open, and my brain. I knew I was likely to be a casualty.' Interview with Edwin Greening, IWMSA 9855/7/2.

38  Letter from J. H. Milanes, acting British Consul in Madrid, to W. J. Sullivan, HM Consul in Valencia, 27 April 1937. FO889/2–118.
39  Interview with Hugh MacKay, IWMSA 12025/5/1. Peter Carroll pointedly makes the same statement about the Americans: 'No official in the Communist Party ever ordered anyone to go to Spain.' Carroll, *The Odyssey of the Abraham Lincoln Brigade*, p. 66.
40  L. B. Shelmerdine, 'Britons in an "Un-British" War: Domestic Newspapers and the Participation of UK Nationals in the Spanish Civil War', p. 31.
41  Buchanan, *Britain and the Spanish Civil War*, p. 127.
42  Salamanca, PS-Aragón, R Carp. 7.
43  Anon, *In Spain with the International Brigade: A personal narrative*, p. 25.
44  For example, see the interview with Charles Bloom in which he states that 'we were offered nothing, and I will further state that when we were offered our salaries a lot of comrades refused to accept it.' Interview with Charles Bloom, IWMSA 992/6/3.
45  Buchanan, *Britain and the Spanish Civil War*, p. 127.
46  Watson and Corcoran, *An Inspiring Example*, p. 64.
47  Watkins, *Britain Divided*, p. 168.
48  See Corkhill and Rawnsley, *Road to Spain*, p. xii: 'Only one in eight of the volunteers was out of work at the time of leaving for Spain and many abandoned regular and sometimes well-paid employment.' And Shelmerdine, 'An "Un-British" War', p. 35: 'Whilst undoubtedly experience of unemployment was for many volunteers a formative influence, it had been estimated that more than 75 per cent of volunteers were actually in work at the time of their recruitment.'
49  For example, Bill Rust presents a straightforward analysis: 'Who were these men of the International Brigade, and why did they volunteer? For the most part they were workers, though some were intellectuals from the middle classes.' However, he does go on to admit that 'it would be a fruitful study to analyse the motives of each volunteer and the exact reasons which led him at a given moment to offer his services.' Rust, *Britons in Spain*, p. 6.
50  Interview with George Baker, cited in Francis, *Miners Against Fascism*, p. 213.
51  Miles Tomalin's unpublished diary, cited in Thomas, *Spanish Civil War*, p. 455.
52  Buchanan, *Britain and the Spanish Civil War*, pp. 127–128.
53  As Hywel Francis notes: 'The Civil War was merely a defensive action to save a bourgeois Popular Front Government from fascism and a struggle for national independence.' Francis, *Miners Against Fascism*, p. 210.
54  Interview with Jud Colman, IWMSA 14575/3.
55  Alexander, *British Volunteers*, pp. 30–31.
56  Romilly, *Boadilla*, p. 50.
57  Ibid., p. 22.
58  At the same time, of course, the rebels referred to the opponents as *Los Rojos*, 'the Reds'.
59  *News Chronicle*, 2 September 1936, p. 2. Most volunteers saw the war as 'the anti-fascist war', rather than as a civil war.
60  Thus there was little quarter given to the enemy. There is no doubt that many of those in the rebel army were neither fascists nor even supporters of the Nationalist cause. Many were victims of the geographical division of Spain and left with little choice but to fight. Nevertheless, Bill Alexander is scathing of George Orwell's refusal to shoot at a rebel soldier with his trousers down, for, Alexander claims, 'this man . . . might have fired machine guns to butcher 4,000 in the Badajoz bullring.' Bill Alexander, 'George Orwell and Spain', p. 97.
61  R. Benewick, *The Fascist Movement in Britain*, p. 301.
62  Alexander, *British Volunteers*, p. 30.
63  Interview with Sam Wild, in Corkhill and Rawnsley, *Road to Spain*, pp. 18–19.
64  Introduction by Jack Jones in Cook, *Apprentices of Freedom*, pp. vii–ix.
65  As Mussolini himself admitted, fascist ideology needed to be flexible: 'The ideology aimed to be pragmatic.' Thus fascism can be seen as an ideology without a political

theory, 'completely wanting in ideological concepts'. Zeev Sternhell, 'Fascist Ideology', in Walter Laqueur, ed., *Fascism – A Reader's Guide*, pp. 315–316 and p. 319.

66  *The Times*, 24 October 1936, p. 13.

67  Interview with David Goodman, in Corkhill and Rawnsley, *Road to Spain*, p. 95.

68  Hynes, 'The British Battalion of the XVth International Brigade', p. 40.

69  Gurney, *Crusade in Spain*, p. 36.

70  As Lloyd Edmonds, an Australian attached to the transport unit of the 14th and later the 15th International Brigade, remarked: 'The war here is the one that will decide the history of Spain and of Europe for the next few years. If the myth of fascist invincibility is destroyed, ordinary folks can sleep quiet.' Edmonds, *Letters from Spain*, p. 172.

71  For example, more than 20 Welsh volunteers, including the political commissars Harry Dobson and Will Paynter, had served prison terms for political activities. Francis, *Miners Against Fascism*, p. 193. Wilf McCartney, the first commander of the British Battalion, had recently served a term in prison for supplying secrets to the Russians. Alexander, *British Volunteers*, p. 65.

72  Leaders of the 'Co-ordinating Committee for Anti-fascist Activity', formed on 25 July 1936 at Conway Hall, in Red Lion Square, London, called on all members of the working class to demonstrate at Mosley's next meeting in Hyde Park in September. The Labour Party executive and the TUC General Council called for their affiliated bodies to have nothing to do with the counter-demonstration. Noreen Branson, *History of the Communist Party of Great Britain 1927–1941*, p. 121.

73  Interview with Wally Togwell, in Hynes, 'British Battalion', p. 27.

74  Interview with Joe Garber, IWMSA 14277/4.

75  Interview with Charles Goodman, IWMSA 16612/4.

76  *Daily Worker*, 9 June 1936, p. 3.

77  'Very brave – high political development. Best Bn. Commissar in Brigade. Work among Spanish very weak in Bn. Very party conscience [*sic*]'. Unsigned, probably by Bill Rust. Moscow 545/6/118, p. 34.

78  Cook, *Apprentices of Freedom*, p. 19.

79  The *Daily Worker* frequently carried stories alleging that the police were not even-handed in their treatment of members of the BUF and those opposing them. Whilst the anti-fascist demonstration at Cable Street is the best-known example, others, such as the rally at the Albert Hall in March 1936, also produced outraged coverage over several days. See 'Crowds Tussle with Police', *Daily Worker*, 23 March 1936, p. 1, 'Police Violence Against Prisoner Alleged', 24 March 1936, p. 1, and 'Protest in Commons', 31 March 1936, p. 1.

80  Gregory, *The Shallow Grave*, p. 178.

81  A. J. P. Taylor, *English History 1914–1945*, p. 395. In another of his works, Taylor explained how 'It was universally believed at the time that this Rebellion was the next stage in a deliberate Fascist strategy of conquest – Abyssinia the first step; reoccupation of the Rhineland the next; and now Spain. The Spanish rebels were supposed to be puppets of the two Fascist dictators.' Taylor, *The Origins of the Second World War*, p. 156.

82  Interview with Bob Cooney, in Cook, *Apprentices of Freedom*, p. 148.

83  Watson and Corcoran, *An Inspiring Example*, p. 29.

84  For the British labour movement's responses to the civil war in Spain, see Jim Fyrth, *The Signal Was Spain*, and two works by Tom Buchanan: *The British Labour Movement and the Spanish Civil War* and *Britain and the Spanish Civil War*.

85  Buchanan, *Britain and the Spanish Civil War*, p. 93.

86  In two letters to Harry Pollitt, dated 29 March and 3 April 1937, Fred Copeman states: 'We send you four of our best comrades, although at this time we can do with every available man in the line. We feel that it is of the utmost importance that the British working-class be given the news direct from men of the Battalion.' NMLH Manchester, CP/IND/POLL/2/5-6. See also Alexander, *British Volunteers*, pp. 137–138.

87  Whether or not the numerous organisations raising aid for Spain constitute 'a movement' is a matter of some contention. For this debate, see Buchanan, 'Britain's Popular Front?'

and *Britain and the Spanish Civil War*, and Jim Fyrth, 'The Aid Spain Movement in Britain 1936–1939'.

88   In 1939, 1,100 people were asked on what they based their opinions. Over a third, by far the largest proportion, said newspapers. The basis of opinion was: newspapers 35 per cent; friends 17 per cent; radio 13 per cent; 'own opinion' 8 per cent; recent history or travel 8 per cent; books 5 per cent; other factors 10 per cent; negative 4 per cent. Charles Madge and Tom Harrisson, *Britain by Mass Observation*, p. 30.

89   In the main, the reporting of the war in the British press infuriated the British volunteers in Spain. Whilst the *Daily Worker* and *News Chronicle* could be relied upon to put across the Republican line, including regular attacks on the 'farce' of non-intervention, most could not. Both William Forrest of the *News Chronicle* and Sefton Delmer of the *Daily Express* visited the battalion in April 1938. They were popular with the volunteers because they 'could be relied upon for their authentic reporting, in contrast to so much unfounded, ill-informed and partial rubbish which all too often passed for objective coverage of the war in the British press.' Gregory, *The Shallow Grave*, p. 114.

90   George Orwell, 'Looking back on the Spanish War', in *The Penguin Complete Longer Non-Fiction of George Orwell*, p. 478. Stephen Spender also criticised the 'heroics' printed in many left-wing newspapers. See *New Statesman and Nation*, 1 May 1937, pp. 714–715.

91   Supporters of both parties in the civil war accused the British press of biased coverage in favour of their opponents. Brian Crozier, a Nationalist sympathiser, was just as critical of the coverage of the war: 'The dreadful fact is that the reporting of the war in the Western press was overwhelmingly pro-Republican and indelibly coloured by Comintern fabrications.' Toynbee, *The Distant Drum*, p. 59.

92   Shelmerdine, 'An "Un-British" War', p. 30. The *Daily Worker* was the one exception to this consensus.

93   Though still a regional newspaper, the *Manchester Guardian* was regarded by many as a national, despite a circulation even lower than that of the *Daily Worker*.

94   Gannon, *The British Press*, p. 40.

95   The reporting of the 'rising' in Barcelona in early May 1937 provides a good example of how the *News Chronicle* often uncritically reported the Communist Party line. John Langdon-Davies, writing in the paper on 10 May 1937, p. 5, described the event as 'a frustrated POUM putsch', though events had clearly been instigated by the attempted eviction by force of members of the Confederación Nacional del Trabajo from the Barcelona telephone exchange. However, it should be said that Claude Cockburn/Frank Pitcairn's reporting in the *Daily Worker* made the often blinkered coverage in the *News Chronicle* seem positively benign by comparison. See, for example, 'Pitcairn Lifts Barcelona Veil', *Daily Worker*, 11 May 1937, p. 1, which claimed that German and Italian agents, 'in cooperation with the local Trotskyists', were preparing 'a situation of disorder and bloodshed'. Pitcairn went on to state that: 'The POUM, acting in cooperation with well known criminal elements . . . planned, organised and led the attacks in the rearguard, accurately timed to coincide with the attack on the front at Bilbao . . . In the plainest terms the POUM declares it is the enemy of the People's Govt.' See also James Pettifer, ed., *Cockburn in Spain*, pp. 182–188.

96   John Langdon-Davies, *Behind the Spanish Barricades*, and Arthur Koestler, *Spanish Testament*. Koestler describes how he deliberately contrived atrocity stories as part of the propaganda campaign. Koestler, *Invisible Writing*, pp. 333–335.

97   See, for example, 'Behind the Censorship in Spain', which describes how 'what is going on in Spain is extremely important for the rest of the world.' *News Chronicle*, 20 July 1936, p. 8.

98   'What the Fall of Irun means to Spain and Us', *News Chronicle*, 7 September 1936, p. 1.

99   Corkhill and Rawnsley, *Road to Spain*, p. 30.

100  Interview with Dougal Eggar, IWMSA 9426/4/3.

101  *News Chronicle*, 7 April 1938, p. 10.

102  Alexander, *British Volunteers*, p. 44.

103 Interview with Jud Colman, IWMSA 14575/3.

104 See, for example, Stanley Harrison, *Good to be Alive: The Story of Jack Brent*, p. 6.

105 This was 14 October 1936, when the front page was taken over by reports of the Communist Party conference, in particular a long statement by Harry Pollitt.

106 The news to vie with the abdication was 'Loyalists Advance Six Miles', *Daily Worker*, 11 December 1936, p. 1.

107 *Daily Worker*, 19 February 1936, p. 5.

108 See, for example, 'Ralph Fox Killed in Action', *Daily Worker*, 5 January 1937, p. 1.

109 See, for example, *Daily Worker*, 15 May 1936, p. 5.

110 'Look I'm Rich', *Daily Worker*, 11 November 1936, p. 1.

111 'You Should Join the Communist Party', *Daily Worker*, 8 April 1936, p. 4.

112 *Daily Worker*, 10 July 1936, p. 4.

113 Ibid.

114 *Daily Worker*, 23 July 1936, p. 2.

115 'How Atrocity Stories Are Faked', *Daily Worker*, 18 August 1936, p. 4. The paper repeatedly denied the stories of church burnings and killing of nuns and clergy, enrolling luminaries such as Dr Montessori and various members of the church to support their claims. See *Daily Worker*, 11 August 1936, p. 4, and 'I Saw Nuns Quietly Sewing', *Daily Worker*, 15 August 1936, p. 5. Indeed, Pitcairn later wrote how it was in fact the rebels who were murdering clergy, not the Republicans. See 'Fascists Murder Pastors in Spain', *Daily Worker*, 17 October 1936, p. 3.

116 See 'Communists to Fore', *Daily Worker*, 24 July 1936, p. 5, and 'How Communists Saved Spain', *Daily Worker*, 11 August 1936, p. 5.

117 See, for example, John Strachey's weekly column 'Looking at the News' on 5 January 1937, cited in Francis, *Miners Against Fascism*, p. 162. 'An ever growing stream of British workers is leaving this country to join the Column. Are we doing enough to support them? We cannot do too much.'

118 'Democracy v Fascism', *Daily Worker*, 5 August 1936, p. 4.

119 *Daily Worker*, 28 August 1936, p. 1.

120 'You Can Help Spain's Wounded with Bandages', *Daily Worker*, 20 October 1936, p. 7.

121 '"Neutrality" Farce Drags On', *Daily Worker*, 21 October 1936, p. 1.

122 For two conflicting assessments of the extent of British aid for the Spanish Republic, see Fyrth, *The Signal Was Spain*, and Buchanan, *The British Labour Movement*.

123 'I wasn't interested in politics at all until the rise of Hitler and when Mosley came into the picture in England . . . There were people from the Manchester area who we know personally, that were in Spain, but nobody from my branch. We took a big part in the Youth Foodship for Spain Campaign.' Interview with Josh Davidson, in Corkhill and Rawnsley, *Road to Spain*, p. 159.

124 'Medical Unit "a Godsend"', *Daily Worker*, 12 September 1936, p. 1.

125 Skoutelsky, 'French Combatants of the International Brigades', p. 7.

126 'English Sculptress Killed in Spain', *Daily Worker*, 4 September 1936, p. 5.

127 *Daily Worker*, 9 November 1936, p. 1.

128 'Men of Four Nations Stem Advance', *Daily Worker*, 12 November 1936, p. 1.

129 'How Madrid Dug in its Heels – and Struck Back', *Daily Worker*, 21 November 1936, p. 2.

130 *Daily Worker*, 24 November 1936, p. 1.

131 'Support Them', *Daily Worker*, 2 December 1936, p. 1.

132 See, for example, 'Italian Troops Land in Spain', *Daily Worker*, 7 December 1936, p. 1, and 'Italian Troops for Franco – Army Pilots Promised 20,000 lire Salary', *Daily Worker*, 9 December 1936, p. 3.

133 'Spain – A Second Abyssinia', *Daily Worker*, 22 August 1936, p. 4.

134 'German Troops March on Madrid', *Daily Worker*, 2 December 1936, p. 1, and 'Nazi Legions Join Franco', 5 December 1936, p. 1, which reported how '20,000 German troops are reliably reported to have reached Spain to fight for the fascist rebels.'

135  Whilst estimates of German aid to the rebels vary greatly, from *c.*17,000 in Thomas, *Spanish Civil War*, p. 985, to 'some 50,000', in Alexander, *British Volunteers*, p. 22, there is little doubt that the reports in the *Daily Worker* of thousands of German troops involved in the attack on Madrid are false.

136  Corkhill and Rawnsley, *Road to Spain*, p. 37.

137  Ibid., pp. 42–43.

138  Interview with James Brown, ibid., pp. 48–49.

139  'Britain's Answer to 20,000 Nazi Troops', *Daily Worker*, 5 December 1936, p. 3.

140  'British Unit Tops 300', *Daily Worker*, 12 December 1936, p. 1.

141  'British Fighters Now Pouring into Spain', *Daily Worker*, 15 December 1936, p. 1.

142  'British Best of Battalion', *Daily Worker*, 13 December 1936, p. 1.

143  *Daily Worker*, 19 December 1936, p. 1.

144  *Daily Worker*, 21 December 1936, p. 1.

145  *Daily Worker*, 23 December 1936, p. 1.

146  *Daily Worker*, 24 December 1936, p. 1.

147  *Daily Worker*, 28 December 1936, p. 5.

148  Hugo Dewar, *Communist Politics in Britain: The CPGB from its Origins to the Second World War*, p. 109.

149  Many of the British volunteers hailed from 'Red Rhondda', including influential figures such as the political commissars Will Paynter and Harry Dobson, plus Billy Griffiths, the battalion party secretary in the summer and autumn of 1938.

150  Stevenson and Cook, *Britain in the Depression*, p. 154.

151  The Americans numbered approximately 2,600, plus perhaps 150 more who served in Republican medical units. Carroll, *Odyssey*, pp. 13–14.

152  Dewar, *Communist Politics in Britain*, pp. 121–122. John Strachey penned a regular feature in the paper, 'Looking at the News'.

153  Branson, *History of the Communist Party*, p. 214.

154  Stevenson and Cook, *Britain in the Depression*, p. 155.

155  Hopkins, *Into the Heart*, pp. 119–120.

156  Interview with Len Crome, IWMSA 9298/4/1.

157  Hopkins, *Into the Heart*, p. 211.

158  Ronald Blythe, *The Age of Illusion*, p. 115.

159  Stevenson and Cook, *Britain in the Depression*, p. 163.

160  Hynes, 'British Battalion', p. 17. See also, Francis, *Miners Against Fascism*, pp. 80–81, which outlines the connection between the NUWM and Spain. Four of the leaders of the march which left South Wales for London later fought in Spain: Tim Harrington, D. R. Llewellyn, Will Paynter and J. S. Williams.

161  Interview with Lance Rogers, South Wales Miners' Library, cited in Francis, *Miners Against Fascism*, p. 161.

162  Hopkins, *Into the Heart*, p. 107.

163  Alexander, *British Volunteers*, p. 37.

164  IBA Box 39, File A/29.

165  Cook, *Apprentices of Freedom*, p. 25.

166  Interview with Frank Graham, IWMSA 11877/6/1.

167  Interview with Sidney Quinn, IWMSA 801/3/1.

168  Watson and Corcoran, *An Inspiring Example*, p. 53.

169  Ibid., p. 64.

170  Interview with Sidney Quinn, IWMSA 801/1/1, and Cook, *Apprentices of Freedom*, pp. 17–18.

171  Hugh Sloan, 'Why I Volunteered', p. 31.

172  Lipman, *Social History of the Jews in England 1850–1950*, pp. 84–87.

173  Stevenson and Cook, *Britain in the Depression*, p. 144.

174  As Kevin Morgan points out, 'The SWMF was, perhaps, the most political of all British unions, and during the Spanish Civil War – the Colliers Crusade – the South Wales

miners demonstrated a sense of urgency and commitment unequalled elsewhere in Britain.' Morgan, *Against Fascism and War: Ruptures and Continuities in British Communist Politics 1935–1941*, p. 135.

175 See *Daily Worker*, 13 July and 7 and 9 December 1936, and Francis, *Miners Against Fascism*, p. 94.
176 Ibid., p. 94.
177 Stevenson and Cook, *Britain in the Depression*, p. 157.
178 Francis, 'Welsh Miners and the Spanish Civil War', p. 179.
179 'Miners Bomb Fascists', *Daily Worker*, 11 August 1936, p. 1.
180 'Welsh Miners Want Aid for Spain', *Daily Worker*, 3 September 1936, p. 1.
181 Francis, *Miners Against Fascism*, p. 107.
182 Corkhill and Rawnsley, *Road to Spain*, pp. 147–149.
183 Stradling, *The Irish and the Spanish Civil War*, p. 140.
184 Romilly, *Boadilla*, pp. 40–41.
185 Interview with Phil Gillan, IWMSA 12150/4/1.
186 Corkhill and Rawnsley, *Road to Spain*, p. 8.
187 Interview with Jud Colman, IWMSA 14575/3/1.
188 The sculptor Felicia Browne, the first British volunteer to be killed in Spain, was already painting in Spain. See the following chapter.
189 Ibid.
190 Tom Buchanan, 'A Far Away Country of Which We Know Nothing?', p. 3.
191 Interview with Leslie Preger, in Corkhill and Rawnsley, *Road to Spain*, p. 30.
192 Soviet War Veterans' Committee, *International Solidarity with the Spanish Republic, 1936–1939*, p. 64 and Wintringham, *English Captain*, p. 26.
193 Alexander, *British Volunteers*, p. 41.
194 Watson and Corcoran, *An Inspiring Example*, p. 64.
195 Thomas, *Spanish Civil War*, p. 606, and Brome, *The International Brigades*, pp. 18–20. See also the following chapter.
196 The others were Joseph, who fought with the Americans, and David, known in Spain as Danny. IBA Box D-7, Files A/1 and A/2.
197 Interview with Walter Greenhalgh, IWMSA 10356/3/1.
198 IBA Box D-7, File A/2, and see Chapter 4.
199 Ian MacDougall, 'Tom Murray: Veteran of Spain', p. 16.
200 Ibid.
201 IBA Box D-7, File A/1, Box C, File 1/2a, and interview with Anne Murray, IWMSA 11318/2/1–2.
202 Cook, *Apprentices of Freedom*, p. 25.
203 Alexander, *British Volunteers*, p. 41.
204 Angus, *With the International Brigade*, p. 2.
205 Ibid.
206 Interview with David Marshall, IWMSA 9330/4/1.
207 Ibid.
208 Cook, *Apprentices of Freedom*, p. 32.
209 Corkhill and Rawnsley, *Road to Spain*, pp. 101–102.
210 Ibid., pp. 138–139.
211 Eluard Luchelle McDaniels from Mississippi, cited in Carroll, *Odyssey*, p. 18.

## 3 Madrid, 1936: manning the Spanish barricades

1 Esmond Romilly, *Boadilla*, p. 51.
2 Preston, *A Concise History of the Spanish Civil War*, p. 89.
3 John Tunnah, a postman from Edinburgh who served in Spain from November 1936 to May 1937, stated that 'the earlier people tended to be more intellectual than those who came later.' Interview with John Tunnah, IWMSA 840/9/3. Likewise, Bill Alexander says

of the early volunteers: 'The early units contained a high proportion of intellectuals. They proved to be less tolerant, at first, than workers from the factory floor, of unexplained delays, of incomprehensible orders from above, and of other such irritations which regular soldiers regard as quite normal.' Alexander, *British Volunteers for Liberty*, p. 54.

4  IBA Box 21, File A, Box D-7, File A/2; Alexander, *British Volunteers*, p. 43; Romilly, *Boadilla*, pp. 40–31; and Keith Scott Watson, *Single to Spain*, p. 36.

5  Alexander, *British Volunteers*, p. 36. A good example of this myth is the description by a British volunteer who later stated that: 'The men of the International Brigades were, for the most part, intellectuals and numbered many scholars amongst them; it was common for them to be proficient in four or five languages besides holding high degrees in science, the law and a multitude of other subjects.' Interview with John Anthony Myers, in the *West London Observer*, 24 February 1939, p. 5.

6  The age profile of the early volunteers also differs considerably from that of those who arrived in Spain after Christmas 1936. The average age was just under 25 years, with the most common age being 20 years. This compares with 29 years and 23 years respectively for the British volunteers as a whole. Source of age data: IBA D-7, File A/2, and Moscow 545/6/91.

7  See IBA Box A15. For Felicia Browne, see Tom Buchanan, 'The Lost Art of Felicia Browne'.

8  Bennett went to work for Barcelona Radio, the voice of the Partido Socialista Unifacado de Cataluña (PSUC), the Catalan socialist party. Alexander, *British Volunteers*, p. 51.

9  Cornford returned to Spain with six other volunteers in mid-October, when he joined the 11th International Brigade. The group was formed into the No. 4 Section of the Machine-Gun Company of the Commune de Paris Battalion.

10  After being wounded, Cohen was repatriated to Britain, Tom Wintringham claims in November 1936, Alexander in April 1937. Wintringham, *English Captain*, p. 41, and Alexander, *British Volunteers*, p. 46. Masters was killed at Brunete in July 1937. IBA Box 21, File A, and Box D-7, File A/1.

11  These were Richard Kisch, Tony Willis and Paul Boyle. IBA Box C, File 5/2.

12  Ibid.

13  See Thomas, *The Spanish Civil War*, 3rd edn, pp. 381–383, and Alexander, *British Volunteers*, p. 51.

14  In a letter Harry Pollitt on 5 September 1936, Tom Wintringham asks Pollitt to 'look after this boy and use your well-known disciplinary powers to make him look after himself for a bit.' IBA Box C, File 5/2. See also Richard Kisch, *They Shall Not Pass*.

15  Interview with David Marshall, IWMSA 9330/1/2.

16  Marshall had little good to say about Keith Scott Watson, who, he claimed, had only 'come for the sensation . . . certainly he was a shit and he pissed off quickly.' Interview with David Marshall, IWMSA 9330/4/1. Esmond Romilly was rather more tactful, but believed Watson was 'over-cynical' and did not take any of the rules and regulations seriously enough. Romilly, *Boadilla*, p. 43. Watson puts his side of the story in his memoir, though he readily admits that he found the discipline of the communists too much for him. Regular arguments with the 'orthodox' Lorimer Birch meant that 'I began to take the war less and less seriously.' Watson, *Single to Spain*, p. 53.

17  Bill Rust recounts that the attempt 'did not come off as he had just explained the real role of the Communists. The fellow is just poison.' Letter to Harry Pollitt, 26 May 1938, IBA Box C, File 22/6.

18  Alexander, *British Volunteers*, p. 52.

19  IBA Box C, File 5/4, and Alexander, *British Volunteers*, p. 52.

20  IBA Box C, File 5/4.

21  Interview with David Marshall, IWMSA 9330/1/2.

22  Phil Gillan was the 'Jock' referred to in Esmond Romilly's *Boadilla*.

23  Interview with Phil Gillan, IWMSA 12150/4/1.

24  They were: Albert Bentley, a seaman, George Middleton and John Beale, both students,

Bruce Campbell, Sid Morton and a Scot, David Mackie. See James Albrighton's diary, IBA Box 50, File L.

25  Pat O'Malley and Frank O'Connor from Dublin, Sidney Lloyd Jones from Wales, John Henderson and Frank Garland from London and the South-East, and Michael Harris from Birmingham. Ibid.

26  Ibid. The only other diaries to have appeared are by Ralph Cantor(ovitch), who died fighting with the British Battalion at Brunete in July 1937, and Fred Thomas, a member of the British Anti-Tank Battery. See Cantor diary, WCML, Manchester, and Thomas, *To Tilt at Windmills: A Memoir of the Spanish Civil War*. Hugh Sloan, another member of the battery, also kept a diary, but had to leave it behind during the Aragon retreats in the spring of 1938. Interview with Hugh Sloan, in MacDougall, *Voices from the Spanish Civil War*, p. 227. However, questions remain over the veracity of Albrighton's account. For example, in the questionnaire he completed when he later joined the International Brigade, he makes no reference at all to his time spent in the centuria in 1936. See Moscow 545/6/101. No International Brigader I have spoken to recalls meeting Albrighton in Spain, though there is some evidence of his being there: his Spanish ID card, showing the date of entry into the country (2 August 1936) and a photograph of him in Spain are held in the WCML in Manchester, and a photograph of him in Spain taken later in the war and his name are in a file held in Moscow. Moscow 545/6/39.

27  Bill Alexander's work is the only one to include a reference to Albrighton. See Alexander, *British Volunteers*, p. 53. The role of Albrighton and his comrades in the Muerte es Maestro has been largely overlooked. According to correspondence between Albrighton and Alexander held in the IBA, his diary was not typed up until the early 1980s. See IBA Box 50, File Al/1–8.

28  Official histories of the International Brigades have, not surprisingly, played down accounts of executions. In later correspondence with Bill Alexander, James Albrighton asks whether to include any mention of executions in which the MM Centuria were involved in his diary: 'I have now typed out the few cases in which the MM company was involved and will appreciate it if you will after reading these extracts from my diaries advise me if you think it would be best for me to delete them or retain them.' IBA Box 50, File Al/5. Bill Alexander's reply is not enclosed, but Albrighton's following letter clearly illuminates Alexander's reluctance to face these rather awkward issues: 'I appreciate your advice regarding the performance of some of MM's "Special Duties", your comments were very much what had been going through my own mind and it has been for that reason that I have been rather reluctant to write about them.' IBA Box 50, File Al/6.

29  Alexander, *British Volunteers*, p. 53.

30  Photographs of the victims were later used in Republican propaganda to demonstrate the vicious nature of the Nationalists. This was the basis of the 'If you tolerate this, your children will be next' poster (and the song by the Manic Street Preachers) that appears on the rear cover of Colin Williams, Bill Alexander and John Gorman, *Memorials of the Spanish Civil War*.

31  Albrighton recalls that this bombing made a deep impact on the Republican forces to the south of Madrid. For some time after the bombing an oft-heard battle cry was 'Recuerdos Getafe.' Albrighton diary, 30 October 1936.

32  Jan Kurzke, a German volunteer who fought with H. Fred Jones and the other British in the 11 International Brigade in the University City, later recalled the bemusement created by the volunteers' international origins. The volunteers were welcomed by Spaniards crying, '"Viva la democracia." "Viva Rusia." "Where are you from?" someone shouted. "London" we shouted back, "Paris, Marseille, Warsaw." "But Russia," they cried, "Are you not from Russia?" They seemed baffled by our "No."' Kurzke, MS, p. 8.

33  Albrighton diary, 9 November 1936.

34  'Walter' was yet another pseudonym. His real name was Świerczewski and he later became the commander of the 35 Republican Division. For Walter's role in Spain, see Len Crome, 'Walter, 1897–1947: A Soldier in Spain'.

35  A decree formalising this was published later on 22 October. Alexander, *British Volunteers*, p. 53.
36  Moscow 33987/3/832, cited in Ronald Radosh, Mary M. Habeck and Grigory Sevostianov, eds, *Spain Betrayed: The Soviet Union in the Spanish Civil War*, p. 104.
37  Several observers, such as the *New York Times* journalist Herbert L. Matthews and the Soviet journalist Mikhail Koltzov, have suggested that Miaja was anything but the courageous and determined figure of his reputation and that, on the contrary, he was 'weak, unintelligent [and] unprincipled'. Certainly, rebel generals such as Franco and Quiepo de Llano considered him an 'incompetent coward'. Preston, *Concise History*, p. 130.
38  Cox, *The Defence of Madrid*, p. 106.
39  'Kleber' was a pseudonym for Lazar or Manfred Stern, a Hungarian with a colourful history. See Thomas, *Spanish Civil War*, p. 459.
40  Rust, *Britons in Spain*, p. 22.
41  Interview with Sam Russell, IWMSA 9484/2.
42  Bernard Knox, *Essays Ancient and Modern*, p. 267.
43  Interview with Sam Russell, IWMSA 9484/2.
44  Jan Kurzke, MS, p. 15. The five British scorning the use of political commissars included H. Fred Jones, who was to command the contingent at Madrid, where he was killed, and Jock Cunningham and Joe Hinks, later to be commanders of the British Battalion. Kurzke described the final two as 'George [possibly Sowersby], a pale thin young man with a red beard which made him look like Christ, and Pat [T. Patton], a young Irishman.'
45  Russell, whose real name was Manassa Lesser, was repatriated to Britain after the battle of Jarama in February 1937. He returned to Spain as *Daily Worker* correspondent, where he succeeded Peter Kerrigan, and as the British Communist Party representative.
46  Interview with Sam Russell, IWMSA 9484/6/2.
47  Knox, *Essays Ancient and Modern*, p. 266.
48  Interview with Sam Russell, IWMSA 9484/6/6.
49  John Sommerfield, *Volunteer in Spain*, p. 31.
50  Knox, *Essays Ancient and Modern*, p. 263. Later arrivals from Britain would also criticise the level of training, as indeed did General Walter, the commander of the 35th Division. 'A month ago I was with the English and Canadian battalions of the 15th Brigade. It is difficult to convey in words the state of weapons and how dirty, especially the rifles. The bores of their barrels were not much different from a seventeenth-century musket barrel found at Belchite. No fewer than 95 per cent of the rifles had no bayonet or cleaning rod, all lost since time immemorial. There was only a handful of cleaning rags in the brigade.' But Walter went on to state that the 15th Brigade improved dramatically after Teruel, 'That the 15th sometimes seems completely different from what it was a short time ago.' Report by General Walter, commander of the 35th Division, 14 January 1938, Moscow 35082/1/95, cited in Radosh *et al.*, *Spain Betrayed*, pp. 440–444. However, not all volunteers feel that the training was insufficient. Jack Edwards, a CP activist in Liverpool, arrived in Spain with no military experience, yet believed his training at Madrigueras, supervised by Joe Harding who had served in the British Army for ten years, was, in the circumstances, very good. When Edwards later volunteered for the RAF during the Second World War, his proficiency with a rifle was noted by an NCO, who was somewhat puzzled by Edwards's claim that he had never served in the military. Interview with Jack Edwards, IWMSA 808/3/2.
51  Bernard Knox, who witnessed the arrival of the volunteers, claims that the descriptions of the march down the Gran Via that appeared in the contemporary newspapers are mostly wrong. He believes that they were getting confused with the arrival of the 12th International Brigade a few days later. Knox, *Essays Ancient and Modern*, p. 256.
52  This was where the battalion spent 'the night by the lonely river' described by John Sommerfield. On the other side of the River Manzanares was the estate, which the Army of African soldiers had occupied. Sommerfield, *Volunteer in Spain*, pp. 113–121.
53  Ibid., p. 43.

54 Alexander, *British Volunteers*, p. 57, and IBA Box 21a, File A.
55 Hearst, MS, pp. 160–161; IBA Box 21a, File A; and Alexander, *British Volunteers*, p. 57.
56 Thomas, *Spanish Civil War*, p. 481.
57 'Freddie' was actually the leader of the British section, H. Fred Jones, a communist who had served in the Grenadier Guards. Kurzke, MS, p. 57.
58 Sommerfield, *Volunteer in Spain*, pp. 135–139.
59 Ibid., p. 139.
60 Here Knox met the first leader of the International Brigades, General Kleber, the 'Russian' (who was actually Hungarian and whose real name was Stern) who managed to get their obsolete and dangerous French St Etienne machine-guns replaced with Lewis guns. Knox, *Premature Anti-Fascist*, p. 7.
61 Alexander, *British Volunteers*, p. 58
62 Rust, *Britons in Spain*, p. 22.
63 Romilly, *Boadilla*, pp. 44–45.
64 Romilly differentiated himself from those volunteers he termed 'Real Communists', such as John Cornford and Lorimer Birch. A 'Real Communist', he claimed, could be defined as 'A serious person, a rigid disciplinarian, a member of the Communist Party, interested in all the technical aspects of warfare, and lacking in any such selfish motive as fear or reckless courage.' Ibid., p. 64.
65 Interview with Chris Thornycroft, IWMSA 12932/3/1.
66 Romilly, *Boadilla*, p. 66.
67 Ibid., p. 72.
68 In Romilly's account of these skirmishes he changes the names of many of the villages caught up in the fighting. It seems likely that the village he refers to as Melilla was in reality Villaconejos, which is roughly 10 miles south of Madrid.
69 Alexander, *British Volunteers*, p. 54.
70 Interview with David Marshall, IWMSA 9330/4/2.
71 Chris Thornycroft soon became the Battalion armourer, for, as Romilly recounts, he was 'a first rate technician'. Thornycroft repaired machine-guns for the Thaelmann Battalion, who refused to allow him to become an ordinary militiaman. Romilly, *Boadilla*, p. 138, and interview with Chris Thornycroft, IWMSA 12932/3/1.
72 Interview with Phil Gillan, in McDougall, *Voices*, p. 15.
73 Interview with David Marshall, IWMSA 9330/4/2-3, and Alexander, *British Volunteers*, p. 60.
74 Romilly, *Boadilla*, p. 143.
75 Rust, *Britons in Spain*, p. 22.
76 Kurzke, MS, p. 103.
77 Knox, *Premature Anti-Fascist*, p. 9.
78 Romilly, *Boadilla*, p. 191; letter dated 4 January 1937 from Peter Kerrigan to Harry Pollitt, NMLH Manchester, CP/IND/POLL/2/5-6.
79 Romilly, *Boadilla*, p. 191.
80 'Nazi Troops Kill Six Britons In Madrid', *Daily Worker*, 28 December 1936, p. 1.
81 Interview with Phil Gillan, IWMSA 12150/4/4.
82 'On Leave from Spain', *Irish Times*, 4 January 1937, p. 3. A photograph of the two back in Britain was taken at the *Daily Worker* offices on 9 January 1937. IBA Box A2, File A/3.
83 'They fight with the International Column', *News Chronicle*, 21 December 1936, p. 8.
84 See, for example, Thomas, *Spanish Civil War*, p. 480. 'The example of the International Brigades fired the populace of the capital with the feeling that they were not alone.'
85 Richardson, *Comintern Army*, p. 61.
86 'It has been argued that the International Brigades saved Madrid . . . This 11th International Brigade, however, comprised only about 1,900 men. The 12th International Brigade, which arrived on the Madrid front on the 13th November, comprised about 1,550. This force was too small to have turned the day by numbers alone. Furthermore, the Republican Army had checked Varela on 7th November, before the arrival of the

Brigade . . . The bravery and experience of the Brigades was, however, crucial in several later battles.' The discovery of the rebel plans in the pocket of a Spanish officer found dead inside an Italian tank also played a part. Thomas, *Spanish Civil War*, pp. 477–480.

87  Interview with Phil Gillan, IWMSA 12150/4/2.

88  Knox, *Essays Ancient and Modern*, p. 260.

89  Wintringham, *English Captain*, p. 135.

90  Ibid. This view is supported by R. Dan Richardson, for example, who states that 'In all these battles the International Brigades played the major role.' Richardson, *Comintern Army*, p. 83.

91  IBA Box C, File 8/3.

92  Figure cited in a report from Peter Kerrigan to Harry Pollitt, undated, CP/IND/POLL/2/5–6, NMLH Manchester.

93  In fact, Nathan had a somewhat chequered past, which would later create political difficulties within the English-speaking battalion. See note 123 below.

94  Alexander, *British Volunteers*, p. 86.

95  Interview with Mike Economides, IWMSA 10428/5/2.

96  'The First British Company', *Volunteer for Liberty*, 2: 29, 13 August 1938, p. 4.

97  There are numerous examples of complaints from volunteers in No. 1 Company about the poor training and equipment. See, for example, interviews with Walter Greenhalgh, IWMSA 10356/3/1, and Joe Monks, IWMSA 11303/4/2. To make matters worse, the French Chauchat machine-guns were inherently unreliable and invariably jammed after one or two rounds had been fired. Alexander, *British Volunteers*, p. 87.

98  Interview with John Tunnah, IWMSA 840/9/5.

99  Report from Peter Kerrigan to Harry Pollitt, undated, NMLH Manchester, CP/IND/POLL/2/5-6.

100  Nathan estimated that, by 31 December, between 12 and 15 British had keen killed, 28 were wounded, and 12 had deserted. This reduced No. 1 Company to 82 men in the line, plus another 25 on guard duties. Ibid.

101  Interview with Walter Greenhalgh, IWMSA 11187/9/3-4.

102  Thomas, *Spanish Civil War*, p. 490.

103  Interview with Walter Greenhalgh, IWMSA 11187/9/4, and Alexander, *British Volunteers*, p. 88.

104  Kerrigan had an exceptional party pedigree: he studied at the Lenin School in Moscow from 1929 to 1930 and was a delegate to the Seventh World Congress of Comintern in 1935. He was heavily involved in the NUWM and acted as election agent for Willie Gallagher, the Communist Party's only MP, in Fife.

105  See Hopkins, *Into the Heart*, p. 421, n.90. However, Bill Alexander claims that he was accused of working for the French intelligence service. Alexander, *British Volunteers*, p. 88.

106  See Wintringham, *English Captain*, pp. 83–86 and Maurice Levine, *Cheetham to Cordova: Maurice Levine, A Manchester Man of the Thirties*, p. 36. Unfortunately Sid Quinn is able to shed little light on this issue. See interview with Sidney Quinn, IWMSA 801/3/1.

107  Albrighton's claims regarding Delasalle must be treated with scepticism. Albrighton also claims that Delasalle accusing Marty of being responsible for the deaths of hundreds of innocent members of the International Brigades. This seems somewhat unlikely, at least in December 1936, and, even if Marty had been responsible for the deaths of hundreds, Delasalle was in no position to have known about it. Albrighton diaries, IBA Box 50.

108  Interview with Walter Greenhalgh, IWMSA 11187/9/4.

109  Hopkins, *Into the Heart*, p. 421, n.93.

110  Interview with Joe Monks, IWMSA 11303/3/4.

111  Conversation with Richard Baxell, 10 March 2001.

112  'The boys were glad he was shot, that I'll say, that I'll say.' Interview with James Brown, IWMSA 824/5/3.

113  Alexander, *British Volunteers*, p. 88.

114  Interview with Walter Greenhalgh, IWMSA 11187/9/4.

115 Sollenberger had saved the lives of Esmond Romilly and 'Babs' Ovenden at Boadilla, not with his medical skills, but by picking up a rifle and covering their retreat. Alexander, *British Volunteers*, p. 61.

116 They were: Denis Coady from Ireland, James Hyndman and James Kermode, both from Scotland, James Knottman, one of many Manchester communists, Robert Coutts from North Shields, and George Palmer and H. Wise from London and the South-East.

117 Alexander, *British Volunteers*, p. 89.

118 IBA Box C, File 8/5.

119 Alexander, *British Volunteers*, p. 65.

120 Rust, *Britons in Spain*, p. 28.

121 Interview with John Dunlop, IWMSA 11355/13/4. How true this tale was is difficult to tell; churches and priests often featured as exponents or victims in atrocity stories told by both sides during the civil war.

122 Alexander, *British Volunteers*, p. 69. Thus Dave Springhall, the brigade commissar, was removed from his post 'because of his grave political mistake in helping the Irish section of the British Battalion to transfer to the American Battalion'. IBA Box C, File 1/77.

123 Nathan had served, probably as an auxiliary, with the Black and Tans in Ireland in the 1920s, and strong rumours linked him to involvement in a hit squad that in May 1921 murdered two prominent members of Sinn Féin; George Clancy, the former lord mayor of Limerick, and George O'Callaghan, the ex-mayor. See Richard Bennett, 'Portrait of a Killer'. According to Joe Monks, one of the Irish volunteers, Nathan admitted to having worked for British intelligence in Limerick. Interview with Joe Monks, IWMSA 11303/4/1. (However, as Kieron Punch points out, Irish hatred of Nathan has probably been exaggerated. During his time in Spain, Nathan gained the reputation as a brave, efficient and talented officer, which, for most volunteers, probably more than compensated for his murky past. Kieron Punch, 'Did Irish Recoil from a "Black and Tan" in the International Brigades?' Abraham Lincoln Brigade Archive, on-line posting, http://forums.nyu.edu. 6 December 2002.) McCartney was also rumoured to have served in the Black and Tans in Ireland. Richard Bennett, in *The Black and Tans*, p. 147, states that the Black and Tan auxiliaries 'used the Long Bar at the Trocadero as their headquarters, where they were advised by their ringleader, who later achieved a certain notoriety as a Soviet agent, to threaten to "blow the gaff" about conditions in Ireland.' This may be a reference to McCartney.

124 Hopkins, *Into the Heart*, p. 174.

125 Stradling, *The Irish and the Spanish Civil War*, p. 131, and Alexander, *British Volunteers*, pp. 68–69. For the background on Frank Ryan, see Seán Cronin, *Frank Ryan: The Search for the Republic*.

126 Joe Monks, a volunteer with a strong IRA background, later criticised both the name of the battalion and the title of Bill Alexander's book on the battalion. Monks felt that the volunteers were 'international' and should have been labelled as such. Interview with Joe Monks, IWMSA 11303/4/3.

127 Interview with John Tunnah, IWMSA 840/9/4.

128 'The friction that existed between the English and Irish was so great that the separation was welcome[d] by both groups.' Moscow 545/3/467, p. 20.

129 Ibid., p. 21.

130 Moscow 545/3/99, p. 8.

131 Alexander, *British Volunteers*, p. 36.

132 Ibid., p. 69.

133 Interview with Phil Gillan, IWMSA 12150/4/2.

134 Ibid.

135 Romilly, *Boadilla*, p. 86.

136 Interview with Phil Gillan, IWMSA 12150/4/2.

137 Interview with Walter Greenhalgh, IWMSA 10356/3/1.

138 Letter from H. O'Donnell to R. Robson, 8 January 1937. IBA Box C, File 9/5.

## 4  Cerca de Madrid, 1937: the battle of Jarama and 'the furnace of Brunete'

1  Interview with Frank McCusker in MacDougall, *Voices from the Spanish Civil War*, p. 43.
2  Also known as the 14 February Battalion.
3  Gal's real name was actually Janos Galicz. He was a naturalised Russian, born in Austro-Hungary. Thomas, *The Spanish Civil War*, 3rd edn, pp. 590–591, and Richardson, *Comintern Army*, p. 72.
4  Walter Gregory states of Čopić that, 'As an intelligent man with a good appreciation of the tactics and strategy of warfare, Čopić was ideally suited to take command of the brigade. His expertise, coupled with his popularity, assured him of our respect and admiration. Indeed, I cannot remember Čopić being the subject of criticism.' Gregory, *The Shallow Grave*, p. 58.
5  J. Delperrié de Bayac, *Les Brigades internationales, 1936–1938*, p. 226. Barthel had been the secretary of the Communist Party of Algeria before his arrival in Spain. Richardson, *Comintern Army*, p. 73.
6  Alexander, *British Volunteers for Liberty*, p. 65.
7  As John Halstead and Barry McGoughlin state, 'Of the 11 battalion political commissars in the 57th, British Battalion of the 15th Brigade, nine, if not all, had been sent to the ILS [International Lenin School in Moscow] or had worked in the Comintern bureaucracy in Moscow. They were, in chronological order: Douglas Springhall, George Aitken, Bert Williams, George Coyle, Jack Roberts, Ernest Torrance, James Bourne, Eric Whalley, Harry Dobson, Walter Tapsell and Bob Cooney.' John Halstead and Barry McLoughlin, 'British and Irish Students at the International Lenin School, Moscow, 1926–37', p. 3. Ralph Fox, the intellectual founder of the *Left Review*, with Tom Wintringham and the *Daily Worker* journalist who was killed at Lopera in December 1936 and other senior party figures, such as the brigade commissar Peter Kerrigan, had also studied at Moscow.
8  Figure quoted in a letter of 4 January 1937, from Peter Kerrigan to Harry Pollitt. NMLH Manchester, CP/IND/POLL/2/5-6.
9  According to Jud Colman, who had fought with No. 1 Company both at Las Rozas and at Lopera, the veterans of No. 1 Company were mainly kept together and became the brigade guard charged with guarding the headquarters, and thus didn't fight as much at Jarama as many other groups. 'I was very relieved. I'm not that sort of a hero. I'd be a fool if I was.' Interview with Jud Colman, IWMSA 14575/3/2.
10  Alexander, *British Volunteers*, p. 93. An estimate appearing in the *Daily Worker* in February 1937 put the number slightly higher, at 800. 'They Fight for Freedom', *Daily Worker*, 17 February 1937, p. 5. At least 30 earlier arrivals, including Richard Kisch, David Marshall, Esmond Romilly and 'Babs' Ovenden, had been sent home.
11  Hugh Thomas states that it was his leg rather than his arm that was injured by the bullet. Thomas, *Spanish Civil War*, p. 591, n.1
12  See, for example, interview with Walter Greenhalgh, IWMSA 11187/9/3.
13  Alexander, *British Volunteers*, p. 91.
14  Hopkins, *Into the Heart of the Fire*, p. 170.
15  On 4 January 1937, Peter Kerrigan wrote to Harry Pollitt that 'Com[rade] McCartney has been appointed Battalion commander and I feel it is a very good appointment.' NMLH Manchester, CP/IND/POLL/2/5-6.
16  IBA Box C, Files 9–10.
17  Interview with Fred Copeman, IWMSA 794/13/1.
18  Interview with George Leeson, IWMSA 803/4/2.
19  Interview with John Tunnah, IWMSA 840/9/5.
20  Any study of Copeman's interview would suggest that his claims should be treated with caution. Copeman also claimed, without any real supporting evidence, that Tom Wintringham deliberately shot himself and that the British political commissar Walter Tapsell and the American commander Robert Merriman were assassinated by the Russians. See final chapter.

21 Fred Copeman and Walter Tapsell were also recalled, but allowed to return to Spain. See following chapter.
22 Rust, *Britons in Spain*, p. 62.
23 The Republican government had 'divisively and controversially' moved itself to Valencia on 6 November 1936, when it looked as though the capital city might well fall to the rebels. Preston, *A Concise History of the Spanish Civilisation*, p. 117.
24 Thomas, *Spanish Civil War*, p. 588.
25 Ibid., p. 589.
26 Interview with Patrick Curry, IWMSA 799/3/1, and Alexander, *British Volunteers*, p. 94.
27 Gregory, *The Shallow Grave*, pp. 43–44.
28 Moscow 545/3/466, pp. 12–13. 'Estamos dispuestos a sacrificar nuestra vida, porque este sacrificio no se hace solo para lograr la pax y la libertad del pueblo español, sino que, tambien para la paz y la libertad de los pueblos franceses, alemanes, ingleses, italianos, checos, croatos, y para todos los demas pueblos del mundo.' The identity of the speaker remains uncertain, for the battalion political commissar, George Aitken, was not a Spanish speaker.
29 Gregory, *The Shallow Grave*, p. 44.
30 Interview with Albert Charlesworth, IWMSA 798/4/1.
31 Gurney, *Crusade in Spain*, p. 101.
32 Ibid.
33 Interview with James Maley, IWMSA 11947/3/1.
34 Tom Wintringham's description of the engagement contains a useful sketch map of the positions during the morning of 12 February 1937. See Wintringham, *English Captain*, p. 62.
35 As battle-hardened crack soldiers, the Moroccan soldiers were used as shock troops by the rebels, just as the International Brigades were for the Republicans. Many other volunteers refer to the terror of coming up against the Moors. See for example, interview with David Anderson, in MacDougall, *Voices*, p. 94.
36 Gurney, *Crusade in Spain*, p. 104 and p. 108.
37 According to James Hopkins, 'Those who had five weeks training, as many did, felt supremely confident, despite the deficiencies of their weapons and the sudden replacement of their battalion commander.' Hopkins, *Into the Heart*, p. 187. Hopkins's recent work on the British volunteers is unusual in that it devotes very little time to the battle at all; as one reviewer pointed out, 'despite claiming familiarity with the battle-fields, he covers this central aspect of the volunteers' experiences in about twenty pages.' See Robert Stradling's review of James Hopkins's *Into the Heart*, in *English Historical Review*, 115: 460, February 2000, pp. 164–166.
38 'It was very much on the lines of the British Army. Long route marches of 10 to 15 miles . . . rifle practice . . . machine-gun practice, though we had very few machine-guns.' Interview with Charles Bloom, IWMSA 992/6/2.
39 Interview with James Maley, IWMSA 11947/3/1.
40 H. Stratton, *To Anti-Fascism by Taxi*, p. 35.
41 Interview with John Tunnah, IWMSA 840/9/3.
42 For a meticulous analysis of the shenanigans surrounding arms procurement for the Republic, which ensured they were equipped with sub-standard armaments, see Howson, *Arms for Spain*.
43 Interview with Eddie Brown, in MacDougall, *Voices*, p. 110.
44 The problem was a symptom of the Republican Army's forced dependence on antiquated military supplies. The belts were the correct type for Maxim machine-guns, and the bullets were also for Maxims, but for guns of a more modern design than the German Maxims with which the British were equipped. Wintringham, *English Captain*, p. 69.
45 The sergeant had been drinking to steady his nerves and had crashed the truck a few miles from the British positions, killing a man. Charles West, one of the captured members of the Machine-Gun Company, described how he had found the sergeant 'sitting by the road-side holding his head in his hands, completely drunk'. NMLH

Manchester, CP/IND/POLL/2/5-6. The sergeant's Moscow file states, 'Conduct in line not good. Absolute drunkard'. Moscow 545/3/99, p. 8.

46  No.1 Company was made up of a combination of those who had fought at Las Rozas and new untrained volunteers who arrived shortly before the battle. According to Jud Colman, who had fought with No. 1 Company at Lopera and Las Rozas, the members of No. 1 Company were mainly kept together and became the brigade guard charged with guarding the headquarters, and didn't fight as much at Jarama as many other groups. 'I was very relieved. I'm not that sort of a hero. I'd be a fool if I was.' Interview with Julius Colman, IWMSA 14575/3/2.

47  Interview with Tom Clarke, in MacDougall, *Voices*, p. 61.

48  Gurney, *Crusade in Spain*, p. 109.

49  The Scottish Ambulance Unit was run by a woman by the name of Fernanda Jacobsen, who believed that the unit's role was to help both sides. She had close links with the British government and used the ambulance unit to ferry rebel sympathisers from embassies in Madrid to Valencia. Not surprisingly, many members of the unit, such as Len Crome, Maurice Linden, Roddy MacFarquar and George Burleigh, were firmly opposed to the use of the unit for this purpose, and three of them left in March 1937 to join the International Brigades. The other – Burleigh – returned to Britain. See interviews with Len Crome, IWMSA 9298/4/1, and Roddy MacFarquar, in MacDougall, *Voices*, pp. 80–83.

50  Interview with Frank Graham, IWMSA 11877/6/2.

51  Gurney, *Crusade in Spain*, p. 107.

52  Rust, *Britons in Spain*, p. 45.

53  As Charlesworth retreated he also joined the long list of casualties when he was blown into the air by an artillery shell. After a spell in hospital he rejoined the battalion and became its postman. Interview with Albert Charlesworth, IWMSA 798/4/1.

54  Fred Copeman was officially second-in-command of No. 1 Company and had been in the Franco-Belge Battalion when the British Battalion had been transferred to Jarama. He rejoined them at Jarama and attached himself to the Machine-Gun Company. Rust, *Britons in Spain*, p. 46.

55  Interview with Fred Copeman, IWMSA 794/13/2.

56  Interview with Joe Garber, IWMSA 12291/10/5.

57  Alexander, *British Volunteers*, p. 97. Rust estimates that, including officers and members of the Machine-Gun Company, a total of 275 British were still in action by the end of the first day. Rust, *Britons in Spain*, p. 46.

58  Gurney, *Crusade in Spain*, pp. 113–114.

59  Interview with George Aitken, IWMSA 10357/3/1. One disgruntled volunteer later wrote his memoirs anonymously and referred significantly to this event in an attempt to discredit the battalion. Anon, *In Spain with the International Brigade*, p. 24.

60  Fred Copeman was also sympathetic to those who cracked under the intense pressure of combat in Spain. Interview with Fred Copeman, IWMSA 794/13/4. See final chapter for a discussion of this issue.

61  Interview with George Aitken, IWMSA 10357/3/2.

62  Rust, *Britons in Spain*, p. 47.

63  See written reports from members of the Machine-Gun Company captured that day: Harold Fry, Bert Levy, Donald Renton, Charles West and Basil Abrahams, undated, NMLH Manchester, CP/IND/POLL/2/5–6. They are bitterly hostile and critical of Overton, describing how he withdrew his company after two shells had fallen to their right and claiming Overton had stated, 'God Damn it! It is too bloody hot here; I am getting out of it.' See also interview with George Aitken, IWMSA 10357/3/1. Aitken claims that it was later rumoured that Overton threw a Mills bomb into the company's ammunition dump to justify the retreat. Clearly Overton panicked at Jarama, but some responsibility must also lie with his commanders, for Overton's weakness had been recognised before the battle. Tom Wintringham described him as 'a fool, a romantic, a

bluffer who wanted to be courageous but had lived too easily, too softly', and went on to admit that, 'Macartney, myself, Springhall – we had already to some extent seen through O. at Madrigueras.' Wintringham, *English Captain*, pp. 109–110.

64  CP/Ind/Poll/2/6, Manchester.

65  There are discrepancies between differing accounts over the numbers captured at Jarama on 13 February 1937. Bill Alexander states that there were 30 captured (*British Volunteers*, p. 183), whereas James Maley – who was himself captured that day – states that the number was 28. Interview with James Maley, IWMSA 11947/3/2. My research support's Alexander's findings. Carl Geiser lists 27 of the 30 in his study of the American prisoners of war *Prisoners of the Good Fight*, pp. 270–271, n.7. The three he missed were a volunteer named Struthers or Stuhldeer, John Bruce from Alexandria, and S. J. Giles from Liverpool. In addition, two volunteers, Jack Flynn and Fred Jones, were captured at the end of February.

66  This version is by Bill Meredith and appears in the battalion diary of the battle of Jarama. See Fred Copeman collection, Imperial War Museum. It also appears in Rust, *Britons in Spain*, pp. 48–49, and Frank Graham, *The Battle of Jarama*, pp. 15–21.

67  *Workers Weekly*, 21 May 1937.

68  Frank Ryan, ed., *The Book of the XVth Brigade: Records of British, American, Canadian and Irish Volunteers in the XV International Brigade in Spain 1936–1938*, pp. 54–55.

69  Moscow 545/3/467, pp. 12–13. It seems likely that this version was also written by Bill Meredith. The last three volunteers mentioned were probably Elins, Plumb and Katsaronas.

70  James Hopkins's recent study of the British Battalion also claims that Fry's Machine-Gun Company was infiltrated and captured by Moors. Hopkins, *Into the Heart*, p. 190.

71  Fred Copeman always insisted that this version was correct: 'Well, I know bloody well they were because I was there . . . They got our uniforms from blokes who were killed.' Interview with Fred Copeman, IWMSA 794/13/1.

72  Interview with Donald Renton, in MacDougall, *Voices*, p. 25.

73  See Interview with George Leeson, IWMSA 803/4/3.

74  Interview with George Leeson, IWMSA 803/4/3.

75  Interview with John Tunnah, IWMSA 840/9/7.

76  Ibid. However, James Maley, a member of the Machine-Gun Company, believed that his company was in a good tactical position. Maley states that 'after the first day there was a lull. We stayed where we were . . . We knew we had a good field of fire.' Interview with James Maley, IWMSA 11947/3/2. As a map of the battle site shows, though the company may have had a good field of fire, Tunnah is right to point out that the position was extremely vulnerable to having any line of retreat cut off.

77  Ibid.

78  See report on the battle of Jarama, Moscow 545/3/467, p. 11.

79  Wintringham, *English Captain*, p. 99.

80  This total includes the remaining few remaining members of the Machine-Gun Company.

81  Unknown to many of the British at the time, there were also no troops to their left, where a Spanish cavalry regiment was supposed to be. This made their desperate defence extremely critical for the Republic. 'There were no troops to the south of the English . . . all our reserves were up to the north . . . It would have been impossible to stop a Fascist attack south of us. There was our weak spot.' Gurney, *Crusade in Spain*, pp. 113–114. Fortunately for the British Battalion, and for the Spanish Republic, the rebel forces, 'did not find this weak spot until February 14th or 15th, when it was no longer very weak'. As Tom Wintringham argues, 'That is the justification, the achievement, of the defence of Suicide Hill. We held our own half-mile or more; we masked the utter weakness, emptiness, of the three miles south of us.' Wintringham, *English Captain*, p. 82.

82  Here too, George Aitken describes using his pistol to encourage a small number of reluctant volunteers back to the front. Interview with George Aitken, IWMSA 10357/3/1.

83  Different accounts name Jock Cunningham, Frank Ryan, George Aitken and George Nathan as the leaders of the march back to the line. The two most likely were Cunningham and Ryan, so Garber is probably confusing Nathan with Ryan.

84  Interview with Joe Garber, IWMSA 12291/10/6.

85  An account by Frank Graham appears in his book on Jarama. It states: 'The events which followed were some of the most glorious in British working-class history. As these men began to climb the hill again, they broke spontaneously into the Internationale. These soldiers who had previously left the front line and gone some distance stopped in surprise, and those who were sitting on the sides of the slope, jumped up to look at this strange band of men, bearded, dirty, ragged, covered with blood, who after three days' hard fighting were proudly marching along. They broke into applause and they too began to sing. The whole mountainside echoed with their song, the song of struggle. More and more men began to join the marching column. It was a real regrouping!' Frank Graham, *The Battle of Jarama*, p. 24. Similar accounts of 'the Great Rally' appear in Rust, *Britons in Spain*, pp. 51–54, and Ryan, *Book of the XVth Brigade*, pp. 58–61.

86  Thomas, *Spanish Civil War*, p. 592. Robert Stradling agrees: 'Although the British Battalion was neither significantly outnumbered nor outgunned by the forces actually facing it, its achievement was nonetheless an epic one. The assertion may ultimately be incapable of proof, but this writer is confident that its conduct – especially on 12 February – represents the greatest single contribution to the victory of Jarama, and thus to the survival of Madrid.' Stradling, *Irish and the Spanish Civil War*, p. 166.

87  Interview with Frank Graham, IWMSA 11877/6/3.

88  If the Irish fighting with the Lincolns are included, the number killed could be as high as 166. A number of others working in medical units were also killed.

89  Moscow 545/3/467, p. 32. At least 20 more British were killed on the same day.

90  Interview with Charles Morgan, IWMSA 10362/2/1.

91  Interview with Jud Colman, IWMSA 14575/3/3.

92  News of the battle of Jarama appeared as early as 15 February: 'Franco Fails. The Battle East of Madrid', *Daily Worker*, 15 February 1937, p. 2. The Jarama casualty list was important enough to be taken back to London personally at the end of February 1937 by Sam Russell, who had been wounded the previous December at Lopera. Interview with Sam Russell, IWMSA 9484/6/4.

93  *Daily Worker*, 6 March 1937, p. 1.

94  As James Hopkins describes, 'The furious bloodletting that month in the valley of the Jarama, caused in no small part by the ineptitude of the higher command, and the long, slow attrition that took place in the trenches in the Spring and early Summer, had encouraged that cynicism felt by every soldier.' Hopkins, *Into the Heart*, p. 239.

95  Moscow 545/6/93, p. 1.

96  Matters would come to a head in August–September and five senior figures of the battalion would be called home. See Chapter 5, pp. 87–108.

97  See orders of 11 April 1937, which stated, 'The attention of all comrades is drawn to the regulations concerning the use of latrines. Only the latrines provided must be used. The co-operation of all comrades in this connection will do much to preserve the health of the battalion.' Moscow 545/3/495, p. 4.

98  Moscow 545/3/467, p. 40.

99  See battalion orders of 11 April and 15 May 1937. Moscow 545/3/495, p. 6.

100 Basil Abrahams, one of the 15th Brigade Staff, further alleged in a later report completed after his repatriation that, on 13 February, Overton had been responsible for filling ammunition belts with the incorrect ammunition. NMLH Manchester, CP/IND/POLL/2/5-6.

101 See report by members of the Machine-Gun Company, undated, NMLH Manchester, CP/IND/POLL/2/5-6, and Wintringham, *English Captain*, p. 113.

102 Alexander, *British Volunteers*, p. 107.

103 Ibid.

104 Hopkins, *Into the Heart*, p. 268. See the final chapter for a discussion of this issue.

105 Alexander, *British Volunteers*, p. 111. The section included two later commanders of the British Battalion, the Irishmen Peter Daly and Patrick 'Paddy' O'Daire.

106 Alexander, *British Volunteers*, pp. 114–115.

107 Whilst at Chimorra, Joe Monks met an American, Max Evershuk, who vehemently believed that German and Italian workers were sabotaging shells. Much to his comrades' horror, Evershuk was in the habit of hammering off the tips of shells and bombs looking for goodwill notes. Monks, *With the Reds in Andalusia*, pp. 35–36.

108 IBA Box 50, File Mk.

109 As Alexander states: 'The plan was bold and imaginative. However, in hindsight, and considering the level of training and the reserves available to the Government, it was clearly over-ambitious.' Alexander, *British Volunteers*, p. 119.

110 Preston, *Concise History*, p. 198.

111 The Anti-Tank Battery was formed in May 1937 and comprised 40 men who had been training at the British headquarters at Madrigueras. They were something of an elite unit and were issued with three Soviet 45 mm guns, capable of firing both armour-piercing and high-explosive shells. They were instructed how to use the new guns by a number of Russian instructors, for at that time the guns represented state-of-the-art military technology. Alexander, *British Volunteers*, p. 219.

112 Cunningham had been hit in the side by a machine-gun bullet in an action to clear a rebel-occupied trench at Jarama. Rust, *Britons in Spain*, pp. 57–58.

113 Interview with Fred Copeman, IWMSA 794/13/6.

114 Brome, *The International Brigades*, p. 199.

115 Gregory, *The Shallow Grave*, p. 67 and Carroll, *Odyssey*, p. 141.

116 Interview with Fred Copeman, IWMSA 794/13/7.

117 As Sid Quinn stated: 'Under the rules of war we had no option. We shot everything in front of us. And they took a few of our men as well.' Interview with Sidney Quinn, IWMSA 801/3/2.

118 Interview with Albert Charlesworth, IWMSA 798/4/1. In Robert Stradling's recent study of the British in Spain, he suggests that this story of rebel soldiers hiding behind civilians may be a myth, invented in order to justify a massacre of rebel prisoners of war after the capture of Villanueva de la Cañada. Whilst there appears to be a certain amount of circumstantial evidence to suggest that a summary execution of rebel prisoners may have taken place, Stradling's theory seems little more than conjecture. See Robert Stradling, *History and Legend. Writing the International Brigades*, pp. 130–141.

119 Alexander Tudor-Hart had been one of the founders of the Spanish Medical Aid Committee (SMAC) in Britain. He arrived in Spain in December 1936 and remained until he was repatriated in October 1938. Fyrth, *Signal was Spain*, pp. 62–67.

120 P. D. Harrisson, MS, p. 117.

121 Interview with Albert Charlesworth, IWMSA 798/4/2.

122 Interview with Frank Graham, IWMSA 11877/6/3.

123 Harrisson, MS, p. 117.

124 Williams's description of his experiences of the mortally wounded at Brunete is a powerful epithet: 'A badly wounded man is . . . a less concerned man you'll never meet. He's very, very quiet. Terribly quiet. Never says a word . . . A badly wounded man is the most silent person you'll ever come across. Next to a dead man.' Interview with Huw Alun Menai Williams, IWMSA 10181/5/3.

125 In David Anderson's company, numbers were reduced from 106 to 24. Interview with David Anderson, in MacDougall, *Voices*, p. 92.

126 Interview with Fred Copeman, IWMSA 794/13/6.

127 Interview with Frank Graham, IWMSA 11877/6/3.

128 Brome, *The International Brigades*, p. 90.

129 Hopkins, *Into the Heart*, p. 256. Walter Gregory agrees that 43 remained, but claimed 600 had gone into the attack on 6 July. Gregory, *The Shallow Grave*, p. 74. One of the

casualties was Major George Nathan, who was killed by a shell on the last day of the battle.

130   Matthew Hughes and Enriqueta Garrido, 'Planning and Command: the Spanish Republican Army and the Battle of the Ebro, 1938', pp. 107–108.

## 5  Into Aragon, 1937–1938: Teruel, 'the great retreat' and the Ebro offensive

1    Walter Gregory, *The Shallow Grave*, p. 121.
2    As a report drawn up by Georgi Dimitrov on 30 July 1937 depicted, '[The International Brigades] are experiencing great difficulties. Many brigades and battalions lost many wounded and killed. In several military units, soldiers and cadres have overstrained themselves. The new contingents are too insignificant to make it possible to carry out serious changes in composition. Relations with the Spanish military powers are not entirely good. Many wounded men and invalids remain without support or the right to it. The commander of the Albacete base [probably Vital Gayman] was in such a state of depression that we were forced to dismiss him immediately.' Moscow 33987/3/1015, cited in Radosh *et al.*, *Spain Betrayed*, p. 233.
3    Gallo estimated that, of the 2,144 troops of the 15th International Brigade taking part in the Brunete offensive, 293 were killed, 735 wounded and 167 missing. Moscow 35082/1/42, cited in ibid., p. 238.
4    The report was drawn up in August 1937 for Marshal Voroshilov, who passed it on to Stalin. Marty believed that the International Brigades' major problem was the lack of personnel following the high casualties sustained at Brunete. He argued for recruitment to be channelled into the existing brigades, rather than creating any further international units, and against intermingling internationals and Spaniards at battalion level or lower. More frequent and longer rests were necessary, and stronger political and military leadership was also required. See Moscow 35082/1/90 and 33987/3/1033, cited in ibid., pp. 241–249.
5    See IBA Box C, Files 8/2, 16/1, 16/3, 17/1 and 17/7.
6    Tapsell argued, as did Fred Copeman, that the capture of Villanueva de la Cañada achieved little apart from allowing the rebels enough time to bring up reinforcements on to the Romanillos Heights overlooking Brunete and Madrid. Malcolm Dunbar, then commander of the Anti-Tank Battery, later promoted to the 15th Brigade staff, admitted as much to Fred Thomas, one of the British members of the battery. Thomas, *To Tilt at Windmills*, p. 36.
7    Hopkins, *Into the Heart of the Fire*, p. 242.
8    *Reynolds News*, 23 July 1961, cited in Brome, *The International Brigades*, p. 205.
9    Brome, *The International Brigades*, p. 206.
10   Letter from Walter Tapsell, 9 August 1937, IBA Box C, File 16/1.
11   Ibid.
12   Ibid. An official report published in April 1937 was also not very complimentary about Aitken. Describing him as 'a good comrade who works hard', it continued: 'nevertheless, I found surprisingly bad outbursts against him expressed by some of the soldiers in the line. These outbursts, I believe, are due firstly to the high nervous tension among the comrades, and secondly because Comrade Aitken himself does not seem to have the best manner of approach to the comrades. I believe that comrade Aitken could work better in the brigade than in the battalion.' Moscow, 545/6/93, p. 1.
13   Letter from George Aitken to Political Bureau, IBA Box C, File 17/7.
14   Ibid.
15   IBA Box C, File 17/1.
16   Bill Rust claimed that 'Copeman refers, almost without exception, to the Brigade in a disparaging fashion . . . he has also been successful in infecting Cde. Alexander his adjutant with this same attitude. Wild has a long established anti-brigade tradition.' 'Report and recommendations re. the English Battalion', December 1937, P5 AR6, Salamanca.

17 It was claimed that Copeman had been removed from his command by Gal because of his 'irrational behaviour', that Bert Williams had been an ineffective political commissar, that Cunningham was unable to complete his duties on the brigade staff and that Aitken had failed to challenge brigade orders which forced the battalion into impossible positions. Alexander, *British Volunteers for Liberty*, p. 131.

18 Copeman has a rather egocentric view of his own role: 'Now, Jock was a bit of a problem. Jock didn't get on with Harry Pollitt, by the way. Harry Pollitt literally worshipped Fred Copeman. He was the boy for Harry. You know what I mean? I couldn't do anything wrong where Harry Pollitt was concerned.' Interview with Fred Copeman, IWMSA 794/13/7-8.

19 Letter from George Aitken to the Political Bureau, undated, IBA Box C, File 17/7. Aitken bitterly resented suggestions that he was only made brigade commissar because he was an old friend of Čopić, whom he had met in the Lenin School in Moscow.

20 Angus, *With the International Brigade in Spain*, p. 7.

21 Even though many had been told they would only be in Spain for a maximum of six months. See final chapter.

22 By the end of 1937, Internationals made up approximately half of the 15th Brigade as a whole. Report by General Walter, Moscow 35082/1/95, cited in Radosh *et al.*, *Spain Betrayed*, p. 452.

23 Brome, *The International Brigades*, pp. 219–220.

24 Thomas, *Spanish Civil War*, pp. 725–726.

25 Gregory, *The Shallow Grave*, p. 78.

26 Peter Daly, 'from a long line of Irish revolutionary stock' was mortally injured at Pulburrel Hill, and replaced by Patrick 'Paddy' O'Daire, another Irish activist. Ryan, *The Book of the XVth Brigade*, p. 287.

27 Gregory, *The Shallow Grave*, p. 80.

28 Alexander, *British Volunteers*, p. 150.

29 Gregory, *The Shallow Grave*, p. 81.

30 Alexander, *British Volunteers*, p. 151.

31 After the end of the war, Franco left the town as a ruin in order to demonstrate the damage caused by '*Los Rojos*'. The American battalion suffered extremely heavy casualties in the offensive; so did the defending rebel forces. Captured prisoners told Ernest Hemingway that over 1,200 were killed defending Belchite. Brome, *The International Brigades*, p. 223.

32 Gregory, *The Shallow Grave*, p. 82.

33 Thomas, *Spanish Civil War*, p. 969.

34 Interview with Hugh Sloan, in MacDougall, *Voices from the Spanish Civil War*, p. 215.

35 Interview with Bill Williamson, IWMSA 12385/18/17.

36 These were Eric Whalley from Mansfield, C. Larlham from Chelsea, Frederick McCulloch from Glasgow, Arthur Robinson from Hartlepool and George Westfield from Liverpool. IBA Box C, File 2/1.

37 However, these numbers were only ever used for official purposes. The British Battalion was usually referred to as *el batallón ingles*.

38 Based at 1 Litchfield Street in London, the Dependents' Aid Committee was responsible for looking after the families of the British volunteers, many of whom were in dire financial hardship. The committee was often accused, erroneously, of being a front for recruitment for the International Brigades. In fact Robson worked on the floor above but, as Alexander admits, the 'close liaison . . . gave rise to difficulties.' Alexander, *British Volunteers*, p. 141.

39 Hopkins, *Into the Heart*, p. 196, and Alexander, *British Volunteers*, pp. 135–136.

40 Alexander, *British Volunteers*, p. 161.

41 Rust, *Britons in Spain*, p. 101.

42 As with the Brunete offensive, one of the aims of the action was to pre-empt a rebel offensive, this time at Guadalajara. Thomas, *Spanish Civil War*, p. 788.

43  'Teruel: The Turn of the Tide', *News Chronicle*, 23 December 1937, p. 8.

44  Alexander, *British Volunteers*, p. 165.

45  As the Welsh medical orderly and first-aider Huw Williams remembers, it was 'very, very cold. [Teruel was] a cruel battle.' Interview with Huw Alun Menai Williams, IWMSA 10181/5/4.

46  Rust, *Britons in Spain*, p. 109.

47  Garry McCartney, a Scottish volunteer in the Machine-Gun Company, observed the barrage from the hillside overlooking the valley. He described how the artillery 'landed shells marking a square of quite large dimensions and then saturated the square not only with shell fire and machine-gun fire, but they sent across their aircraft to bomb it.' Interview with Garry McCartney, in MacDougall, *Voices*, p. 247.

48  Alexander, *British Volunteers*, p. 166. General Walter, the commander of the 35th Division, of which the British Battalion was part, praised highly the actions of the 15th Brigade at Saragossa, stating that their discipline had improved dramatically since the previous year. Report by General Walter, Moscow 35082/1/95, cited in Radosh *et al.*, *Spain Betrayed*, p. 440.

49  Rust, *Britons in Spain*, pp. 113–114.

50  Alexander, *British Volunteers*, p. 167.

51  Corkhill and Rawnsley, *The Road to Spain*, pp. 116–118.

52  Cooney was lauded as 'very brave – high political development. Best battalion commissar in brigade'. Moscow 545/6/118, p. 34. Similarly, Peter Kerrigan described him as one 'whose work it is impossible to speak [of] too highly. Through the whole of this two months without a break of any kind and in every action, his steadiness has been a sheet anchor for others.' Letter from Peter Kerrigan to Harry Pollitt, 27 September 1938, IBA Box C, File 25/5.

53  Rust, *Britons in Spain*, pp. 115–116, and Alexander, *British Volunteers*, pp. 167–168.

54  Brome, *The International Brigades*, p. 245.

55  Thomas, *Spanish Civil War*, p. 798.

56  Rust, *Britons in Spain*, p. 142.

57  Interview with Hugh Sloan, in MacDougall, *Voices*, pp. 222–223.

58  Report by Sam Wild, Moscow 545/3/497, p. 22.

59  Alexander, *British Volunteers*, p. 172.

60  Thomas, *Spanish Civil War*, p. 798.

61  Rust, *Britons in Spain*, pp. 144–145.

62  Interview with Frank Graham, IWMSA 11877/6/5.

63  Interview with David Stirrat, in MacDougall, *Voices*, p. 267.

64  Report by Sam Wild, Moscow 545/3/497, p. 23.

65  Peter Kemp, 'I Fought for Franco', p. 1608.

66  Rust, *Britons in Spain*, pp. 146–147.

67  Alexander, *British Volunteers*, p. 176, and Thomas, *Spanish Civil War*, p. 800.

68  Rust, *Britons in Spain*, p. 148.

69  Report by Sam Wild, Moscow 545/6/495, p. 27.

70  As Hugh Thomas describes: 'The fronts hardly existed. There were isolated acts of resistance by one or other of the republican units, as well as confusion, breakdown of communication, suspicion of treachery.' Thomas, *Spanish Civil War*, p. 801.

71  Alexander, *British Volunteers*, p. 173.

72  Ibid., p. 178. However, it should be remembered that by far the majority of this number were Spaniards. By March 1938 there were barely enough British to form a company of 200, let alone a battalion of 1,000.

73  Interview with Joseph Leo Byrne, IWMSA 12930/3/2.

74  Official report compiled by Jack Jones and Garry McCartney on Calaceite and San Pedro. IBA Box C, File 3/1a.

75  Gregory, *The Shallow Grave*, p. 108, and report by Bob Cooney, Moscow 545/3/497, pp. 17–18.

76 Report by George Fletcher, Moscow 545/3/497, p. 33.

77 Interview with Harold Collins, IWMSA 9481/4/3.

78 Interview with David Stirrat, in MacDougall, *Voices*, p. 269.

79 IBA Box C, File 3/1a.

80 Geiser, *Prisoners of the Good Fight*, pp. 60–61.

81 Rust, *Britons in Spain*, p. 154. See also Rust's obituary of Tapsell in the *Daily Worker*, 26 July 1938, p. 3.

82 Carl Geiser refers to him as 'Tony', the name by which he was known in the battalion.

83 As an officer, Frank Ryan was fortunate not to have been shot on the spot, particularly as he identified himself as such. Ironically, as Seán Cronin explains, Ryan's bravery was probably one of the factors that saved his life. Cronin believes the other factors were the Italian commander's orders against summary executions and that Ryan's rank was sufficiently high that the question of his execution was passed up to senior rebel officers. Cronin, *Frank Ryan*, p. 136.

84 Interview with Joseph Leo Byrne, IWMSA 12930/3/2.

85 Interview with David Stirrat, in MacDougall, *Voices*, p. 268. Thirteen divisions of the rebel army, plus a huge number of tanks, artillery pieces and anti-tank guns, backed up with over 900 aircraft, were massed for the push through Aragon to the Mediterranean. The defending Republican forces were outnumbered in the region of five to one. Alexander, *British Volunteers*, pp. 169–170.

86 Gregory, *The Shallow Grave*, p. 109.

87 Interview with George Drever, in MacDougall, *Voices*, p. 281.

88 'For example, the first time we caught a rabbit. Now that's your dinner, but what do you do with it? It's kicking about and it's got fur on. And how do you get it into a pot?' Interview with David Stirrat, in ibid., p. 270.

89 Angus, *With the International Brigade*, pp. 10–11.

90 Gregory, *The Shallow Grave*, pp. 110–111.

91 Rust, *Britons in Spain*, p. 157, and Gregory, *The Shallow Grave*, p. 112.

92 Interview with David Stirrat, in MacDougall, *Voices*, p. 272.

93 Thomas, *Spanish Civil War*, p. 803.

94 Alexander, *British Volunteers*, p. 201.

95 Other British commanders also received promotions: Malcolm Dunbar, originally commander of the British Anti-Tank Battery, was promoted to the post of 15th International Brigade chief of staff, and his erstwhile number two and replacement commander, Hugh (Humphrey) Slater, was promoted brigade chief of operations.

96 A large number of recruits joined the battalion in the spring of 1938. Interview with Garry McCartney, in MacDougall, *Voices*, p. 249.

97 Though one section of the Anti-Tank Battery remained, armed with an antiquated replacement gun. Thomas, *To Tilt at Windmills*, pp. 104–105.

98 Gregory, *The Shallow Grave*, p. 116.

99 Report by Comrade Gómez, the head of the International Brigade base at Albacete [real name Wilhelm Zeisser], 26 July 1938, Moscow 33987/3/1149, cited in Radosh *et al.*, *Spain Betrayed*, p. 464.

100 Part of these preparations included the British volunteer Lewis Clive, an Olympic oarsman and strong swimmer, swimming across the Ebro at night to reconnoitre the rebel positions. Clive was later killed attempting to capture Hill 481 at Gandesa. See p. 104.

101 Hughes and Garrido, 'Planning and Command', p. 107.

102 George Wheeler, *To Make the People Smile Again*, pp. 60–61.

103 'Hitting Back', *News Chronicle*, 28 July 1938, p. 8.

104 'Republicans' Surprise Drive Across Ebro', *Daily Worker*, 27 July 1938, pp. 1–3.

105 'The atmosphere of enthusiasm and determination, as revealed by their talk, has to be seen to be believed. They fully realise all this battle means to Spain and to democracy throughout the world. Many of these men . . . were in the Aragon retreat.' 'Republicans Sweep On', *Daily Worker*, 26 July 1938, p. 1.

106 George Wheeler, MS, p. 43. Another volunteer said, 'I remember well the recrossing of the Ebro because it was a very, very dramatic moment in time for everybody.' Interview with Hugh Sloan, in MacDougall, *Voices*, p. 227.

107 Ibid., p. 228. Though the offensive was delayed when a vehicle became stuck on one of the pontoon bridges. Interview with Peter Kerrigan, IWMSA 810/6/3, and Brome, *The International Brigades*, p. 256.

108 Despite attempts by the rebels to collect military intelligence, all of the Republican offensives of 1937–1938 caught the rebels somewhat unawares. Stanley Payne, *The Franco Regime*, p. 138. However, as Hugh Thomas points out, the front in the Spanish Civil War stretched for over 1,000 miles and, though rebel reports had described the movement of Republican units, it was impossible for the rebel command to investigate every rumour. Thomas, *Spanish Civil War*, p. 840.

109 Alexander, *British Volunteers*, p. 206.

110 'Key Franco Town Surrounded on Three Sides', *Daily Worker*, 29 July 1938, p. 1.

111 Hughes and Garrido, 'Planning and Command', pp. 109–110.

112 Peter Kerrigan's reports for the *Daily Worker* become less triumphant as July moved to August, stressing the determination of the Republicans' advance despite increasing rebel opposition. See, for example, *Daily Worker*, 4 August 1938, p. 1, which admitted that 'the Government attacks during the last few days have been met by a new concentration of artillery and machine-gun fire, assisted almost continuously by aviation.' Coverage then shifted in tone, carrying a laudatory interview with General Modesto, calls for more donations for Spain (*Daily Worker*, 8 August 1938, p. 1, and 9 August, p. 3), and demands that France should open the border with Spain. *Daily Worker*, 11 August 1938, p. 3.

113 Chris Henry, *The Ebro 1938: The Death Knell of the Republic*, p. 37.

114 Interview with Steve Fullarton, in MacDougall, *Voices*, p. 298.

115 Ibid.

116 For a revealing description of the unequal levels of artillery and air support, see Hughes and Garrido, 'Planning and Command', pp. 110–111.

117 Thomas, *To Tilt at Windmills*, p. 115.

118 Ibid., p. 112.

119 'Rowing Blue Dies for Democracy in Spain', *Daily Worker*, 8 August 1938, p. 1.

120 Wheeler, *To Make the People Smile Again*, pp. 76–78. A monument to the Republican soldiers who were killed in the Sierra Pandols region was recently unearthed in Spain, having lain undiscovered throughout the Franco years. On the monument appear the names of four British volunteers killed in the Ebro offensive – Lewis Clive, David Guest, Harry Dobson, killed on Hill 481, and Morris Miller, killed on Hill 666 – together with one killed in the retreats through Aragon – the battalion commissar Walter Tapsell. The monument was constructed by Republican engineers including Percy Ludwick, a British civil engineer who served on the 15th Brigade staff from September 1937 to December 1938. See Percy Ludwick, MS, p. 10.

121 Gregory, *The Shallow Grave*, p. 126.

122 Wheeler, MS, p. 43.

123 The Lincolns had held the position consisting mainly of solid rock for ten days, sheltering behind stone parapets as the rebels poured artillery and aircraft fire on them. Carroll, *The Odyssey of the Abraham Lincoln Brigade*, p. 199.

124 Alexander, *British Volunteers*, p. 210. Following the British defence of Hill 666, it took the rebels until November 1938 finally to capture it. Henry, *The Ebro 1938*, p. 60.

125 Wheeler, MS, p. 61.

126 Gregory, *The Shallow Grave*, p. 131. During the rebel counter-attack, rebel aircraft were dropping over 5,000 kg of bombs on the Republican lines every day. Hugh Thomas's description of the rebels' air superiority gives some level of understanding of the desperate circumstances in which Gregory and his comrades found themselves: 'All day and every day the nationalist aeroplanes, sometimes two hundred at the same time, circled over the Republican lines, with hardly any interference from the inadequate anti-

aircraft defences and badly managed fighters of their opponents. Many of their Moscas and Chatos were destroyed; many were damaged, and many pilots were either dead or wounded; by this time, most of the best Russian pilots had been withdrawn.' Thomas, *Spanish Civil War*, p. 843.

127 As Bill Rust described to Harry Pollitt in a letter dated 26 May 1938, it had been decided previously that the foreign volunteers were now in such small numbers that they could be withdrawn. 'According to our old froggie friend [André Marty] there is no longer an I. B. there are only foreign soldiers mixed with Spanish Brigades. Also, after a couple of victories, everyone will go.' IBA Box C, File 22/6. A report from Dimitrov to Marshal Voroshilov in Moscow confirms that the decision to withdraw the brigades originated with Premier Negrín, who believed they were 'exhausted', 'their military efficiency had fallen off' and 'the influx of new volunteers is negligible.' Thus the withdrawal of the brigades should not necessarily be seen as evidence for Stalin's withdrawal of support for the Republic. See Moscow 33987/3/1149, cited in Radosh *et al.*, *Spain Betrayed*, p. 469. A copy of the Spanish resolution for withdrawal of non-Spanish combatants from Spain put to the League of Nations in September 1938 resides in the PRO. See FO371/22696 W12789.
128 Wheeler, MS, p. 81.
129 By 23 September, only 106 of the battalion were British. Alexander, *British Volunteers*, p. 215.
130 Letter from Peter Kerrigan to Harry Pollitt, 27 September 1938, IBA Box C, File 25/5.
131 Peter Kerrigan listed the casualties between 22 and 24 September as: dead 14, wounded 24, missing 132, deserters 31. Ibid. A number of British, including Frank West, George Wheeler and John Dunlop, were captured and later joined the comrades at the prison camp of San Pedro de Cardeña, near Burgos. See the following chapter.
132 Letter from Peter Kerrigan to Harry Pollitt, 27 September 1938, IBA Box C, File 25/5.
133 Carroll, *Odyssey*, p. 162.
134 Alexander, *British Volunteers*, p. 239.
135 There has been some confusion over the exact date of the farewell parade in Barcelona. It is often listed as having taken place on 29 October. See, for example, Alexander, *British Volunteers*, p. 239, and Arthur Landis, *History of the Abraham Lincoln Brigade*, pp. 592–593. In fact it actually took place on 28 October, as coverage of the event in the British press on 29 October demonstrates. See, for example, 'A Last Parade in Barcelona – Cheers and Flowers', *The Times*, 29 October 1938, p. 14. I am grateful to Fred Thomas for bringing this to my attention.
136 Thomas, *To Tilt at Windmills*, p. 164.
137 Alexander, *British Volunteers*, p. 240.
138 This number includes British volunteers with 15th Brigade staff and other units. Ibid., p. 241.
139 As has been noted, it was hardly surprising that the British right-wing press chose not to report the welcome at Victoria for the 305 that arrived on 7 December 1938. 'Clearly to report the return of British volunteers would have proved anathema to newspapers which had consistently condemned the International Brigades as the embodiment of that Bolshevik threat.' Shelmerdine, 'Britons in an "Un-British" War', p. 40.

## 6 Prisoners of war

1 Interview with James Maley, IWMSA 11947/3/1.
2 Gregory, *The Shallow Grave*, pp. 134–135. While most British prisoners were held together, a handful were kept in other jails. John Firman Danson from Chatham, actually Canadian, and Archibald Bartlett from Pontypridd (whose real name was Archibald Yemm) were both prisoners at Duesto prison in Bilbao. So too was Tom Picton, an ex-boxer from Wales, who was shot whilst in prison. See IBA Box 28a, File A/6, and Alexander, *British Volunteers for Liberty*, p. 187.

3  See Chapter 4.

4  Telegram from George Ogilvie-Forbes, Counsellor in Madrid. PRO PRO371/20584-W15462. Like many others, Ogilvie-Forbes was expecting the capital to fall shortly to the rebel forces.

5  Ibid.

6  PRO FO371/21287 W6098.

7  Peter Kemp, *Mine Were of Trouble*, p. 162. Kemp later recounts how, on 14 March 1938, his superior officer, Colonel Peñaredora, ordered him to execute a deserter from the International Brigades, an Irishman from Belfast. Peñaredora insisted that Kemp execute the prisoner and sent two legionnaires after him to make sure that the order was obeyed. Ibid., pp. 170–173. The date suggests that the executed brigader could have been either Ben Murray, a Communist Party branch secretary born in County Tyrone, or Joseph Murray (no relation), also from County Tyrone.

8  As Peter Carroll states: 'With very few exceptions, fascist policy was to take no prisoners.' He cites Carl Geiser's figure of 173 shot out of a total of 287 Americans captured. Carroll, *The Odyssey of the Abraham Lincoln Brigade*, pp. 155 and 175.

9  See, for example, interview with George Drever, IWMSA 841/2/1, and interview with Tom Murray, in MacDougall, *Voices from the Spanish Civil War*, p. 318. Bill Rust later claimed that 'the fascists never allow a captured political commissar to remain alive.' Rust, *Britons in Spain*, p. 154. Carl Geiser, an American officer and political commissar, also believed that 'all officers of the International Brigade were executed upon capture.' Geiser, *Prisoners of the Good Fight*, p. 67.

10  How much of this was based on racial stereotyping – not unknown among the volunteers' descriptions of the Moors – is difficult to establish. John Myers, who was a prisoner at San Pedro de Cardeña, gave a colourful interview to the *West London Observer* on 24 February 1939, p. 6, which described how the Moors' 'horribly ferocious treatment of prisoners was only too well known . . . in appearance they were a revolting spectacle, with their long ugly teeth "like Dracula", saliva streaming from the corners of their mouths and their eyes ablaze with an insane lust.'

11  Report on International Brigades by M. V. Miller, Barcelona, 5 April 1939. PRO FO371/24124–7458.

12  For an account of the shooting of prisoners at Quinto, see Geiser, *Prisoners*, pp. 30–31 and Carroll, *Odyssey*, p. 156.

13  See, for example, Stradling, *History and Legend*, pp. 130–141.

14  As recounted to Giles Romilly. IBA Box 28. See also Geiser, *Prisoners*, p. 15.

15  IBA Box 28.

16  Carl Geiser states that Dickenson was enraged at the shooting of Elias, and his contemptuous reaction towards the Nationalists led them to halt the column and shoot him. Geiser, *Prisoners*, p. 15: 'Stood against a tree Dickenson realized he was about to be executed. He smiled, raise his clenched fist, and called out "Salud" as they fired.' Whether Dickenson's smile and calm acceptance of the situation is an exaggeration is impossible to verify. Geiser admits that his version originated with Bill Alexander, so is at least third hand. The original version is probably the one in Moscow: 'The men were ordered to march down the valley to a spot 400 metres off. The Spanish officer, mad with delight, ordered Ted Dickenson, second in command of the Machine-Gun Company, out of their ranks. Dickenson, knowing what was coming, displayed marvellous courage. He stepped smartly out of the ranks, marched towards the tree indicated by the fascist officer, turned about, and with the words "Salud Comrades" fell with fascist bullets in him.' Moscow 545/3/467, p. 13.

17  Interview with Tommy Bloomfield, in MacDougall, *Voices*, p. 49.

18  Ibid.

19  Alexander, *British Volunteers*, p. 184.

20  'Britons Captured in Spain', *Daily Mail*, 31 March 1937, p. 20.

21 Nationalists claimed that the two were caught having deserted from the Republican lines. They were later released with the other British prisoners. IBA Box D-7, File A/7.

22 Many of the volunteers were badly wounded following their capture. Donald Renton had been wounded in the legs, Harold Fry had a broken arm and both Jimmy Rutherford and George Watters had been beaten virtually unconscious. Interview with Donald Renton, in MacDougall, *Voices*, p. 26; Alexander, *British Volunteers*, p. 184 and Geiser, *Prisoners*, pp. 15–16.

23 Geiser, *Prisoners*, p. 16.

24 IBA Box 28, File A/18.

25 Ibid.

26 IBA Box 28 and Alexander, *British Volunteers*, p. 184.

27 See 'Prisoners Released by Franco: A Generous Parting Gesture', *The Times*, 29 May 1937, p. 13.

28 IBA Box 33, File 16/6.

29 'Jimmy Rutherford Died for Freedom', *Challenge*, 20 February 1939, p. 7.

30 IBA Box 28, Files A2 and A/56, and Alexander, *British Volunteers*, p. 185.

31 Alexander, *British Volunteers*, p. 185.

32 Geiser, *Prisoners*, p. 17.

33 Alexander, *British Volunteers*, p. 186.

34 Interview with Joseph Leo Byrne, IWMSA 12930/3/2, and Morien Morgan, IWMSA 9856/4/2.

35 Anon., *They Fought in Franco's Jails*, pp. 3–4.

36 IBA Box C, File 3/1a. Carl Geiser reported that many of the American prisoners felt likewise. Geiser, *Prisoners*, p. 142. As Bill Alexander further acknowledges, morale was, not surprisingly, very low, and he states that many volunteers felt they had 'dishonoured' their cause by being captured and that others had been shattered by their experiences of war. Although he admits that 'all were uncertain, having heard of the cruelty and terror experienced by the earlier group of prisoners', he makes no mention of the 'violent reactions to the party and battalion leadership' mentioned in the official report. Alexander, *British Volunteers*, p. 186.

37 IBA Box C, File 3/1a.

38 Nigel West and Oleg Tsarev, *The Crown Jewels: The British Secrets at the Heart of the KGB Archives*, London: HarperCollins, 1998, p. 154, cited in Halstead and McLoughlin, 'British and Irish Students at the International Lenin School, Moscow, 1926–37', p. 4. Other members of the British Battalion were also involved with Soviet espionage. Nigel West identifies Douglas 'Dave' Springhall as the centre of a Soviet spy ring. He was arrested and convicted in 1943 for possession of classified papers. Wilf McCartney is also named as a reliable USSR agent. West further suggests that Charlotte Haldane became a member of the CPGB's underground in 1937 and that her husband, J. B. S. Haldane, may have been 'Intelligencia', the leader of the spy ring. Nigel West, *Venona: The Greatest Secret of the Cold War*, pp. 60–78.

39 IBA Box C, File 3/1a; *They Fought in Franco's Jails*, p. 5; and Alexander, *British Volunteers*, pp. 186–187.

40 Geiser, *Prisoners*, pp. 95–96. Garry McCartney later described the display as resembling 'a hundred tic-tack men at a racecourse, all waving their arms about in different directions.' Interview with Garry McCartney, in MacDougall, *Voices*, p. 250.

41 Ibid., p. 257.

42 Interview with George Wheeler, IWMSA 11442/8/7. On first sight this appears a fairly typical gloss on the prisoners' response to the camp authorities, in keeping with the 'official' history, and, indeed, the story features in Alexander, *British Volunteers*, p. 191. However, it should also be remembered that some rather iconoclastic British volunteers had been shouting 'No bloody pan' as an alternative to '*No pasaran*' and referring to political commissars as 'comic stars'. See the following chapter.

43  Alexander, *British Volunteers*, p. 187.

44  According to James Maley, the prisoners captured at Jarama in February 1937 had all been fingerprinted, which would have made Rutherford's discovery inevitable. However, no other volunteer makes any reference to their fingerprints having been taken, so this seems inconclusive. See interview with James Maley, IWMSA 11947/3/2.

45  Letter from the Foreign Office to J. Rutherford, father of James. PRO FO371/24122–W2027 and IBA Box 28, File 4/4. The dates here are incorrect: in fact Rutherford was repatriated in May 1937 and recaptured in March 1938 after returning to Spain.

46  Letter from Foreign Office to Willie Gallagher, PRO FO371/24122-W1565.

47  Interview with George Leeson, IWMSA 803/4/3.

48  According to the official record there were 102 British prisoners at Saragossa on 3 April 1938. This number soon increased to 146.

49  The official report, IBA Box C, File 3/1a, lists Kim Philby as working for the *Daily Telegraph*. In fact Philby was assigned to the Nationalists and was working for *The Times* to build up his Conservative credentials, whilst all the time secretly reporting back to Moscow.

50  Interview with Dougal Eggar, IWMSA 9426/4/4.

51  Jimmy Moon, who was a prisoner at Saragossa and San Pedro, blames William Carney for recognising Jimmy Rutherford, thus virtually ensuring his execution. Interview with Jimmy Moon, IWMSA 15729/4/2. However, other volunteers recount that it was Merry de Val who recognised Rutherford. (See, for example, interview with Dave Goodman, IWMSA 16621/5/4.) As he had interviewed individually all the British captured at Jarama it seems probable that, whether or not Carney did pick Rutherford out, Merry del Val would have recognised him anyway.

52  IBA Box C, File 3/1a.

53  *They Fought in Franco's Jails*, p. 7, and Alexander, *British Volunteers*, p. 187.

54  Interview with Frank West, IWMSA 9315/8/6.

55  Walter Gregory and George Wheeler were captured at the same time. Alexander, *British Volunteers*, p. 191 The machine-gun group, including George Green, the husband of Nan Green, was surrounded at the same time and was never seen again. Gregory, *The Shallow Grave*, p. 134.

56  Interview with George Wheeler, IWMSA 11442/8/6.

57  IBA Box C, File 3/1a, and *They Fought in Franco's Jails*, p. 8.

58  Cyril Kent, 'I Was in a Franco Prison', *Challenge*, 5 January 1939, pp. 10–11, and Alexander, *British Volunteers*, p. 188.

59  Interview with George Wheeler, IWMSA 11442/8/6.

60  Interview with Joe Norman, IWMSA 818/4/3.

61  Interview with Morien Morgan, IWMSA 9856/4/3.

62  Interview with George Wheeler, IWMSA 11442/8/6.

63  For example, Kearney 'Castles' (real name Cassells), a volunteer from Liverpool, was suffering from constipation but was treated for diarrhoea for several days before the mistake was recognised. Chris Hall, *Disciplina Camaradas: Four English Volunteers in Spain*, p. 103.

64  Interview with Harold Collins, IWMSA 9481/4/4.

65  Interview with Maurice Levitas, IWMSA 16358/5/4.

66  Interview with Joseph Leo Byrne, IWMSA 12930/3/3.

67  Interview with Bruce Allender, IWMSA 11300/4/3.

68  Geiser, *Prisoners*, pp. 102–103.

69  For a short time the white beans were replaced with red kidney beans. Popular at first, the red beans became less so after being served twice daily for a week.

70  Though not all the prisoners agree on this point. One recounts that 'They would throw the bread on the floor, hoping to see us scrabbling for it. But the discipline with these people was very, very good. There was no scrabbling for the food, you know.' Interview with Morien Morgan, IWMSA 9856/4/4.

71 Dolly Shaer-West, MS, p. 22.

72 Cronin, *Frank Ryan*, pp. 139–140, and Geiser, *Prisoners*, p. 113.

73 Interview with Jimmy Moon, IWMSA 15729/4/2.

74 IBA Box C, File 3/1a.

75 Various groups of volunteers, usually Communist Party members, made contact with each other. For example, Garry McCartney, a Scottish member of the CP and YCL, was in close contact with two other prisoners, Willie Collins and Donald Carson, whom he knew from trade union activities in Scotland. Interview with Garry McCartney, in MacDougall, *Voices*, p. 249.

76 IBA Box C, File 3/1a.

77 Ibid.

78 Ibid.

79 *They Fought in Franco's Jails*, p. 11.

80 Interview with Joe Norman, IWMSA 818/4/3.

81 IBA Box C, File 3/1a.

82 Ibid.

83 The report explains that 'sharp divisions arose on the manner of saluting and shouting. Everyone saluted, especially when in front of the officers, and no-one advocated otherwise, but the English speaking comrades were loath to shout "Franco".' Ibid.

84 See ibid. Two non-party prisoners were singled out in the report for opposing the committee's line, as was another prisoner, a party member. The three were George Ives, a member of the Labour Party from Shipley and William Collins from Glasgow. The Communist Party member was Lionel Jacobs from Hackney in London.

85 Ibid.

86 IBA Box D-7, Files A/1 and A/6.

87 IBA Box C, File 3/1a, and Geiser, *Prisoners*, p. 128.

88 IBA Box C, File 3/1a.

89 *They Fought in Franco's Jails*, pp. 12–13.

90 Geiser, *Prisoners*, pp. 188–189, and *They Fought in Franco's Jails*, p. 11.

91 Geiser, *Prisoners*, p. 191.

92 Gregory, *The Shallow Grave*, p. 149. See also Cyril Kent, 'I Was in a Franco Prison', *Challenge*, 5 January 1939, pp. 10–11.

93 Geiser, *Prisoners*, p. 185.

94 Dewar, *Communist Politics in Britain*, pp. 121–122.

95 *They Fought in Franco's Jails*, p. 13, and Alexander, *British Volunteers*, p. 191.

96 IBA Box C, File 3/1a.

97 Interview with George Wheeler, IWMSA 11442/8/7.

98 Geiser, *Prisoners*, p. 128.

99 Seven Americans wrote a letter to *The Times* denying the charges against Ryan. *The Times*, 1 June 1938, cited in ibid., p. 133.

100 Ibid., p. 174.

101 IBA Box D-7, File A/1.

102 Almost without exception, accounts by British prisoners testify to the brutal treatment meted out by the guards at San Pedro de Cardeña. Jimmy Moon, for example, describes how 'people were beaten every day.' Interview with Jimmy Moon, IWMSA 15729/4/2.

103 Geiser, *Prisoners*, p. 129.

104 Interview with Jimmy Moon, IWMSA 15729/4 /3. George Wheeler described 'Tanky' as 'the most evil man that I ever knew . . . Tanky was the enemy, he hated us like mad.' IWMSA 11442/8/6.

105 Alexander, *British Volunteers*, p. 188. By all accounts the feeling was mutual: George Wheeler described 'Froggy' as 'the most disgusting specimen of humanity you will ever see.' Ibid.

106 IBA Box C, File 3/1a.

107 See, for example, interview with William Kelly, IWMSA 819/1/1.

108  Alexander, *British Volunteers*, p. 191.

109  *They Fought in Franco's Jails*, p. 8.

110  Interview with Bob Doyle, IWMSA 806/4/3.

111  Interview with Joe Norman, IWMSA 818/4/4.

112  Interview with Bob Doyle, IWMSA 806/4/3.

113  IBA Box C, File 3/1a.

114  Ibid.

115  Interview with Morien Morgan, IWMSA 9856/4/4.

116  Interview with Joe Norman, IWMSA 818/4/4.

117  Interview with Jimmy Moon, IWMSA 15729/4/3.

118  The blank paper at the back of the books was used for writing paper. The rest was probably used for rather more practical purposes.

119  Maurice Levitas claims the propaganda was totally ineffective: 'We would not respond to any kind of political propaganda.' Interview with Maurice Levitas, IWMSA 16358/5/4.

120  IBA Box C, File 3/1a.

121  George Wheeler describes how Levitas ignored the punctuation and inserted his own. Interview with George Wheeler, IWMSA 11442/8/6. However, Levitas states that he was required to read a fascist pamphlet responding to the Bishop of Teruel's anti-fascist lecture and replaced the fascist responses to the bishop's questions with his own. Interview with Maurice Levitas, IWMSA 16358/5/4.

122  'A Life of Ease', *Spain*, 55, 18 October 1938, pp. 41–43.

123  The caption underneath the photograph reads, 'Do these look as though they were "Beaten every day for six weeks?".' 'Franco's "Hell Prisons"', *Spain*, 58, 8 November 1938, pp. 106–107.

124  *New York Times*, 3 April 1938, cited in Geiser, *Prisoners*, p. 96.

125  *Jaily News*, 11 August 1938, p. 1. The cartoon appears in Alexander, *British Volunteers*, p. 190.

126  *Diario de Burgos*, 1 April 1938, cited in Geiser, *Prisoners*, p. 118.

127  'Notifying you that I am well.' Gradually the restrictions were lifted: by mid-June, prisoners were free to write home and to request money, though it could take months to receive a reply. Geiser, *Prisoners*, p. 131.

128  Letter from Foreign Office to Charlotte Haldane, 11 January 1939. PRO FO371/24122–W22.

129  Letter to T. Moon, 10 January 1939. PRO FO371/24122-W207.

130  Anon., *In Spain with the International Brigade: A Personal Narrative*. The author was probably Alec Alexander, a labourer from Liverpool, who became disaffected with the International Brigade in Spain. I am indebted to Jim Carmody for bringing this to my attention.

131  Geiser, *Prisoners*, p. 141.

132  Many prisoners were also concerned that Jewish volunteers might be targeted. Thus pseudonyms were used by some. See IBA Box D-7, File A/6, and interview with Jimmy Moon, IWMSA 15729/4/2.

133  IBA Box C, File 3/1a.

134  Hall, *Disciplina Camaradas*, pp. 101–102.

135  IBA Box C, File 3/1a.

136  Interview with George Wheeler, IWMSA 11442/8/7.

137  IBA Box C, File 3/1a.

138  Geiser, *Prisoners*, p. 103.

139  Shaer-West, MS, p. 22.

140  IBA Box C, File 3/1a. Carl Geiser states that the escape was on the previous night, 13 November.

141  The official report, IBA Box C, File 3/1a, refers to him as English, though he was actually Scottish. See IBA Box D-7, File A/1.

142  IBA Box C, File 3/1a.

143 'Franco Will Never Conquer the Spanish', *Challenge*, 20 February 1939, p. 6, penned by David Goodman.

144 'General Franco Frees 67 Britons', *Daily Telegraph*, 6 February 1939, p. 7.

145 Geiser, *Prisoners*, p. 198.

146 PRO FO371/24122-W784.

147 Alexander, *British Volunteers*, p. 241.

148 Interview with Morien Morgan, IWMSA 9856/4/4, and with George Drever, in MacDougall, *Voices*, p. 288.

149 Interview with Bruce Allender, IWMSA 11300/4/3.

150 Interview with George Wheeler, IWMSA 11442/8/7-8.

151 Bill Alexander suggests that Jones was a Welsh Nationalist, though there is no other evidence for this. See Alexander, *British Volunteers*, p. 193.

152 Geiser, *Prisoners*, p. 133.

153 A telegram of 10 February 1939, from Burgos to London, stated that there were believed to be 12 British prisoners still at Burgos and another two at Bilbao. The writer remarked: 'I cannot at present get Frank Ryan included in the exchange but I am making further efforts.' PRO FO371/24123-W2491.

154 See Cronin, *Frank Ryan*.

## 7 British volunteers for liberty or Comintern army?

1 Report from Colonel K. Sverchevsky ['General Walter'] to Com. Voroshilov, People's Commissar of the Defence of the USSR, Marshal of the Soviet Union, 20 November 1938, Moscow 33987/3/1149, cited in Radosh *et al.*, *Spain Betrayed*, p. 471.

2 Richardson, *Comintern Army*, p. 177.

3 Hopkins, *Into the Heart of the Fire*, p. xi.

4 The dispute essentially rested on two opposing beliefs; the first, put forward by the communists, was that the first priority was to win the war, thus the revolution should be put on hold. The alternative view, expounded by the anarchists and the POUM, was that this was a revolutionary war, that war and revolution were thus inseparable. Whilst the former argument is seductive, as George Orwell himself recognised, the problem was that it provided an ideological smokescreen for the suppression of those supporting the alternative perspective. See George Orwell, *Homage to Catalonia*, pp. 58–64 for his original analysis.

5 Richardson, *Comintern Army*, p. 1.

6 Ibid, p. 2.

7 Ibid., pp. 14–15. This paragraph is quoted in Hopkins, *Into the Heart of the Fire*, p. 153 and appears to form the basis of much of his interpretation of the role of the Communist Party in the International Brigades and in Spain, though he does go on to admit that both Jason Gurney and Fred Copeman claim that the Communist Party simply took advantage of a popular sympathy for the Spanish Republic: 'Ultimately, Moscow would take possession of this idealism and shape it for its own purposes.' Ibid., p. 156.

8 Richardson, *Comintern Army*, p. 23.

9 Review of Antonio Elorza and Marta Bizcarrondo, *Queridos camaradas: la Internacional Comunista y España 1919–1939*, Barcelona: Planeta, 1999, by Helen Graham, in *The Volunteer*, 23: 5, winter 2001, pp. 17–19.

10 B. R. Mitchell and P. Deane, *Abstract of British Historical Statistics*, p. 66, cited in Stevenson and Cook, *Britain in the Depression*, p. 311.

11 The leaders of the trade union movement were exceedingly reluctant to become embroiled in industrial action on behalf of the Spanish Republic, partly because of the legacy of the General Strike, but also due to the fear and loathing of communism by those such as Walter Citrine, the leader of the TUC, and Ernest Bevin, leader of the powerful TGWU. Citrine advised all trade councils not to provide assistance to the hunger

marchers. The Labour Party was not in a position to challenge the National Government in parliament, who had a majority over the Liberals and Labour of 249 seats. See Buchanan, *The British Labour Movement*, p. 63, and Stevenson and Cook, *Britain in the Depression*, p. 187.

12 As R. E. Dowse argues, by disaffiliating from the Labour Party in July 1932, 'the I.L.P. had, in effect, cut itself completely from the organised working-class.' Dowse, *Left in the Centre: The Independent Labour Party, 1893–1940*, p. 189.

13 Tom Buchanan points out that, 'On Spain, as on most political issues in the later 1930s, the Communist Party was undoubtedly the most energetic force on the British left.' Buchanan, *Britain and the Spanish Civil War*, p. 74.

14 Interview with George Leeson, IWMSA 803/4/1.

15 For example, Radosh *et al.* cite a letter from Marty to Moscow requesting experienced military commanders as evidence of the Comintern's determination to control the brigades, even though the document states that, of the recruits, 'one third have insufficient military training [and] the command staff is extremely small and insufficiently qualified.' Moscow 33987/3/832, cited in Radosh *et al.*, *Spain Detrayed*, pp. 103–105.

16 Helen Graham, *The Spanish Republic at War*, pp. 143–144.

17 Hopkins, *Into the Heart*, p. 213. However, later in his book, Hopkins conversely argues that 'it is hard to believe that at some level the volunteers did not know what was taking place.' Ibid., p. 279. If members of the battalion were denied the means to discover information for themselves, this latter claim seems a little unfair.

18 Ibid., p. 317. However Fred Thomas, who fought with the Anti-Tank Battery, argues that Hopkins places too much reliance on some untrustworthy witnesses. Letter from Fred Thomas to Richard Baxell, 27 September 1999. For example, Thomas states that Hopkins's readiness to accept Fred Copeman's claim, that he created an Anti-Tank Battery composed of 'good looking students' to keep the middle- and working-class communists separated in a kind of apartheid, is disputed by all the ex-members of the British Anti-Tank Battery, who recollect that it was the battery's commander, Malcolm Dunbar, rather than Fred Copeman who chose the members. There certainly seems to be little doubt that many of Copeman's uncorroborated assertions should be treated with caution. They also include claims that Tom Wintringham shot himself at Jarama, that Bob Merriman and Walter Tapsell were executed by the Communist Party to keep them quiet, and that homosexuality was rife in the British Battalion. Interview with Fred Copeman, IWMSA 794/13/2-8.

19 See Andrew Thorpe, 'Comintern "Control" of the Communist Party of Great Britain, 1920–43'; and Thorpe, 'The Communist International and the British Communist Party', in Tim Rees and Andrew Thorpe, eds, *International Communism and the Communist International, 1919–1943*, pp. 67–86.

20 Thorpe, 'The Communist International', p. 80.

21 In a confidential report written in December 1937, Bill Rust stated that '[Fred] Copeman refers, almost without exception, to the Brigade in a disparaging fashion.' Rust also claimed that these sentiments were widespread amongst senior figures in the British Battalion: '[Copeman] has also been successful in infecting C[omra]de [Bill] Alexander his adjutant with the same attitude and S[am] Wild has a long established anti-brigade tradition. Also [Ted] Edwards – battalion sec[retar]y is just a weakling who swims with the tide – in this case against the brigade.' According to the report, only Walter Tapsell, the battalion commissar, spoke up for the brigade staff and was thus 'treated by Copeman and Wild with contempt'. In a clear demonstration of the importance of keeping these critical reports in perspective, Rust still acknowledged that, assuming Copeman could be brought back into line, he possessed many 'sterling qualities as a battalion commander'. AHN Salamanca, PS AR 6, pp. 1–4.

22 Many of these would later leave the Communist Party. Whilst some volunteers maintained their support for the USSR for a number of years after the end of the Spanish war, others did not. Some, like Fred Thomas and John Angus, left when the Soviet

Union's policies no longer coincided with theirs; others, like Leslie Preger, left the party even earlier; he left when he returned home from Spain: 'I just drifted away, especially because of their attitude towards the P. O.U.M.ists and anarchists. The *Daily Worker* had accounts of the P. O.U.M.ists playing football with Franco's troops. I thought there are some things I can't accept and when the trials started and every leading theoretician of the Russian Party suddenly turned out to be a Western spy I just couldn't accept all those things.' Interview with Leslie Preger, in Corkhill and Rawnsley, *The Road to Spain*, p. 33. Likewise, Bernard Knox left the party over the show trials of the old Bolsheviks in 1937 and Russia's brutal annexation of the Balkan states and the war in Finland. He was appalled and disgusted when he heard of the recall of General Kleber and his subsequent execution. Bernard Knox, *Premature Anti-Fascist*, p. 11.

23  Miles Tomalin later claimed that 'promotion in our brigades, and presumably throughout the Republican Army, was based solely on service record.' However, this claim should be seen in the light of his statement which followed: 'The best soldiers were generally the men with the deepest social convictions.' Miles Tomalin, 'Memories of the Spanish War', p. 541.

24  Moscow 545/6/95.

25  Richardson, *Comintern Army*, p. 159.

26  Hopkins, *Into the Heart*, p. 151.

27  Alan Bullock, *Hitler and Stalin*, p. 582.

28  See Cary Nelson's review of James Hopkins's *Into the Heart of the Fire*, in *The Volunteer*, 22: 1, winter 2000, pp. 5–15.

29  Interview with John Longstaff, IWMSA 9299/13/10. Other British volunteers suffered from shell-shock during their time in Spain. It seems that a rather enlightened attitude to the condition was adopted in the battalion, with those affected being moved into positions in the rear, such as the cookhouse. See interview with Frank Graham, IWMSA 11877/6/6.

30  Interview with John Peet, in Corkhill and Rawnsley, *Road to Spain*, p. 111.

31  Interview with John Tunnah, IWMSA 840/9/1.

32  Illness was a major problem for the British volunteers, as, indeed, it was for the Republican Army as a whole. 'Sickness and disease were far more dangerous enemies than Nationalists. For every battle injury, there were four, five, or six who had to be discharged or hospitalized because of illness.' Michael Seidman, 'Quiet Fronts in the Spanish Civil War', p. 830. Olive oil, beans, poor quality meat and wine were not a good mixture. Tom Murray recounts how the brigaders used to help themselves to fruit, particularly grapes. As a result, as Fred Thomas describes, 'most of us, including me, are having tummy trouble.' Fred Thomas, *To Tilt at Windmills*, p. 26. See also Sommerfield, *Volunteer in Spain*, p. 31, Romilly, *Boadilla*, p. 33, and interview with Tom Murray, in MacDougall, *Voices from the Spanish Civil War*, pp. 315–316.

33  Nelson, review of Hopkins's *Into the Heart*, p. 5.

34  Moscow 545/6/96, p. 45.

35  Ibid., p. 1.

36  Brome, *The International Brigade*, pp. 68–69.

37  Hopkins, *Into the Heart*, p. 184.

38  Interview with Donald Renton, in MacDougall, *Voices*, p. 24.

39  IBA Box C, File 16/2. In June 1937 Bill Meredith reported to Fred Copeman that five members of his No. 2 Company were drunk and that 'fighting has been going on in the trench and some drastic action should be taken as an example to the rest of the Battalion.' Copeman sentenced the offenders to ten days in a labour battalion and docked them five days' pay. Moscow 545/3/451, p. 49.

40  For example, George Adamson is listed as 'Brave at front. Drunkard in rear', and Frank Cairns as 'Good, but tendency to drink.' Moscow 545/6/96, pp. 5–7. A report compiled in February 1938 listed 40 deserters, though it admitted that there had been perhaps three times as many. The majority were returned to the front. Moscow 545/3/451, p. 91.

41 Hearst, MS, p. 84.
42 Richardson, *Comintern Army*, p. 165.
43 Moscow 545/6/99, pp. 14–19, is a list of thieves, drunkards, deserters and other undesirables in the English-speaking battalions.
44 Alexander, *British Volunteers for Liberty*, p. 81. As Peter Carroll's study of the American volunteers points out, it is extremely difficult to gauge accurately the numbers of deserters. Most of the volunteers entered illegally, surrendering their passports (if they had them), and were, for obvious reasons, at pains to conceal their tracks. Nevertheless, Carroll estimates the number of American deserters to number around 100, about 4 per cent. Carroll, *The Odyssey of the Abraham Lincoln Brigade*, pp. 147–148.
45 Interview with Walter Greenhalgh, IWMSA 11187/9/7.
46 Report from Albacete, [end of] July 1937. Moscow 35082/1/90, cited in Radosh *et al.*, *Spain Betrayed*, p. 246.
47 Interview with Fred Copeman, IWMSA 794/13/2.
48 Interview with George Aitken, IWMSA 10358/3/2.
49 Angus, *With the International Brigade in Spain*, p. 7. Will Paynter, the Welsh organiser for the Communist Party and base commissar at Albacete, also remarks on the low moral after Brunete: 'The ferocity of the battles, the absence of effective supporting arms, after the first attack – they had been deployed to meet a fascist counter-attack on another section of the front [at Brunete] – and the state of disorganization, all created problems of morale which led to some of the men leaving the battle front.' Will Paynter, *My Generation*, p. 70.
50 Richardson, *Comintern Army*, p. 167.
51 Ibid., p. 169.
52 As many volunteers have recounted, by the summer of 1937 the warning that 'you couldn't volunteer out' was included in Robbie's caution to potential recruits. See, for example, interviews with John Tunnah, IWMSA 840/9/1, and John Longstaff, IWMSA 99219/13/4.
53 IBA Box C 14/5, cited in Hopkins, *Into the Heart*, p. 255. Bill Alexander also acknowledged that 'one of the biggest problems facing the British concerned leave and repatriation.' Alexander, *British Volunteers*, p. 79.
54 James Hopkins claims that 'this impression was fostered both in England and confirmed at Albacete by prominent members of the brigade leadership.' Hopkins, *Into the Heart*, p. 292. Togliatti admitted in a report at the end of August 1937 that many of the American, English and Italian volunteers had been promised they would be in Spain for no more than six months. Report by Togliatti, 29 August 1937, Moscow 33987/3/961, cited in Radosh *et al.*, *Spain Betrayed*, p. 253.
55 As General Walter realistically observed: 'Leave in the army always attracts a great deal of interest, and the problem flares up with a special keenness during a war.' Report by General Walter, Moscow 35082/1/95, cited in ibid., p. 458.
56 Report by Togliatti, 29 August 1937, Moscow 33987/3/961, cited in ibid., p. 253.
57 Letter from Will Paynter, 4 September 1937, IBA Box C, File 17/1.
58 Letter from George Aitken, undated, IBA Box C, File 17/7.
59 Angus, *With the International Brigade*, p. 7. Angus claimed that 'The British chaps included none, or really very few, really bad elements. They were just ordinary chaps who thought they had been conned and whose morale had been reduced by seeing a number of commissars, one after the other, stay with them for a few weeks and then return to England.' Ibid., p. 8.
60 Bert Williams, George Coyle, Jack Roberts, Ernest Torrance, Jim Bourne and Eric Whalley. Moscow 545/6/89, p. 37.
61 Fred Copeman, Joe Hinks, Peter Daley, Paddy O'Daire and Harold Fry. Moscow 545/6/89, p. 37.
62 John Angus was placed in charge of the camp to try and restore morale. He appears to have been popular with the British in the camp, and he was also viewed highly by the battalion military and political leadership. Alexander, *British Volunteers*, p. 81.

63 Interview with Joe Norman, IWMSA 818/4/2.

64 Hopkins, *Into the Heart*, p. 268.

65 Carroll, *Odyssey*, pp. 177–178. Another example of this is recounted by Jack Jones, who came across 'Taffy' Foulkes, a deserter from the British Battalion, in Barcelona. When Jones accompanied Foulkes back to the battalion, Sam Wild 'simply told him not to be a bloody fool again.' Jack Jones, *Union Man*, p. 69.

66 Or in the case of ranking soldiers they might be demoted. See Steve Nelson, *The Volunteers: A Personal Narrative of the Fight against Fascism in Spain*, p. 106.

67 Moscow 545/3/467, p. 46. See also interview with John 'Bosco' Jones, IWMSA 9392/6/5. Jones admits that within his section there was an arrangement that one or two volunteers would slip off to Madrid for a couple of days: 'What we did arrange in Jarama, which was perhaps only 30 miles from Madrid, as it was stalemate, that two at a time could go to the main road and most of the Spaniards couldn't read or write, you could hand them almost any document. "I want a camion to take me to Madrid". And so we were taking unofficial twenty-four hours. So long as they got back next morning, okay. This went on through my section quite well.' Jones's ruse was discovered, however, and he was sentenced to ten nights digging trenches in no-mans land.

68 Report signed by Lieutenant Edwards, 9 December 1937. Boon was stopped three days' pay and Cranfield and Steventon two. Moscow 545/3/495, p. 22 and p. 29.

69 To identify volunteers and prevent them returning to Spain, deserters repatriated via the British consulates had their passports stamped, 'Valid for a single direct journey to the United Kingdom'. As a note explained: 'The object of this procedure is to warn His Majesty's authorities concerned that the persons in question have served with the Spanish forces.' From the tone of the correspondence – the deserters were described as 'thugs' and 'misguided stiffs' it is quite clear that the consular officials harbour a hostile and patronising attitude towards the deserting volunteers. PRO FO889/2/97–125.

  The view that the Spanish war was a 'distraction' from more important matters was widely prevalent amongst members of the British Government and ruling establishment. Randolph Churchill famously remarked that, 'A few excitable Catholics and ardent Socialists [in Britain] think that this war matters, but for the general public it's just a lot of bloody dagoes killing each other.' Arnold Lunn, *Spanish Rehearsal for World War*, p. 43, cited in Buchanan, 'A Far Away Country', p. 23.

70 Moscow 545/6/99, p. 9.

71 IBA Box 21a, File A.

72 IBA Box D-7, File A/1.

73 IBA Box 39, File A/31.

74 Moscow 545/3/99, p. 5.

75 Interview with Albert Charlesworth, IWMSA 798/4/2-3.

76 'There is utterly no reason to believe that any commander, including Jock Cunningham and Fred Copeman, used his pistol against any member of the Brigade.' Interview with Hugh Sloan, in MacDougall, *Voices*, p. 211.

77 'We had an absolute rigid rule when I was commander that none of our men would ever get shot. The worst punishment you could have in our battalion was to be sent home in disgrace if you deserted. And we only had three real deserters . . . all the others [would] be away for a fortnight.' Interview with Fred Copeman, IWMSA 794/13/4.

78 Brome, *The International Brigades*, p. 233.

79 James Hopkins appears to overstate the number of executions by referring to the execution of two volunteers for desertion and later to that of Patrick Glacken in January 1938. In fact, Glacken was one of the two deserters. See Hopkins, *Into the Heart*, pp. 267–268.

80 'The death sentences imposed on the two deserters from the British Battalion received the complete approval of a Battalion meeting yesterday.' *Our Fight*, 10 January 1938, p. 1.

81 Dunlop states that all the members of the execution squad were Communist Party members, and of the rank of sergeant. Interview with John Dunlop, IWMSA 11355/13/7.

82 Alexander, *British Volunteers*, p. 82.

83  Interview with Bob Cooney, in Corkhill and Rawnsley, *Road to Spain*, pp. 120–122.

84  IBA Box 21a, File A.

85  Moscow 545/3/99.

86  Interview with Bob Cooney, in Corkhill and Rawnsley, *Road to Spain*, p. 121.

87  Ibid., pp. 121–122.

88  Interview with John Dunlop, IWMSA 11355/13/7-8.

89  Hugh Sloan refers to meeting a 'Paddy' Ryan in July 1938 in Ian MacDougall's collection of interviews with Scottish volunteers. MacDougall erroneously identifies him as Frank Ryan, who had been captured at Calaceite at the end of March 1938, rather than as Maurice Ryan. Interview with Hugh Sloan, in MacDougall, *Voices*, p. 229, and n.152, p. 349.

90  Dunlop described Ryan as 'a decidedly kenspeckle character'. Interview with John Dunlop, IWMSA 11355/13/7/10.

91  Moscow 545/6/99.

92  See, for example, Tom Murray's accusation that Ryan refused to obey orders and threatened him with a hand grenade. Interview with Tom Murray, in MacDougall, *Voices*, p. 324; also cited in Hopkins, *Into the Heart*, pp. 266–267.

93  Interview with John Dunlop, IWMSA 11355/13/10.

94  Ibid.

95  Interview with Tom Murray, in MacDougall, *Voices*, p. 324.

96  Interview with Fred Copeman, IWMSA 794/13/3.

97  Hopkins, *Into the Heart*, p. 268.

98  Moscow 545/6/171, p. 37.

99  The file shows that Meeke was allocated a repatriation number when he entered a camp in France after the war. Thus he cannot have been executed in Spain. PRO FO371/2696/133-241.

100  Anon, *In Spain with the International Brigade*, p. 8.

101  See Buchanan, 'Death of Bob Smillie', pp. 435–464.

102  Interview with Tony Gilbert, IWMSA 9157/10.

103  There appears to be no mention of Browning in any of the files held in the IBA or Moscow.

104  PRO FO371/6060-10683/6/41.

105  Carroll, *Odyssey*, p. 188.

106  Harvey Klehr, J. E. Haynes and F. I. Firsov, in *The Secret World of American Communism*, also exaggerate the level of disaffection. They list only about 100, and many of those are hardly serious disciplinary issues, especially considering that this was around August 1938, in the wake of what Bill Alexander describes with some justification as the 'disastrous' retreats of the spring of 1938.

107  IBA Box C, File 8/2, p. 2.

108  Report from General Walter to Com. Voroshilov, People's Commissar of the Defence of the USSR, Marshal of the Soviet Union. Moscow 33987/3/1149, cited in Radosh *et al.*, *Spain Betrayed*, p. 471.

109  As Bill Rust admits, many of the volunteers were 'exercising the inalienable British right to grumble'. Rust, *Britons in Spain*, p. 31.

110  See Hopkins, *Into the Heart*, pp. 258–264.

111  Marcovitch had a long history of arguments with Peter Kerrigan in Glasgow and was clearly singled out. However, very few other British brigaders were actually imprisoned for political nonconformity, so-called deviationism, though persistent deserters might be imprisoned. This was, after all, an army.

112  General Walter, the commander of the 35th Division, ruefully acknowledged that 'Being an "antifascist revolutionary" allows you to argue and debate with the commander, as a rule, using the familiar "tú" with your hands in your pockets and a cigarette in your mouth.' Radosh *et al.*, *Spain Betrayed*, p. 446.

113  As Thomas Evans described, political commissars were often referred to as 'comic

stars'. Interview with Thomas Glyndwr Evans, in Hynes, 'The British Battalion of the XVth International Brigade', p. 58.

114 John Booth, one of the contingent of volunteers from Manchester, said that 'when they had us chanting "No Pasaran", the lads would be there, grim-faced, with the old clenched fist firmly up, not a smile among them, all shouting "No Bastard Pan".' Interview with John Booth, in ibid., p. 58.

115 Some of the volunteers were highly critical of the party propaganda, believing it to be self-defeating. For example, James Albrighton claimed that the official communiqués that were distributed to the volunteers deliberately underestimated casualty numbers. 'Whoever is responsible for issuing these communique's and wall newspapers [*sic*] must think that we are fools or children . . . To many of the comrades it is an insult to their intelligence to make such statements.' James Albrighton's diary, Tuesday 5 January 1937.

116 John Peet, *The Long Engagement: Memoirs of a Cold War Legend*, p. 77.

117 Peet goes on to describe how several German commissars and Russian advisors assumed the battalion to be in a state of near-mutiny, 'and would make urgent representations to our political commissars. The political commissars, "comic stars" was the usual brigade term, often did not fully grasp what the complaints were about – they often led the singing themselves.' Ibid., p. 77.

118 As Alexander states: 'It was a difficult time for the army and for the Republic . . . There was some defeatism, some desertion and there were some who drifted from the front.' Alexander, *British Volunteers*, pp. 197–198.

119 Moscow 545/6/93, p. 3. As James Jump recounts, the Republican Army had a puritanical attitude to venereal diseases: 'To get VD for example, you were told it was the equivalent of a self-inflicted wound, you were not only harming yourself but the army.' Interview with James Jump, IWMSA 9524/6/4. Whilst he was in hospital for hepatitis, Jump's medical records were mixed up with those of another patient suffering from a venereal disease. His description of the coldness with which he was treated by all the hospital staff is a good demonstration of how badly the condition was viewed, both politically and morally.

120 Thomas B. Hughes from London is listed as 'Repat. S.I. Wnd. N.G.', and Thomas McColl from Scotland as 'Mataro, S.I. Wound'. Moscow 545/6/97, p. 9 and p. 11.

121 This was also true of the Republican Army as a whole. As Michael Seidman states, 'Madrid Hospital 14, Calle de la Puebla reported so many self-mutilations in the left hand or arm that health care personnel assumed that any injuries in these body parts were self-inflicted. On a quiet sector near Lerida in September 1937, commissars recommended public shaming and severe punishment, including death sentences, for *automutilados*.' Seidman, 'Quiet Fronts', p. 830.

122 Report by General Walter, 14 January 1938, Moscow 35082/1/95, cited in Radosh *et al.*, *Spain Betrayed*, p. 450.

123 Hooper, *No Pasarán!*, p. 32.

124 Interview with Hugh Sloan, in MacDougall, *Voices*, p. 208. George Wheeler, a corporal in the British Battalion, also recalls having to prompt a Spanish comrade forward at bayonet point. However, he was honest enough to admit to his own fears: '"*Adelante*" I yelled at him in righteous indignation, conveniently forgetting that a little earlier I had been almost ready to flee.' Wheeler, MS, p. 79.

125 Angus, *With the International Brigade*, p. 9.

126 Hamish Fraser, *The Truth About Spain*, p. 5.

127 See Moscow 35082/1/90, reproduced in Radosh *et al.*, *Spain Betrayed*, pp. 241–242.

128 See report of 29 August 1937, which describes how, during the fighting round Madrid in 1936 and the first half of 1937, the International Brigades 'represented a force that was significantly superior to the Spanish units from every point of view.' Moscow 33987/3/961, cited in ibid., p. 255.

129 IBA Box C, File 16/1.

130  See Chapter 5, in which the arguments following Brunete that raged between Tapsell, Aitken and others are discussed. One of the central issues was the performance of Spanish members of the battalion.

131  Letter from Peter Kerrigan to Harry Pollitt, 27 September 1938, IBA Box C, File 25/5.

132  In September 1938 the Spanish reinforcements in the British Battalion were 'very young, almost untrained, and a number were prisoners from Franco's army who had accepted the option of joining the Republican forces.' Alexander, *British Volunteers*, p. 211.

133  Togliatti reported critically of the disparaging attitude of the Internationals towards the Spanish units, yet concluded that in many ways the Lister Brigade was at least as professional as any of the International Brigades. Report dated 29 August 1937, Moscow 33987/3/961, reproduced in Radosh *et al.*, *Spain Betrayed*, p. 255.

134  There was, of course, genuine sympathy for the Spanish Republicans. It is important to remember, for example, that all Communist Party members gave a third of their wages to Socorro Rojo (Red Aid).

135  V. B. Johnson, *Legions of Babel: The International Brigades in the Spanish Civil War.*

136  Moscow 545/6/89, pp. 12–13.

137  Ibid. and Alexander, *British Volunteers*, p. 151.

138  Ruskin, whose real name was Doumont Zubchaninov, was of White Russian descent. He had worked as a communications technician in Spain, France and Argentina, and actually spoke eight languages. He was at first used as the brigade interpreter, before being placed in charge of brigade transmission. Ibid., p. 118.

139  Brome, *The International Brigades*, p. 272.

140  Interview with Joe Monks, IWMSA 11303/4/3.

141  In a letter of 23 June 1937, General Stern remarks upon 'the attitude of Spaniards toward them and of them towards the Spaniards . . . the chauvinism of the nationalities [in the International Brigades]'. Moscow 33987/3/1056, cited in Radosh *et al.*, *Spain Betrayed*, p. 240.

142  Moscow 35082/1/90, in ibid., p. 241.

143  For example, Vincent Brome claims that some Spanish soldiers thought little of the foreigners and that they asked when they would be leaving Spain. Brome, *The International Brigades*, p. 253.

144  Interview with James Jump, IWMSA 9524/6/5.

145  Moscow 35082/1/90, cited in Radosh *et al.*, *Spain Betrayed*, p. 260.

146  Report by General Walter, 14 January 1938, Moscow 35082/1/95, cited in ibid., pp. 448–449.

147  See Chapter 3.

148  See, for example, the refusal by the Americans to accept George Wattis as their battalion commander. As James Hopkins states, 'there was always considerable tension between the Americans and the British.' Hopkins, *Into the Heart*, pp. 273–274, n.26, pp. 412–413 and n.69, pp. 419–420.

149  Anon., *In Spain with the International Brigades*, p. 6.

150  Gregory, *The Shallow Grave*, p. 112.

151  Interview with Fred Copeman, IWMSA 794/13/2. Many of the British agreed with Copeman: 'We were the shock battalion of the shock brigades.' Interview with Tommy Bloomfield, in MacDougall, *Voices*, p. 52.

# References and bibliography

## 1. Primary sources

### 1.1 Unpublished memoir material

Albrighton, James, 'Diaries'. IBA Box 50, File Al/12.
Anon., 'The Epic of Arganda Bridge', IBA Box B-4, File L/8.
Cantor, Ralph, 'Diary', WCML, Manchester.
Green, Oliver, Piper, Alec, Aitken, George, Meredith, Bill, Diamont, André, McElroy, James, and McAnaw, T., 'The British Brigade'. Fred Copeman Collection, Imperial War Museum, London.
Griffiths, W. J., 'Spain: Memoirs of the Spanish Civil War'. South Wales Miners' Library, Swansea.
Harrisson, P. D., 'Interesting Times'. Author's copy, courtesy of David Leach.
Hearst, Louis, *The First Twelve*. Author's copy, courtesy of David Marshall.
Kurzke, Jan, *The Good Comrade*, Author's copy
Ludwick, Percy, 'Fortification Work in the XVth International Brigade'. Moscow, 1998.
Murphy, Molly, 'Nurse Molly'. NMLH, Manchester.
Peet, Jon, 'Nuts and Bolts of Spanish War'. IBA Box A-12, File Pe/3.
Steventon, Sydney, 'Impressions of the Spanish War', IBA Box 21, File H-18.
Thompson, W. M., 'Sojourn in Spain', IBA Box 50, File Th/1.
Wheeler, George, 'To Make the People Smile Again'. Author's copy, courtesy of George Wheeler.

### 1.2 Published primary sources

Acier, Marcel, ed., *From Spanish Trenches: Recent Letters from Spain*. New York: Modern Age Books, 1937.
Alexander, Bill, *British Volunteers for Liberty*. London: Lawrence & Wishart, 1982.
Angus, John, *With the International Brigade in Spain*. Loughborough: Loughborough University Press, 1983.
Anon., *In Spain with the International Brigade: A Personal Narrative*. London: Burns, Oates & Washborne, 1938.
Anon., *They Fought in Franco's Jails*. London: CPGB, 1939.
Atholl, Katherine, *Searchlight on Spain*. London: Penguin, 1938.
Belcher, Bill, *Shipwreck on Middleton Reef: The Story of a Tasman Survivor*. Auckland: Collins, 1979.

Bolín, Luis, *Spain: The Vital Years*. London: Cassell, 1967.

Borkenau, Franz, *The Spanish Cockpit*. Ann Arbor: University of Michigan Press, 1963.

Britten, Austin F., *On the Aragon Battlefront*. London: Nicholls, n.d.

Brockway, Fenner, *The Truth About Barcelona*. London: ILP, 1938.

Cardozo, Harold, *The March of a Nation: My Year in Spain's Civil War*. London: Eyre & Spottiswoode, 1937.

Chalmers-Mitchell, Peter, *My House in Malaga*. London: Faber & Faber, 1938.

Churchill, Winston, *Step by Step 1936–1939*. London: Macmillan, 1943.

Clark, Bob, *No Boots to my Feet: Experiences of a Britisher in Spain 1937–38*. Stoke-on-Trent: Student Bookshops, 1984.

Colodny, Robert, *The Struggle for Madrid*. New York: Paine-Whitman, 1958.

Copeman, Fred, *Reason in Revolt*. London: Blandford Press, 1948.

Cornford, John, *Collected Writings*. Manchester: Carcanet, 1986.

Coward, Jack, *Back from the Dead*. Liverpool: Merseyside Writers, *c*.1985.

Cox, Geoffrey, *The Defence of Madrid*. London: Gollancz, 1937.

Deegan, Frank, *There's No Other Way*. Liverpool: Toulouse Press, 1980.

Delmer, Sefton, *Trail Sinister*. London: Secker & Warburg, 1961.

Doyle, Bob, *Memorias de un rebelde sin pausa*. Madrid: AABI, 2002.

Eden, Anthony, *Facing the Dictators: Memoirs, Part 1*. London: Cassell, 1962.

Edmonds, Lloyd, *Letters from Spain*, ed. Amirah Inglis. Sydney: Allen & Unwin, 1985.

Elstob, Peter, *Spanish Prisoner*. London: Macmillan, 1939.

Fischer, Louis, *Men and Politics: An Autobiography*. London: Jonathan Cape, 1941.

Foss, William, and Gerahty, Cecil, *The Spanish Arena*. London: Right Book Club, 1939.

Fraser, Hamish, *The Truth About Spain*. Oxford: Catholic Social Guild, 1949.

Fyvel, Penelope, *English Penny*. Ilfracombe: Arthur Stockwell, 1992.

Geiser Carl, *Prisoners of the Good Fight*. Westport, CT: Lawrence Hill, 1986.

Graham, Frank, ed., *The Battle of Jarama*. Newcastle: Frank Graham, 1987.

—— *Battles of Brunete and the Aragon*. Newcastle: Frank Graham, 1999.

Gregory, Walter, *The Shallow Grave: A Memoir of the Spanish Civil War*. London: Victor Gollancz, 1986.

Guest, Carmel Haden, *David Guest: A Scientist Fights for Freedom 1911–1938*. London: Lawrence & Wishart, 1939.

Gurney, Jason, *Crusade in Spain*. London: Faber & Faber, 1974.

Haldane, Charlotte, *Truth Will Out*. London: Weidenfeld & Nicolson, 1949.

Hooper, David, *No Pasarán! A Memoir of the Spanish Civil War*. London: Avon, 1997.

Horne, Harold, *All the Trees Were Bread and Cheese*. Luton: Owen Hardisty, 1998.

Hyde, Douglas, *I Believed*. New York: G. P. Putnams, 1950.

James, Tommy, 'Pounded Earth', in Brian Lewis and Bill Gledhill, *A Lion of a Man*. Yorkshire: Art Circus, 1985, pp. 31–82.

Jirku, Gusti, *We Fight Death: The Work of the Medical Service of the International Brigades in Spain*. Madrid: Diana (UGT), 1938.

Jones, Jack, *Union Man*. London: Collins, 1986.

Kemp, Peter, *Mine Were of Trouble*. London: Cassells, 1957.

—— 'I Fought for Franco', in A. J. P. Taylor, ed., *History of the Twentieth Century*. London: Purnell, 1968, pp. 1604–1609.

Kisch, Richard, *They Shall Not Pass: The Spanish People at War 1936–9*. Letchworth: Weyland, 1974.

Knox, Bernard, *Essays Ancient and Modern*. Baltimore: Johns Hopkins University Press, 1989.

—— *Premature Anti-Fascist*. New York: New York University Press, 1998.

Koestler, Arthur, *Spanish Testament*. London: Victor Gollancz, 1937.

—— *Invisible Writing*. London: Collins, 1954.

Langdon-Davies, John, *Behind the Spanish Barricades*. London: Secker & Warburg, 1936.

Lee, Laurie, *A Moment of War*. London: Viking, 1991.

—— *To War in Spain*. Harmondsworth: Penguin, 1996.

Lehmann, John, ed., *Ralph Fox: A Writer in Arms*. London: Lawrence & Wishart, 1937.

Levine, Maurice, *Cheetham to Cordova: Maurice Levine, a Manchester Man of the Thirties*. Manchester: privately published, 1984.

Loveday, Arthur F., *World War in Spain*. London: John Murray, 1939.

Lunn, Arnold, *Spanish Rehearsal for World War: An Eyewitness Account of the Spanish Civil War*. London: Hutchinson, 1937.

Macartney, W. F. R., *Walls Have Mouths*. London: Victor Gollancz, 1936.

MacKee, Seamus, *I Was a Franco Soldier*. London: United Editorial, 1938.

McNair, John, *In Spain Now*. London: ILP, 1937.

—— *Spanish Diary*. Leeds: ILP, 1938.

Madge, Charles, and Harrisson, Tom, *Britain by Mass Observation*. London: Penguin, 1939.

Martin, Robert, 'With the International Brigade', *Workers' Liberty*, November 1995, pp. 28–30.

Monks, J., *With the Reds in Andalusia*. London: privately printed, 1985.

Nelson, Steve, *The Volunteers: A Personal Narrative of the Fight against Fascism in Spain*. New York: Masses and Mainstream, 1953.

—— *The Aura of the Cause*. Waltham, MA: Abraham Lincoln Brigade Archives, 1997.

O'Connor, Peter, *Recollections of a Socialist and Anti-Fascist Fighter*. Dublin: MSF, 1996.

O'Donnell, Paedar, *Salud! An Irishman in Spain*. London: Methuen, 1937.

O'Duffy, Eoin, *Crusade in Spain*. Dublin: Brown & Nolan, 1938.

O'Riordan, Michael, *Connolly Column*. Dublin: New Books, 1979.

Orwell, George, *Homage to Catalonia*. London: Secker & Warburg, 1938.

—— 'Spilling the Spanish Beans', *New English Weekly*, 29 July and 2 September 1937.

—— 'Looking Back on the Spanish Civil War', in *The Penguin Complete Longer Non-Fiction of George Orwell*. Harmondsworth: Penguin, 1983.

Paynter, Will, *My Generation*. London: Allen & Unwin, 1972.

Peet, John, *The Long Engagement: Memoirs of a Cold War Legend*. London: Fourth Estate, 1989.

Pitcairn, Frank, *Reporter in Spain*. London: Lawrence & Wishart, 1936.

Pollitt, Harry, *Spain and the T.U.C.* London: CPGB, 1936.

Regler, Gustav, *The Owl of Minerva*. London: Rupert Hart-Davies, 1959.

Rust, William, *Britons in Spain*. London: Lawrence & Wishart, 1939.

Romilly, Esmond, *Boadilla*. London: Hamish Hamilton, 1937.

Ryan, Frank, ed., *The Book of the XVth Brigade: Records of British, American, Canadian and Irish Volunteers in the XV International Brigade in Spain 1936–1938*. Madrid: War Commissariat, 1938.

Sarolea, Charles, *Daylight on Spain*. London: Hutchinson, 1938.

Sloan, Hugh, 'Why I Volunteered', *Scottish Trade Union Review*, 51, July–September 1991, pp. 30–31.

Sommerfield, John, *Volunteer in Spain*. London: Lawrence & Wishart, 1937.

Spender, Stephen, *World Within World*. London: Readers Union, 1951.

Steer, G. L., *The Tree of Gernika*. London: Hodder & Stoughton, 1938.

Stratton, H., *To Anti-Fascism by Taxi*. Port Talbot: Alun Books, 1984.

Thomas, Frank, *Brother Against Brother*, ed. Robert Stradling. Stroud: Sutton, 1998.

Thomas, Fred, *To Tilt at Windmills: A Memoir of the Spanish Civil War*. East Lansing: State University of Michigan Press, 1996.

Tinker, F. G., *Some Still Live*. London: Lovatt Dickson, 1938.
Tomalin, Miles, 'Memories of the Spanish War', *New Statesman*, 31 October 1975, pp. 541–542.
Trench, Chalmers, *Nearly Ninety: Reminiscences*. Ballivor, Co. Meath: Hannon Press, 1996.
Watson, Keith Scott, *Single to Spain*. London: Arthur Baker, 1937.
Wheeler, George, *To Make the People Smile Again*, ed. David Leach, Newcastle: Zymurgy, 2003.
Wintringham, Tom, *English Captain*. London: Faber & Faber, 1939.

## 2 Secondary sources

Aldgate, Anthony, *Cinema and History: British Newsreels and the Spanish Civil War*. London: Scholar Press, 1979.
Alexander, Bill, 'George Orwell and Spain', in Christopher Norris, ed., *Inside the Myth. Orwell: Views from the Left*. London: Lawrence & Wishart, 1984, pp. 85–102.
—— *No to Franco: The Struggle Never Stopped (1939–1975!)*. London: privately published, 1992.
Alpert, Michael, *El ejército republicano en la guerra civil*. Barcelona: Ibérica de Ediciones y Publicaciones, 1977.
—— 'Humanitarianism and Politics in the British Response to the Spanish Civil War, 1936–39', *European History Quarterly*, 14: 4, October 1984, pp. 423–439.
—— 'Uncivil War – the Military Struggle', *History Today*, 39, March 1989, pp. 13–19.
—— *A New International History of the Spanish Civil War*. London: Macmillan, 1994.
Anon., *Images of the Spanish Civil War*. London: Allen & Unwin, 1986.
Anon., *In Defence of Liberty: Spain 1936–9. International Brigade Memorial*. n.p., n.d.
Balfour, Sebastian, and Preston Paul, eds, *Spain and the Great Powers in the Twentieth Century*. London: Routledge, 1999.
Ball, S., 'The Politics of Appeasement: The Fall of the Duchess of Atholl and the Kinross and West-Perth By-Election, December 1938', *Scottish Historical Review*, 187, April 1990, pp. 49–85.
Beevor, Anthony, *The Spanish Civil War*. London: Orbis, 1982.
Benewick, R., *The Fascist Movement in Britain*. London: Allen Lane, 1972.
Bennett, Richard, 'Portrait of a Killer', *New Statesman*, 24 March 1961, pp. 471–472.
—— *The Black and Tans*. London: Edward Hulton, 1959.
Blythe, Robert, *The Age of Illusion*. London: Hamish Hamilton, 1963.
Bolloten, Burnett, *The Grand Camouflage: The Communist Conspiracy in the Spanish Civil War*. London: Hollis & Carter, 1961.
—— *The Spanish Civil War: Revolution and Counter-Revolution*. London: Harvester Wheatsheaf, 1991.
Bradley, Ken, *International Brigades in Spain 1936–39*. London: Osprey, 1994.
Branson, Noreen, *History of the Communist Party of Great Britain 1927–1941*. London: Lawrence & Wishart, 1985.
Brenan, Gerald, *The Spanish Labyrinth*. Cambridge: Cambridge University Press, 1974.
Brendon, Piers, *The Dark Valley: A Panorama of the 1930s*. London: Jonathan Cape, 2000.
Bridgeman, Brian, *The Flyers: The Untold Story of British and Commonwealth Airmen in the Spanish Civil War and other Air Wars from 1919 to 1940*. Swindon: B. Bridgman, 1989.
Brome, Vincent, *The International Brigades: Spain, 1936–1939*. London: Heinemann, 1965.
Broué, Pierre, and Témime, Emile, *The Revolution and the Civil War in Spain*. London: Faber & Faber, 1972.
Buchanan, Tom, *The British Labour Movement and the Spanish Civil War*. Cambridge: Cambridge University Press, 1991.

—— 'Britain's Popular Front? Aid Spain and the British Labour Movement', *History Workshop Journal*, 31, 1991, pp. 60–72.

—— 'A Far Away Country of Which We Know Nothing?', *Twentieth Century British History*, 4: 1, 1993, pp. 1–24.

—— *Britain and the Spanish Civil War*. Cambridge: Cambridge University Press, 1997.

—— 'The Death of Bob Smillie, the Spanish Civil War, and the Eclipse of the Independent Labour Party', *Historical Journal*, 40: 2, 1997, pp. 435–464.

—— 'The Lost Art of Felicia Browne', *History Workshop Journal*, 54, 2002, pp. 181–201.

Bullock, Alan, *Hitler and Stalin*, new edn. London: Fontana, 1993.

Carlton, David, 'Eden, Blum, and the Origins of Non-Intervention', *Journal of Contemporary History*, 6: 3, 1971, pp. 40–55.

Carr, E. H., *The Comintern and the Spanish Civil War*. London: Macmillan, 1984.

Carr, Raymond, ed., *Spain 1808–1975*. Oxford: Clarendon Press, 1966.

—— *Modern Spain 1875–1980*. Oxford: Oxford University Press, 1980.

—— *The Republic and the Civil War in Spain*. London: Macmillan, 1971.

—— *The Spanish Tragedy: The Civil War in Perspective*. London: Phoenix, 2000.

Carroll, Peter N., *The Odyssey of the Abraham Lincoln Brigade*. Stanford, CA: Stanford University Press, 1994.

Castells, Andreu, *Las brigadas internacionales de la guerra de España*. Barcelona: Ariel, 1974.

Chomsky, Noam, 'Objectivity and Liberal Scholarship', in James Peck, ed., *The Chomsky Reader*. New York: Pantheon, 1987, pp. 83–120.

Coker, Christopher, *War and the Twentieth Century*. London: Brasseys, 1994.

Cook, Judith, *Apprentices of Freedom*. London: Quartet Press, 1979.

Cooper, Mike, and Parkes, Ray, *We Cannot Park on Both Sides: Reading Volunteers in the Spanish Civil War 1936–39*. Reading: Reading International Brigades Memorial Committee, 2000.

Cordery, Bob, *La ultima cruzada*. Leigh on Sea: Partisan Press, 1989.

Corkhill, D., and Rawnsley, S., eds, *The Road to Spain: Anti Fascists at War 1936–1939*. Dunfermline: Borderline, 1981.

Coverdale, John F., *Italian Intervention in the Spanish Civil War*. London: Princeton University Press, 1975.

Crick, Bernard, *George Orwell: A Life*. London: Secker & Warburg, 1980.

Crome, Len, 'Walter, 1897–1947: A Soldier in Spain', *History Workshop Journal*, 9, spring 1980, pp. 116–128.

Cronin, Seán, *Frank Ryan: The Search for the Republic*. Dublin: Repsol, 1979.

Crowley, Mike, 'Rebels Against Rebels', *North West Labour History*, 22, 1997–1998, pp. 78–81.

Cunningham, Valentine, ed., *Spanish Front: Writers on the Civil War*. Oxford: Oxford University Press, 1986.

Curtis, Michael, *The Press*. London: News Chronicle, 1951.

Delperrié de Bayac, J., *Les Brigades internationales, 1936–1938: l'épopée de la guerre d'Espagne*. Paris: Librairie Arthème Fayard, 1968.

Dewar, Hugo, *Communist Politics in Britain: The CPGB from its Origins to the Second World War*. London: Pluto, 1976.

Dowse, R. E., *Left in the Centre: The Independent Labour Party, 1893–1940*. London: Longmans, 1966.

Durant, Henry, 'Public Opinion Polls and Foreign Policy', *British Journal of Sociology*, 6, 1955, pp. 149–168.

Durgan, Andy, 'Freedom Fighters or Comintern Army?', *International Socialism Journal*, 84, autumn 1999, pp. 1–16.

Eaton, George, *Neath and the Spanish Civil War*. Neath: privately published, 1980.

Eby, C., *Between the Bullet and the Lie: American Volunteers in the Spanish Civil War*. New York: Holt, Rinehart & Winston, 1969.

Edwards, Jill, *The British Government and the Spanish Civil War*. London: Macmillan, 1979.

Ellwood, Sheelagh M., *The Spanish Civil War*. Oxford: Blackwell, 1991.

——*Franco*. Harlow: Longman, 1994.

Engel, Carlos, *Historia de las brigadas mixtas del ejército popular de la República*. Madrid: Almena, 1999.

Fernbach, David, 'Tom Wintringham and Socialist Defence Strategy', *History Workshop Journal*, 14, autumn 1982, pp. 63–91.

Fleay, C., and Saunders, M. L., 'The Labour Spain Committee: Labour Party Policy and the Spanish Civil War', *Historical Journal*, 28: 1, 1985, pp. 187–197.

Flint, J., 'Must God Go Fascist? English Catholic Opinion and the Spanish Civil War', *Church History*, 56, 1987, pp. 264–274.

Francis, Hywell, 'Welsh Miners and the Spanish Civil War', *Journal of Contemporary History*, 5: 3, 1970, pp. 177–191.

——*Miners Against Fascism: Wales and the Spanish Civil War*. London: Lawrence & Wishart, 1984.

——'"Say Nothing and Leave in the Middle of the Night": The Spanish Civil War Revisited', *History Workshop Journal*, 32, autumn 1991, pp. 69–76.

Fraser, Ronald, *Blood of Spain*. London: Allen Lane, 1979.

Fyrth, Jim, *The Signal Was Spain*. London: Lawrence & Wishart, 1986.

——'The Aid for Spain Movement in Britain', in Joyce M. Bellamy and John Saville, eds, *Dictionary of Labour Biography*. London: Macmillan, 1993, pp. 25–32.

——'The Aid Spain Movement in Britain 1936–1939', *History Workshop Journal*, 35, 1993, pp. 153–164.

Fyrth, Jim, and Alexander, Sally, *Women's Voices from the Spanish Civil War*. London: Lawrence & Wishart, 1991.

Gallagher, Tom, 'Scottish Catholics and the British Left', *Innes Review* 34: 1, 1983, pp. 17–42.

Gannes, Harry, and Repard, Theodore, *Spain in Revolt*. London: Victor Gollancz, 1936.

Gannon, Franklin Reid, *The British Press and Germany 1936–1939*. Oxford: Clarendon Press, 1971.

Gartner, Lloyd P., *The Jewish Immigrant in England 1870–1914*. London: Simons, 1973.

Graham, Helen, *The Spanish Republic at War, 1936–1939*. Cambridge: Cambridge University Press, 2002.

Graham, Helen, and Labanyi, Jo, eds, *Spanish Cultural Studies: An Introduction: The Struggle for Modernity*. Oxford: Oxford University Press, 1995.

Graham, Helen, and Preston, Paul, eds, *The Popular Front in Europe*. London: Macmillan, 1987.

Greene, Thomas R., 'The English Catholic Press and the Second Spanish Republic, 1931–1936', *Church History*, 45: 1, 1976, pp. 70–84.

Haigh, R. H., Morris, D. S., and Peters, A. R., *The Guardian Book of the Spanish Civil War*. Aldershot: Wildwood House, 1987.

Hall, Christopher, *Disciplina Camaradas: Four English Volunteers in Spain 1936–39*. Pontefract: Gosling Press, 1994.

——*Revolutionary Warfare: Spain 1936–39*. Pontefract: Gosling Press, 1996.

Harrison, Stanley, *Good to be Alive: The Story of Jack Brent*. London: Lawrence & Wishart, 1954.

Hemingway, Ernest, *For Whom the Bell Tolls*. New York: Scribner, 1940.

Henry, Chris, *The Ebro 1938: The Death Knell of the Republic*. Oxford: Osprey, 1999.

Heywood, Paul, 'Why the Republic Lost', *History Today*, 39, March 1989, pp. 20–27.

Hills, G., *The Battle for Madrid*. London: Vantage, 1976.

Hoar, Victor, *The Mackenzie-Papineau Battalion*, Vancouver: Copp Clark, 1969.

Hopkins, James K., *Into the Heart of the Fire: The British in the Spanish Civil War*. Stanford, CA: Stanford University Press, 1998.

Howson, Gerald, *Arms for Spain: The Untold Story of the Spanish Civil War*. London: John Murray, 1998.

Hughes, Matthew, and Garrido, Enriqueta, 'Planning and Command: The Spanish Republican Army and the Battle of the Ebro, 1938', *International Journal of Iberian Studies*, 12: 2, 1999, pp. 107–115.

Imperial War Museum, *The Spanish Civil War Collection*. London: Imperial War Museum, 1996.

Inglis, Amirah, *Australians in the Spanish Civil War*. Sidney: Allen & Unwin, 1987.

Jackson, Angela, *British Women and the Spanish Civil War, 1936–39*. London: Routledge, 2002.

Jackson, Gabriel, ed., *The Spanish Civil War: Domestic Crisis or International Conspiracy?* Boston: D. C. Heath, 1967.

—— *A Concise History of the Spanish Civil War*. London: Thames & Hudson, 1974.

—— *The Spanish Republic and the Civil War, 1931–1939*. Princeton, NJ: Princeton University Press, 1976.

Jackson, Michael, *Fallen Sparrows: The International Brigades in the Spanish Civil War*. Philadelphia: American Philosophical Society, 1994.

Johnson, V. B., *Legions of Babel: The International Brigades in the Spanish Civil War*. University Park: Pennsylvania University Press, 1967.

Klaus, H. Gustav, ed., *Strong Words, Brave Deeds: The Poetry, Life and Times of Thomas O'Brien, Volunteer in the Spanish Civil War*. Dublin: O'Brien Press, 1994.

Klehr, Harvey, Haynes, J. E., and Firsov F. I., *The Secret World of American Communism*. London: Yale University Press, 1995.

Krammer, Arnold, 'Germans Against Hitler: The Thaelmann Brigade', *Journal of Contemporary History*, 4: 2, 1969, pp. 65–83.

Landis, Arthur, *History of the Abraham Lincoln Brigade*. New York: Citadel Press, 1967.

Laqueur, Walter, ed., *Fascism – A Reader's Guide*. Aldershot: Scholar Press, 1991.

Lending, Edward I., 'Jews Who Fought', *Horizons*, January–February 1992, pp. 15–19.

Lewis, Brian, and Gledhill, Bill, *A Lion of a Man*. Yorkshire: Art Circus, 1985.

Lipman, V. D., *Social History of the Jews in England 1850–1950*. London: Watts, 1954.

Little, Douglas, *Malevolent Neutrality: The United States, Great Britain and the Origins of the Spanish Civil War*. Ithaca, NY: Cornell University Press, 1985.

—— 'Red Scare, 1936: Anti-Bolshevism and the Origins of British Non-Intervention in the Spanish Civil War', *Journal of Contemporary History*, 23, 1988, pp. 291–311.

MacDougall, Ian, 'Tom Murray: Veteran of Spain', *Cencrastus*, 18, autumn 1984, pp. 16–19.

—— ed., *Voices from the Spanish Civil War: Personal Recollections of Scottish Volunteers in Republican Spain, 1936–1939*. Edinburgh: Polygon, 1986.

McGarry, Fearghal, *Irish Politics and the Spanish Civil War*. Cork: Cork University Press, 1999.

Mackenzie, S. P., 'The Foreign Enlistment Act and the Spanish Civil War, 1936–1939', *Twentieth Century History*, 10: 1, 1999, pp. 52–66.

McLachlan, Donald, 'The Press and Public Opinion', *British Journal of Sociology*, 6, 1955, pp. 159–168.

McLoughlin, Barry, 'Colder Light on the Good Fight: Revisiting Volunteers in the Spanish Civil War', *Yearbook of the Irish Labour History Society*, 24, 1999, pp. 67–71.

Manning, Maurice, *The Blueshirts*. Dublin: Gill & Macmillan, 1970.

Mendlesohn, Farah, *Quaker Relief Work in the Spanish Civil War*. New York: Edwin Mellen Press, 2002.

Miller, John, ed., *Voices Against Tyranny*. New York: Charles Scribner, 1986.

Mitchell, B. R., and Deane, P., *Abstract of British Historical Statistics*. Cambridge: Cambridge University Press, 1971.

Mitchell, David, *The Spanish Civil War*. London: Granada, 1982.

Moradiellos, Enrique, 'The Origins of British Non-Intervention in the Spanish Civil War: Anglo-Spanish Relations in early 1936', *European History Quarterly*, 21: 3, July 1991, pp. 339–364.

——'Appeasement and Non-Intervention: British Policy during the Spanish Civil War', in Peter Catterall and C. J. Morris, eds, *Britain and the Threat to Stability in Europe, 1918–47*. London: Leicester University Press, 1993, pp. 94–104.

——*La perfidia de Albión: El Gobierno británico y la guerra civil española*. Madrid: Siglo veintiuno editores sa, 1996.

——'The British Government and the Spanish Civil War', *International Journal of Iberian Studies*, 12: 1, 1999, pp. 4–13.

Morgan, Kevin, *Against Fascism and War: Ruptures and Continuities in British Communist Politics 1935–1941*. Manchester: Manchester University Press, 1989.

——*Harry Pollitt*. Manchester: Manchester University Press, 1993.

Mowat, Charles L., *Britain Between the Wars*. London: Methuen, 1955.

Payne, Stanley G., *The Spanish Revolution*. London: Weidenfeld & Nicolson, 1970.

——*The Franco Regime: 1936–1975*. Madison: University of Wisconsin Press, 1987.

Pettifer, James, ed., *Cockburn in Spain*. London: Lawrence & Wishart, 1986.

Preston, Paul, *The Coming of the Spanish Civil War: Reform, Reaction and Revolution in the Second Republic, 1931–1936*. London: Macmillan, 1978.

——ed., *Revolution and War in Spain 1931–1939*. London: Methuen, 1984.

——*The Spanish Civil War 1936–1939*. London: Weidenfeld & Nicolson, 1990.

——*Franco: A Biography*. London: HarperCollins, 1993.

——*A Concise History of the Spanish Civil War*. London: Fontana, 1996.

Preston, P. and Mackenzie, A., eds, *The Republic Besieged: Civil War in Spain 1936–1939*. Edinburgh: Edinburgh University Press, 1996.

Radosh, Ronald, Habeck, Mary M., and Sevostianov, Grigory, eds, *Spain Betrayed: The Soviet Union in the Spanish Civil War*. London: Yale University Press, 2001.

Rees, Tim, and Thorpe, Andrew, eds, *International Communism and the Communist International, 1919–1943*. Manchester: Manchester University Press, 1999.

Richardson, R. Dan, *Comintern Army*. Lexington: University of Kentucky Press, 1982.

Riddell, Neil, 'The Catholic Church and the Labour Party, 1918–1931', *Twentieth Century British History*, 8: 2, 1997, pp. 165–193.

Robinson, R., *The Origin of Franco's Spain: The Right, the Republic and Revolution, 1931–1936*. Newton Abbot: David & Charles, 1970.

Romerstein, Herbert, *Heroic Victims: Stalin's Foreign Legion in the Spanish Civil War*. Washington: Council for the Defence of Freedom, 1994.

Sandoval, Jose, and Azcárate, Manuel, *Spain 1936–1939*. London: Lawrence & Wishart, 1966.

Schauff, Frank, 'The NKVD in Spain: Questions by Stanley Payne, Answers by Alexander Orlov', *Forum für osteuropäische Ideen- und Zeitgeschichte*, 4: 2, 2000, pp. 229–250.

Seidman, Michael, 'Quiet Fronts in the Spanish Civil War', *The Historian*, summer, 1999, pp. 821–841.

Shelden, Michael, *Orwell: The Authorised Biography*. London: Heinemann, 1991.

Shelmerdine, L. B., 'Britons in an "Un-British" War: Domestic Newspapers and the Participation of UK Nationals in the Spanish Civil War', *North West Labour History*, 22, 1997–1998, pp. 20–47.

Skoutelsky, Rémi, *L'Espoir guidait leurs pas: les volontaires français dans les Brigades internationales 1936–1939*. Paris: Bernard Grasset, 1998.

—— 'French Combatants of the International Brigades', *The Volunteer*, 20: 3, fall–winter 1998, pp. 8–10.

—— 'The Comintern and the International Brigades', *The Volunteer*, 24: 1, March 2002, pp. 9–13.

Sloan, Patrick, ed., *John Cornford: A Memoir*. London: Jonathan Cape, 1938.

Southworth, Herbert R., *Guernica! Guernica!* London: University of California Press, 1977.

—— *Disinformation and the Spanish Civil War: The Brainwashing of Francisco Franco*. London: Routledge, 2001.

—— 'Julián Gorkin, Burnett Bulloten and the Spanish Civil War', in P. Preston and A. Mackenzie, eds, *The Republic Besieged: Civil War in Spain 1936–1939*. Edinburgh: Edinburgh University Press, 1996, pp. 261–310.

Soviet War Veterans' Committee, *International Solidarity with the Spanish Republic, 1936–1939*. Moscow: Progress Publishers, 1976.

Sperber, Murray, *And I Remember Spain*. London: Hart Davis MacGibbon, 1974.

Squires, M., *The Aid to Spain Movement in Battersea 1936–1939*. London: Elmfield Publications, 1994.

Stansky, Peter, and Abrahams, William, *Journey to the Frontier: Two Roads to the Spanish Civil War*. London: Constable, 1966.

Stevenson, John, and Cook, Chris, *Britain in the Depression: Society and Politics 1929–1939*. New York: Longman, 1994.

Stone, Glyn, 'Britain, Non-Intervention and the Spanish Civil War', *European Studies Review*, 9, 1979, pp. 129–149.

Stradling, R., 'Orwell and the Spanish Civil War: A Historical Critique', in Christopher Norris, ed., *Inside the Myth. Orwell: Views from the Left*. London: Lawrence & Wishart, 1984, pp. 103–125.

Stradling, Robert, 'Franco's Irish Volunteers', *History Today*, 45: 3, 1995, pp. 40–47.

—— *Cardiff and the Spanish Civil War*. Cardiff: Butetown History and Arts Project, 1996.

—— *The Irish and the Spanish Civil War 1936–1939: Crusades in Conflict*. Manchester: Manchester University Press, 1999.

—— *History and Legend: Writing the International Brigades*. Cardiff: University of Wales Press, 2003.

Taylor, A. J. P., *The Origins of the Second World War*. Harmondsworth: Penguin, 1979.

—— *English History 1914–1945*. Oxford: Oxford University Press, 1992.

Thomas, Hugh, *The Spanish Civil War*. London: Eyre & Spottiswoode, 1961; 3rd edn, Harmondsworth: Penguin, 1990.

—— 'The Spanish Civil War', in A. J. P. Taylor, ed. *History of the Twentieth Century*. London: Purnell, 1968, pp. 1598–1603.

Thornberry, Robert S., 'Writers Take Sides, Stalinists Take Control: The Second International Congress for the Defence of Culture', *The Historian*, spring 2000, pp. 589–605.

Thorpe, Andrew, ed., *The Failure of Political Extremism in Inter-War Britain*. Exeter: Department of History and Archaeology, University of Exeter, 1989.

—— *Britain in the 1930s*. Oxford: Blackwell, 1992.

—— 'Comintern "Control" of the Communist Party of Great Britain, 1920–43', *English Historical Review*, June 1998, pp. 637–662.

Thurlow, Robert, 'The Failure of British Fascism 1932–1940', in A. Thorpe, ed., *The Failure of Political Extremism in Inter-War Britain*. Exeter: Department of History and Archaeology, University of Exeter, 1989, pp. 67–84.

Thwaites, Peter, 'The ILP Contingent in the Spanish Civil War', *Imperial War Museum Review*, 1987, pp. 50–61.

Toynbee, Philip, ed., *The Distant Drum: Reflections on the Spanish Civil War*. London: Sidgwick & Jackson, 1976.

Vidal, César, *Las Brigadas Internacionales*. Madrid: Espasa Fórum, 1998.

Viñas, Angel, 'Gold, the Soviet Union, and the Spanish Civil War', *European Studies Review*, 9, 1979, pp. 105–129.

Walton, John K., 'British Perceptions of Spain and their Impact on Attitudes to the Spanish Civil War: Some Additional Evidence', *Twentieth Century British History*, 5: 3, 1994, pp. 283–299.

Watkins, K. W., *Britain Divided: The Effect of the Spanish Civil War on British Political Opinion*. London: Nelson, 1963.

Watt, D. C., 'Soviet Aid to the Republic', *Slavonic and East European Review*, 38, June 1960, pp. 536–540.

Watson, Don, and Corcoran, John, *An Inspiring Example: The North East of England and the Spanish Civil War 1936–1939*. n.p.: McGuffin, 1996.

Weintraub, Stanley, *The Last Great Cause: The Intellectuals and the Spanish Civil War*. London: W. H. Allen, 1968.

West, Nigel, *Venona: The Greatest Secret of the Cold War*. London: HarperCollins, 1999.

Whealey, Robert, 'Foreign Intervention in the Spanish Civil War', in Raymond Carr, ed., *The Republic and the Civil War in Spain*. London: Macmillan, 1971, pp. 213–238.

—— 'Nazi Propagandist Joseph Goebbels looks at the Spanish Civil War', *The Historian*, winter 1999, pp. 341–360.

Williams, Colin, Alexander, Bill, and Gorman, John, *Memorials of the Spanish Civil War*. Stroud: Sutton, 1996.

Wolff, Milton, *Another Hill*. Urbana and Chicago: University of Illinois Press, 1994.

Wood, Ian S., 'Scotland and the Spanish Civil War', *Cencrastus*, 18, autumn 1984, pp. 14–16.

Worley, Matthew, 'The British Communist Party 1920–1945', *The Historian*, 55, 1997, pp. 26–28.

## 3 Unpublished material

Bagon, Paul, 'Anglo-Jewry and the International Brigades: A Question of Motivation', BA dissertation, University of Manchester, 2001.

Errock, Heather Mary, 'The Attitude of the Labour Party to the Spanish Civil War', MA thesis, University of Keele, 1980.

Halstead, John, and McLoughlin, Barry, 'British and Irish Students at the International Lenin School, Moscow, 1926–37', conference paper given at University of Manchester, April 2001.

Hynes, M. J., 'The British Battalion of the XVth International Brigade', BA dissertation, University of Manchester, 1985.

O'Shaughnessy, Michael, 'Far from Home or Glory: New Zealanders in the Spanish Civil War', conference paper given at University of Auckland, August 2001.

Pike, David Wingeate, 'Conjecture, Propaganda and Deceit in the Spanish Civil War', PhD thesis, California Institute of International Studies, 1968.

Shaer-West, Dolly, 'Frank West: A Biography'.

Suart, Natalie, 'The Memory of the Spanish Civil War and the Families of British International Brigaders', PhD thesis, De Montfort University, 2001.

Sugarman, Martin, 'Against Fascism – Jews who served in the Spanish Civil War', 2000.

# Index

O'Connor, Frank **51**, 171n
O'Connor, Peter 42, 44
O'Daire, Patrick 90, 91, 92, *101*, 146;
    British battalion commander **150**, 183n
O'Donnell, Hugh 65
O'Duffy, General Eoin 161n
Oldershaw, Thomas, battalion commissar
    **151**
O'Malley, Patrick **51**, 171n
Ondarreta prison, San Sebastian 121, 128
Orwell, George (Eric Blair) 4, 12, 15; on
    press reports 35; view of War 130, 134,
    193n
Ovenden, Arthur 'Babs' 44, 48, **57**, 58, *59*
Overton, Bert: as company commander 66,
    180n; death of 80, 142; at Jarama 74, 76,
    80, 178–9n

Paester, Samuel **57**
Palencia PoW camp 121
Palmer, George 175n
Paris 6
Partido Obrero de Unificación Marxista
    (POUM) 15, 36, 166n, 193n;
    Communist Party and 130
*Pasionaria, La see* Ibarruri, Dolores
Patton, Thomas 18, **54**
Paynter, Will 14, 37, 82, 136; commissar at
    Albacete 88, 138, 196n; and repatriation
    problem 138–9
Peet, John 46, 144, 199n
Peñaredora, Colonel 188n
Philby, Kim 115, 190n
Picton, Tom 187n
Pitcairn, Frank *see* Cockburn, Claude
Plymouth, Earl of 4
Poland, volunteers from 53
police, British, Special Branch 5–6
political commissars 53, 172n, 176n, 199n
Pollitt, Harry, general secretary of CPGB
    13, 14, 79; and British volunteers 38–9,
    40, 67, 155n; as candidate for Rhondda
    20, 40–1; and Comintern 133–4; and
    leadership of British Battalion 80, 88–9,
    139, 183n; view of deserters 140; visits
    to British Battalion 92, 100
'Popular Frontism' 37, 132
Portugal, fascism in 3
Power, John 107
Pozoblanco sector 80
Pozorrubio, officer training school 66, 89
Preger, Leslie 36, 44, 195n
press: coverage of Spanish civil war 35,
    36–8, **36**, 166–8nn; reports of atrocities

167n; reports of PoW camp life 125–6;
    and reports of volunteers 38–9
Price, Bill 156n
Price, Goff 156n
Price, Leo 156n
prisoner-of-war camps 12, 108; *see also* San
    Pedro de Cardeña
prisoners 108, 189nn; attempts to
    indoctrinate 124–5, 192nn; deaths
    among 128; escape attempts 127–8;
    execution of 110–11, 181n, 188nn;
    German volunteers 119, 127–8;
    psychological questionnaire 126–7;
    punishments 121–2; repatriated 121,
    128; taken at Calaceite 99, 109, 112,
    114; taken at Caspe 96; taken at Jarama
    74–6, 109, *113*, 179nn, 190n; treatment
    of 111–12, 114–15; *see also* San Pedro de
    Cardeña
pseudonyms, use of 12–13
Pugh, James, as PoW 112
Pulburrel Hill (near Saragossa) 90–1
Pyrenees 6

Quinn, Sidney 42, 43, 62
Quinto (near Saragossa) 89, 91; execution
    of prisoners at 110–11

Rabone, Albert 140
Radosh, Ronald, Mary M. Habeck and
    Grigory Sevostianov, *Spain Betrayed* 132,
    133
Rae, Jimmy 44
Ramelson, Baruch 163n
Ramona, in Tom Mann Centuria *59*
recruitment: by CPGB 4, 5–6, 162n; effect
    of casualty rate on 9–10, 89, 155–6nn;
    methods 162–3nn; organised by
    Comintern 3–4; quotas 9
Red Army exercises 91
Red Cross, visit to San Pedro 125
'Relief Committee for the Victims of
    Fascism' 38
Renton, Donald 75, 189n
repatriation 58, 121, 128, 138–9, 197n
Republican Army 2, 52; 5th Regiment 86;
    11th Division 105; 35th Division 89,
    102–5, (Medical services 42, 107);
    Madrileños 47, 52; relations with
    International Brigades 8, 89, 91, 92,
    144–7, 199–200nn; use of executions
    50–1, 171n
Republican Party 134; and 1936 elections 2
Rhondda, mining district 20, 43, 168n